CW00821494

CUISINIER
GASCON

First published in Great Britian in 2009 by:

Absolute Press
Scarborough House
29 James Street West
Bath BA1 2BT
Phone: + 44 (0) 1225 316013
Fax: + 44 (0) 1225 445836
E-mail: info@absolutepress.co.uk
Website: www.absolutepress.co.uk

Photography copyright
© Jean Cazals
www.jeancazals.net

Publisher Jon Croft
Commissioning Editor Meg Avent
Editor Roz Denny
Design and Art Direction Matthew le Maistre Smith
www.joinedupthinking.eu
Food styling Pascal Aussignac & Jean Cazals
Cover illustration Evelyn Shifflett

Original antique French tableware and textiles supplied by
Anthea Quick Antique Textiles

The Fell Types used in this book are digitally reproduced by
Igino Marini

A catalogue record of this book is available from the
British Library.

ISBN 9781906650209

Printed and bound in Italy by Printer Trento

CUISINIER
GASCON
PASCAL *AUSSIGNAC*

A.

4

CUISINIER *GASCON*

FOREWORD
By PIERRE KOFFMANN

The news that reached me in 1998 that a French chef from
Toulouse was to open a restaurant in London's Smithfield
celebrating the cuisine of the South West of France, warmed
my Gascon blood. I had been flying the flag for Gascony in
my restaurant La Tante Claire for many years and was
intrigued to discover what this 'new boy' would be sending
out from his kitchen. I visited soon after Pascal opened
Club Gascon in 1998 and to my utmost joy discovered that
this was cooking of a very special quality, immersed in the
traditions of Gascony yet accented with new and imaginative
twists. Pascal had decided to produce tapas-style plates of
food, which at that time was a brilliant innovation, indeed
this set the trend for many restaurants in London and
around the country for years to come and continues to
do so to this day.

Soon, his one restaurant became two, and then three, four
and five. Each had a particular twist and style of eating
but all derived their inspiration from Gascony and its close
neighbours. Pascal gained a well-deserved Michelin star for
Club Gascon, his flagship restaurant, and won many plaudits
and awards from the critics and food guides alike. But always
at the heart of his food remained the produce and cuisine of
his beloved Gascony.

Now, in his first book, he once again manages to be truthful
to the food that has inspired him and with which he grew up.
It is charmingly written and beautiful to look at. And it seems
to me to be very much a love letter to his homeland. A very
special book from a very special chef celebrating very
special food.

I am immensely happy to have been asked to write the
foreword to Pascal's wonderful book, Cuisinier Gascon,
and feel sure that it will instantly become the benchmark
for those in search of the glories and delights of culinary
South West France.

Vincent Labeyrie co-founder &
Director Club Gascon Group.

Pascal Aussignac co-founder &
chef patron Club Gascon Group.

CUISINIER GASCON

INTRODUCTION

It all started in 1965. My father worked in construction in Mali, whilst my mother, Simone, tried hard to adapt to a new and exotic life totally different to that in the villages along the Garonne. However, in spite of their rich and interesting life together in Africa, they decided that it would be better if I were born in Toulouse. In truth, both sides of my family live in South West France, so I was returning to their roots, and in joining them became 'Gascon'. In the event, my father was posted to La Rochelle, where the family settled. I was three months old.

Four years later my parents divorced, and I became a member of the growing number of single-parent families: my mother, a shop assistant, had little spare time and that is why, in trying to help, my hands turned to the saucepans. Together, every Sunday, we would shop for the week and start cooking. We would begin with a *pot-au-feu*: I would peel the vegetables, cut the shin and the shoulder and Simone would assemble everything in a large pan and bring it slowly to the boil on the cooker. The stock from the *pot-au-feu* we would use each evening as a simple broth or with noodles or as a base for a soup or *garbure*. As the seasons changed, my work progressed to making the mayonnaise for the white asparagus or cutting the new local potatoes into chips. I have to tell you that my mother's chips, from L'Île de Ré potatoes, are by far the best I have ever eaten. We also made pizzas, but not like the original. The dough was *pâté sablée*, the tomatoes stewed gently with lots of sugar and garlic; the anchovies were added later together with *petit luques* olives...sensational! Without a doubt it was this weekly ritual of learning and cooking that drove me to inform my family at the age of nine, 'I shall be a chef'.

My family were surprised but my decision was final. Every school holiday became a new training stage in local restaurants, graduating at the age of thirteen to work in a brasserie in Bordeaux. My first day there was marked by a visit to the cellar where I managed to drop three bottles, and three days later I spilt soup on the clothes of some foreign clients. My boss forgave me but agreed the kitchen should be my environment. At fourteen I was accepted for training at the Lycée Hotelier de Talence where the *directrice* Madame Guyot terrified me but, at the same time, taught me to concentrate. I respected her enormously and so worked hard and well.

After graduation my first official 'stage' was at Chez Darroze at Villeneuve de Marsan which is in the country and for me, a town boy, it was a shock: preparing wood pigeon, cooking ortolan, collecting your own mushrooms, discovering foie gras. Those were three very intensive months but followed by the chance, thanks to a close friend of my mother, Madame Heuline, to work for Gerard Vie of the Trois Marches at Versailles. So now, at the age of seventeen, and complete with diploma, I was a *commis* working with a much respected chef who was very important for my future. He never ceased to challenge me, to lead me and to give me the very best advice. As my experience widened I was lucky enough to work with and be trained by Alain Dutournier, Jacques Le Divellec, Jacques Cagna, Guy Savoy – and it is thanks to them that I managed to learn, understand and evolve my own culinary identity. National Service found me cooking for General Lanatta and his family in his official residence on the place Victor Hugo in Paris. I loved the Air Force without seeing a single aircraft! At twenty-five, I really wanted my own restaurant and spent the next four years working with talented individuals who gave me a lot, and pestering the banks with business plans. Whilst awaiting their decisions I travelled the world, learning how to manage cocktail parties, receptions and extraordinary dinners for wealthy people in St Tropez, Beiruthand, Greece, St Barth, Lisbon...

By good luck one day I met Fabienne Labeyrie and through her Vincent Labeyrie, her brother. Vincent, lover of good food, oenologue and experienced businessman, asked me to join him in his ambition to open a specialist restaurant in London. Club Gascon was born and opened on 13 September 1998, beginning a magic adventure which projects the values of South West France to a knowledgeable clientele.

Pascal Aussignac, *Londres, Octobre,* 2009

GASCONY
The COUNTRY
& its CUISINE

The variety of landscape in Gascony is the keynote for the entire culinary repertoire of the area and it helps to have an outline of its geography.

For almost every kind of topography is found in Sud–Ouest (South–West) France, from the mountainous Basque Pyrenees in the south, to Europe's longest reclaimed dune coastline of Les Landes in the west. The area we still refer to loosely as Gascony stretches roughly from Bordeaux in the north, south and west to Bayonne and east to Toulouse. Sandwiched in the middle are the lush pastures, orchards, meadows, river banks and estuaries of the Dordogne, Garonne and Gironde, cradling the great wine lands of Bordeaux. These are now divided into the Aquitaine region and Midi–Pyrenees regions with further divisions, or departments such as Landes, Gers and Haut–Pyrenees.

Gascony no longer technically exists, but it was once a large province of south–west France with a proud and long history. It was the land of swash buckling heroes where fact and fiction blended into romantic legends – Henri of Navarre who became King of all France, d'Artagnan and his Muske-teers and the love lorn Cyrano de Bergerac. It was inhabited by the Vascones, or Basques, people from the mountains, who set up the duchy of Vasconia or Gascony in 601 replacing the Roman province of Novempopulana. After various invasions, wars, fluctuating borders and ultimately anarchy, most of what was Gascony was taken over in the 11th century by the Duchy of Aquitaine.

When Henry Plantagenet (the future English King Henry II) married the great heiress Eleanor of Aquitaine in 1152, a large part of south–west France, including Gascony, came under the English crown. As a result there have been centuries' long cultural and commercial associations between England and Gascony. Gascony as a region continues to be recognised in France, particularly in the south–west!

Over 800 years later, Gascony still retains firm links with the British, although now this includes welcoming tens of thousands of English-speaking tourists who flock every year to eat our delicious Gascon food, to enjoy the wines of Bordeaux or to simply relax in the peace and tranquillity of our many and varied landscapes.

In the following chapters, I hope to introduce you to some of the joys of Gascon foods and recipes which reflect their landscapes. Some are traditional, some modern, and some I have given a Club Gascon twist. I see my Gascon food, in all its manifestations, as a refinement of the original Gascon *cuisine de terroir*, a cuisine which reflects and respects its origins, which remains close 'to the earth'. In the dishes I have borrowed and created I may have made subtle alterations, replacing heartiness with a more modern lightness, for instance, but they are all still anchored firmly in the strength of local produce. Some of the ingredients may surprise you: treacle, Baileys and Fishermen's Friends – aniseed lozenges which may not be traditionally Gascon – but they are used in a gutsy Gascon context.

My past ten years in London have helped me strengthen my emotional ties with Gascony and I have never felt so close to home.

CUISINIER GASCON

I

'SNACKINGS'

LA ROUTE *DU* SEL

We all need a little salt in our diet not only to enhance flavour but also for healthy body functions. Thousands of years ago, early man found he could survive long cold winters without starving by preserving fresh fish and meats using salt from the sea or rock salt mines. So it is a pretty safe bet that salt was probably one of the first commodities to be traded great distances along what came to be known as 'salt roads' or *routes du sel*.

In traditional South West French cooking, salt is very important for curing hams, in confit, caviar, salt cod, cured salmon, olives and lemons and consequently, over the centuries the region was criss-crossed by *routes du sel*. These old roads are the inspiration for first courses on my menus – a route into the treasures and pleasures of Gascon cooking.

The dishes in this chapter, which I nickname 'Snackings', have salted or cured food at their core, from salted fish with piquillos peppers to crunchy grapes with bacon, home-cured treacly salmon and perhaps my favourite – a dish of 'piggy treats' presented on a platter with the small Gascon yellow-green guindilla peppers (see page 20). Perfect for starters to bring a taste of Gascony to your table or drinks party. And certainly nothing could be more chic then handing around a tin of caviar for your guests to spoon on to little crisp waffles.

LA ROUTE DU SEL

"Crazy Salt" – a mix of sea
salt and Espelette pepper

Black ham slices (Noir de Bigorre)
with guindilla peppers

CUISINIER GASCON

1) OYSTERS & CHIPOLATAS

Cool, creamy, fresh oysters are delicious served with a hot (roasted, pan-fried or, best, barbecued) spicy chipolata (buy French or Spanish, British are not the same). On the side you could have a small dish of chopped shallot in red wine vinegar to drizzle on the oysters. This is a classic *terroir* recipe from Arcachon and the Gironde, happily enjoyed by friends for lunch or pre-dinner, great with a glass of a nice Sauvignon Blanc.

2) PRESERVED LEMON

Cut a cross in the top of 10 lemons about a third of the way down and open up slightly. Mix together 250g sugar and 250g rock salt together and press into each lemon.

Arrange lemons in a large heatproof bowl and pour over boiling water to cover (about 2–3 litres) the lemons completely. Place a heavy plate on top to ensure the lemons are held under and store in the fridge for at least 3 weeks until softened.

To use, scoop out the pulp and dice the shell into small neat cubes. Or for a dressing, whizz a whole lemon in a blender with 100ml cold water and 2–3 tablespoons olive oil. No need for seasoning. Delicious for grilled vegetables, chicken, meats and fish.

3) CAVIAR MIMOSA IN SPOONS

I like presenting things attractively, and this caviar mimosa (with hard-boiled egg yolk and white) looks great in a large teaspoon (you'll fill six to eight with the following ingredients). There is another egg element – a baked egg white meringue, rather like an *île flottante*, or floating island. In the restaurants we sometimes use a little disc of cored apple at the base.

Peel the skins from 6 large red radishes and chop the flesh into neat small dice. Chop a shallot finely and a fistful of parsley leaves. Boil a large free-range egg until hard, peel and then separate the yolk from the white. Rub the yolk and white separately through a sieve with the back of a wooden spoon. Then whisk a raw egg white to soft peaks, spread on a shallow plate and microwave on full power for 20 seconds until firm. Cool, then cut out small discs from this 'meringue' that will fit the teaspoons.

Arrange lines of chopped radish, shallot, parsley, egg yolk and white over the spoon bases. Place a round of whipped meringue on top and finish with some French caviar.

DUCK SCRATCHINGS (not pictured)

Use the skins from duck *magrets* (see page 119, for instance). Cut in diamond shapes about 2–3cm. Rub with rock salt and leave for 30 minutes then rinse, pat dry and lay in a shallow saucepan. Cover with sunflower oil and heat gently on the stove for about 2 hours. Drain, pat well with paper towel and leave in a low oven (150°C/ Gas 2) until crisp. Sprinkle with fine salt before serving.

4) TREACLE-CURED SALMON

Lay a 500g skinned and boned salmon fillet in a shallow dish and sprinkle with 250g coarse sea salt. Chill for 2–3 hours until the liquid seeps out, and drain. Rinse and pat dry, then cut into 2cm cubes. Mix with 5 tablespoons black treacle, marinate for 10 minutes and strain again. Lay the fish cubes on a shallow baking dish and flash under a preheated hot grill for about 1 minute until slightly charred. Serve skewered on sticks.

5) BRANDADE OF SALT COD

Soak 500g thick-cut salt cod fillets in cold water for 24 hours, changing the water two or three times. Put the cod into a saucepan, cover with cold water, bring to the boil and simmer for 5 minutes. Then drain, skin and flake the flesh. Cook 500g of peeled potatoes in unsalted water until just tender, 12–15 minutes. Drain and crush with a fork. Sauté 2 chopped onions and 1 crushed fat garlic clove in 4 tablespoons olive oil for 12–15 minutes until softened. Then mix in to the potatoes and stir in the flaked cod, adding a little milk if necessary for a creamy texture. Season with freshly ground black pepper. Use as a snack with a salad of frisée lettuce or as a stuffing for piquillo peppers.

6) WAFFLES *with* CAVIAR & CLOTTED CREAM

You will need a waffle maker for this with the traditional lattice-shape grid. (Failing that you can buy ready-made waffles and cut these into fingers.) I like the idea of mixing the very Gascon caviar with the very English clotted cream.

Put 85g plain flour, ½ teaspoon salt, 25g melted and cooled butter, an egg yolk, and 130ml milk into a blender or food processor then whizz to a smooth batter. Pour into a bowl.

In another bowl, whisk 1 egg white to soft peaks and fold into the batter. Heat a waffle maker, brush lightly with some oil and pour in a small ladle of batter. Cook until set.

To serve, cut each waffle into finger strips and fill alternate holes with tiny teaspoons of caviar and piped blobs of clotted cream, or a blob of each in each hole, whatever you like.

TEMPURA OF ANDOUILLE *with* SMOKED SALT (not pictured)

Crumble 7g fresh yeast into a bowl and whisk in 125ml tepid water, then mix in 60g plain flour, ½ teaspoon caster sugar and ½ teaspoon sea salt until smooth. Set aside for 2–3 hours until it starts to bubble. Slice 500g andouille sausage into 25g cubes and toss in flour. Heat vegetable oil in a deep frying pan, dip the cubes in the batter and deep-fry until crisp and golden. Drain, sprinkle with smoked salt and serve on skewers.

7) ROLLED SALTED MACKEREL

Lay fillets of fresh mackerel skin-side down on to a flat plate and sprinkle the flesh side with rock salt. Leave for 15 minutes then rinse off in cold water and pat dry. Wrap each fillet in clingfilm and twist the ends, then poach in a pan of water set at 55°C for about 15 minutes. Remove the fillets and cool. Cut each fillet (still in the clingfilm) into discs about 1cm deep. Unwrap and brush each disc with olive oil before laying out to serve.

8) MILLAS FRIES *with* GREEN OLIVES

Put 75g instant polenta (*millas*) in a large non-stick saucepan with 500ml milk, 1½ tablespoons olive oil, 1 chopped garlic clove plus seasoning. Bring to the boil, stirring, and simmer for 5 minutes. Remove and cool then mix in a whole egg plus an egg yolk. Chop 300g pitted green olives and stir into the polenta. Pour out on to a shallow dish and cool until set. When cold, cut in finger-sized sticks and toss with a mixture of 50g polenta and 50g plain flour. Deep-fry in hot oil until golden and crisp.

9) POTTED SHRIMPS À LA FRANCAISE

Chop 2 large shallots and sauté gently in 2 tablespoons olive oil. Add 2 tablespoons pastis and white Lillet or dry Martini and 1½ tablespoons white wine vinegar. Boil down until reduced by half. Stir in 2 tablespoons double cream, the juice of 1 lemon, 150g peeled brown shrimps and 110g chilled, diced butter. Season with salt and some Espelette pepper. Mix in 2 tablespoons chopped fresh parsley then pour into ramekins to chill and set. Serve with hot toasts, sprinkled with chopped fresh dill.

10) CRUNCHY GRAPES & BACON

Roughly crush or chop 2 tablespoons each sunflower seeds and pine nuts. Chop a tablespoon of fresh dill. Sprinkle the base of a medium non-stick frying with about 3 tablespoons caster sugar and heat on the hob, without stirring until it starts to dissolve, but not caramelise. Then stir in about 150g seedless green grapes until coated and mix in the seeds, nuts and dill. Remove and tip out onto some non-stick baking paper. Cool until crunchy. Meanwhile, grill 2-3 rashers lean streaky bacon until crisp, crush finely and toss with the grapes.

NUT AND SEED MEUSLI (not pictured)

Crush a teaspoon juniper berries and 1 star anise in a pestle and mortar. Sprinkle a medium saucepan with 1 tablespoon caster sugar and heat until it begins to dissolve and caramelise. Then remove from the heat and stir in 25g Rice Krispies. Cool on non-stick baking paper.

In another pan, heat 25g pine nuts, 25g unsalted pistachios, 25g sunflower seeds and 25g white and black sesame seeds until golden and toasted. Mix with the Krispies, plus the crushed juniper and star anise, some pinches of fleur de sel and Espelette pepper and if you have them a small handful dried blueberries. Store in an air tight container.

11) ARTICHOKES & DAIRY LEA DIP

Prepare four large artichokes by trimming the tops and snapping off the stems. Boil for 30 minutes in salted lemon-flavoured water, then drain upside down. When cool, pull out the central hairy chokes and scrape the bases with a teaspoon. Put 4 Dairy Lea (or Vache Qui Rit) cheese spreads in a pan with 100ml boiling water. Heat, stirring until melted and creamy, add 1 tablespoon each chopped fresh chives and parsley plus seasoning. Pour into the centre of each artichoke and serve.

12) CHERRY TOMATOES *with* ANCHOVIES, OLIVES & CELERY

Slice the tops off 20 even-sized cherry tomatoes and scoop out the insides. Drain upside down on kitchen towel. Finely chop 5 anchovies, drained of oil, 50g stoned Kalamata olives and one celery stick. Blend with 2 teaspoons olive oil, some crushed sea salt and a little Espelette pepper. Spoon back into the tomato shells and serve lightly chilled with a toothpick skewered through the centre.

13) CURED DUCK MAGRET *with* AILLADE

Pull the skin from 1 large duck *magret* (this can be used to make duck scratchings, see page 15). Mix together 30g coarse rock salt, 1 teaspoon sugar, leaves from a large sprig fresh thyme and a crushed dried bay leaf. Rub this into both sides of the *magret* and chill for 12 hours. Wash and pat dry, then place on a wire rack, sprinkle with 2 teaspoons Espelette pepper, and store in the fridge for up to 6 days. On the last day make an *aillade*, a characteristic Gascon sauce, which is perfect with duck. Crush 10 walnut halves and 10 garlic cloves to a paste in a pestle and mortar and work in 3 tablespoons olive oil. Slice the duck *magret* wafer thin and lay out on four plates. Serve with *aillade* and toast alongside.

14) FROMAGE FRAIS & TAPENADE

My favourite *tapenade* is made by chopping finely and mixing together 100g stoned Kalamata olives, 4 anchovies in oil, 2 tablespoons capers, 1 teaspoon fresh thyme leaves and 1 garlic clove (this can be done in a blender using the pulse button), then blend with 100ml olive oil. Stir into 300g fromage frais and season to taste. Divide between six ramekins and top with sliced piquillo peppers and drizzle with some balsamic vinegar. Alternatively, if you have some leftover *pipérade* (see page 39) then top with that. Delicious with crackers or crisp toasts.

LA ROUTE DU SEL

Smoked Salt

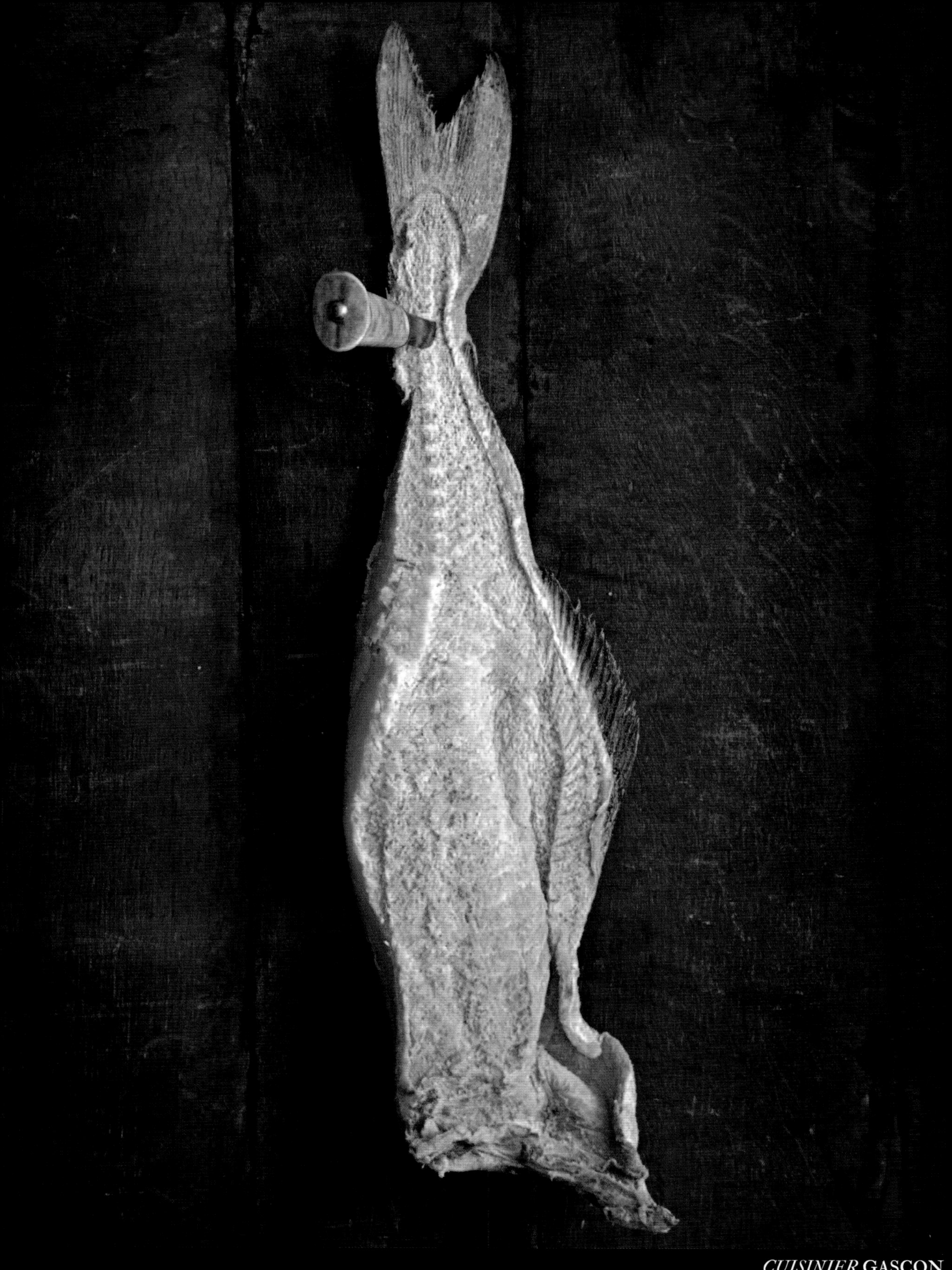

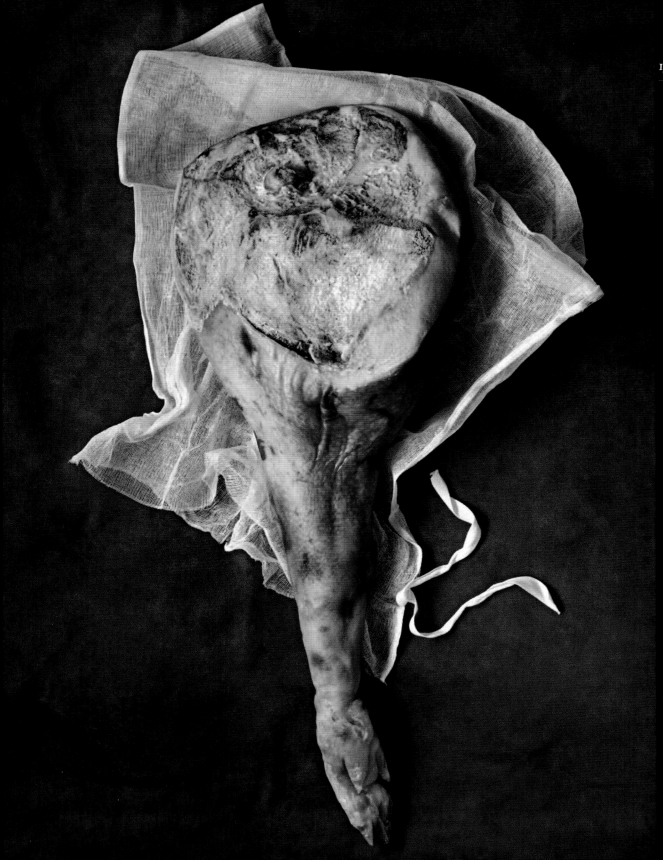

LA ROUTE DU SEL

THE PIGGIE TREATS
various charcuterie served on
a platter with small Gascon
yellow-green guindilla peppers

PIGS' TROTTER CAKE

This is baked in a terrine then sliced and cubed. You will need the meat from two slow-cooked pigs' trotters, but failing that any shredded and chopped slow-cooked ham will do.

Makes 1 x 1kg cake

INGREDIENTS

70g butter, softened

100g plain flour

2 pigs' trotters, cooked

2 free-range eggs, beaten

2 dessertspoons Dijon mustard

½ teaspoon baking powder

100g Parmesan cheese, freshly grated

4 garlic cloves, crushed

3 tablespoons chopped fresh parsley

sea salt and Espelette pepper

a little olive oil or duck fat

1 Preheat the oven to 180°C/Gas 4. Take a medium or 1kg loaf tin and brush the tin with some of the butter and dust with some of the flour.

2 Remove the trotter skin, and pull the meat away from the bones. Chop finely.

3 Then put the eggs, remaining butter, flour, mustard, baking powder, cheese and garlic into a large bowl and mix well. Stir in the chopped pork and parsley, and season well with salt and Espelette pepper.

4 Spoon into the prepared tin and pat down to level. Cover the top with a strip of non-stick baking parchment paper and then foil.

5 Bake in the preheated oven for 35-40 minutes until the top feels firm when pressed. Remove and cool then chill.

6 When ready to serve, cut in 1-2cm slices. Heat some oil or duck fat in a frying pan and sauté each side to brown and reheat. Then cut into cubes about 2cm. Nice with a well-seasoned salad.

PIGS' EARS

Tender cooked pigs' ears are an essential part of our piggy treats platter. Take fresh pigs' ears and using sharp kitchen scissors, cut out and discard the inner ear ridged sections, leaving the larger outer ears intact. Cover with water and simmer for 4–5 hours until very tender. Then drain, cool and pat dry. Sprinkle with crushed sea salt. Cut into thin strips and serve as they are, or dust in some sifted flour and fry in oil or duck fat until crisp and golden.

CAVIAR *D'AQUITAINE*

The sturgeon is a living dinosaur, a primitive living part bone, part cartilage fish that is so old (300 million years) it doesn't have scales. The skin is composed of such hard, lethally sharp plates, handlers need to wear protective gloves. It doesn't exactly look inviting yet its rich, firm flesh makes such good eating that for centuries it was given royal protection by many European monarchs.

Of the 25 or so species world wide, *Acipenser sturio* is native to French and British waters and for centuries was common in the Gironde estuary, and rivers Garonne and Dordogne feeding into it. But then over fishing and pollution took its toll and now the native species have all but disappeared. Ironically, the political upheavals associated with the fall of the Soviet empire in 1991 that lead ultimately to the collapse of the Caspian sturgeon and caviar industry, provided the stimulus for a resurgence in the French sturgeon and caviar industry. A Siberian species *A. baerii* was trialled in the Gironde and, given the fact sturgeon take up to 15 years to mature, eventually became an economic success. The fussy fish liked Garonne waters and began to flourish under farmed conditions.

I was lucky enough to visit one of the major farms, and even went into the water with some of these Russian–French fish! 'Sturgeon' (the name of the enterprise) is run by Claudia and Jean Boucher, who work with Dr Alan Jones, an eminent British aquaculturist. Their Guyenne hatchery, located at Saint Seurin-sur-l'Isle in the Gironde (once the capital of France's original caviar industry), is now Europe's largest sturgeon hatchery, with a potential annual production of 4–5 million eggs. The fish are reared in hectares of re-shaped rivers and ponds; there are vast areas of fresh water, divided into 'tanks' of various sizes, in which they can pursue an almost natural life cycle.

When the successfully bred adult fish reaches maturity, processes are put in place to extract the roes and return the fish to the water and carrying on growing. The roes are lightly salted to turn them into the luxury product esteemed by gourmets the world over. This Caviar d'Aquitaine, which is attracting younger customers into the market, is more consistent, dependable and above all sustainable.

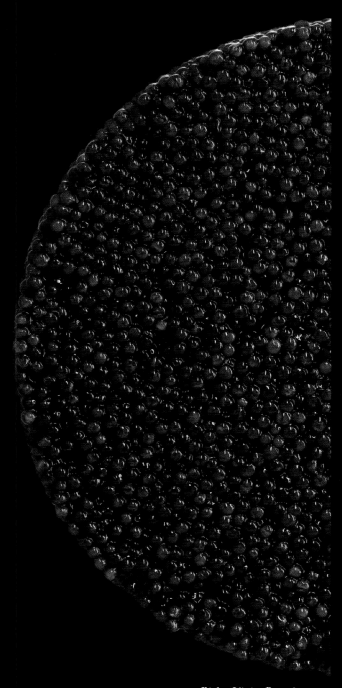

Right: Olivier Brunel, assistant de directeur d'exploitation de la Societe Sturgeon

APERITIFS

Whilst my Snackings first courses that follow are perfect with just a glass of wine or Champagne, may I also suggest you seek out some traditional Gascon aperitifs to accompany your first course? There are quite a few to choose from.

The best known is the Floc de Gascogne, a *vin de liqueur* (about the same strength as a sherry) of one part Armagnac and two parts grape juice. But on occasions I also serve chilled neat Armagnac as an aperitif with foie gras.

Pousse-Rapière, is an Armagnac-based liqueur topped up Kir Royale style with Champagne or sparkling white wine and served with a twist of orange. *Pousse-rapière* means 'rapier thrust' and you may find that in Gascony the drink is served in a special fluted glass with a small moulded rapier on the side.

Not surprisingly, the Bordeaux region produces two wine aperitifs in the vermouth style known as Lillet – blanc and rouge: wines blended with fruit brandy and matured 6–12 months to an 18% alcohol. Both are popular in cocktails over crushed ice; Lillet blanc is perfect for a gin or vodka Martini and rouge for Manhattans or Negronis.

VIN DE FEUILLES DE NOYER

Should you (or your neighbour) have a walnut tree in your garden why not try and recreate a delightful homemade liqueur from a great Gascon cook, Madame Sarran?

Pick 9–10 fresh walnut leaves (Madame recommends this is best done on St John's Day, otherwise known as Midsummer's Day, 21st June) and shred them with a sharp knife. Place in a bowl with 250ml Armagnac, 3 cloves and ¼ stick of cinnamon and leave in a cool place for 9 days, stirring occasionally. Then drain off the liquid into another bowl (discarding the leaves) and add 500ml white wine.

Stir 250ml red wine with 250g sugar in a saucepan, bring to the boil, stirring until dissolved, and simmer for 2–3 minutes, then remove and mix in the spiced walnut leaf-infused Armagnac and white wine.

Cool and pour into a clean and sterilised 1 litre bottle. You can serve the liquid once it is cold, but Madame recommends you stop it with a cork and leave to mature for about a month.

Left: barrels of ageing Armanac at Domaine Boingnères.

2

DISHES *from the* *KITCHEN* GARDEN

LE POTAGER

'Grow your own' may be fashionable nowadays in my adopted country of Britain, but the French have always found room in their back gardens or smallholdings to plant a few rows of vegetables for their *potages* (soups) and there continues to be a connection between the kitchen and garden. And whilst Gascon town markets may display high piles of perfect commercially grown vegetables and fruit there is often space on the side for a lady gardener with her bunches of radishes and herbs or bottles of home-distilled fruit liqueur, (like the Walnut Leaf Wine on page 25).

In the *Sud-Ouest* the beans, peppers, pumpkins, aubergines, courgettes, tomatoes, squashes, chestnuts and of course plump spears of white and green asparagus have inspired most of the traditional recipes we think of as Gascon. The gentle market towns and villages, fields of sunflowers, pine tree woods, and above all rivers and sea coasts, have inspired dishes that are cooked slowly, mostly in one pot, wasting virtually nothing. *La garbure*, a hearty vegetable soup thickened with potatoes or beans, or *cassoulet* using *confit* of duck or goose or gizzards are all complete meals. No surprises then that *poule au pot, pot-au-feu* and *cassoulet* all derive from the same base. But *'Soupe'* still holds centre stage. When it was time to go home my mother, Simone, would ask *'Que preparons pour le souper?'*

But vegetables inspired other South West classics – Salade Landaise from the sandy duned Atlantic coast, Pipérade and Bayaldi, the Basque equivalents of ratatouille using the special long red peppers that grow so prolifically this far south. And I also offer my own dish of stuffed tulip flowers (a take on courgette flowers) using vegetables and sago, a thickener still used in France although long out of fashion across the Channel in the UK where it is still associated with school milk puddings.

LE POTAGER

SOUPES & VELOUTÉS

SMOKED CHESTNUT *POTAGE with* TRUFFLE CREAM

This is a popular soup on our restaurants' menus, especially as autumn and winter approach. We give the chestnuts an extra Gascon touch by smoking them first, *éclade* style over pine needles, but the soup is equally delicious if you haven't time to do this. You can also use ready-cooked whole chestnuts sold in vacuum packs.

Serves 4

INGREDIENTS

300g cooked and peeled chestnuts, ideally smoked (see below)

100g Philadelphia cream cheese

1 teaspoon black truffle oil or ½ teaspoon white truffle oil

sea salt, Espelette pepper and white pepper

STOCK INGREDIENTS

2 medium carrots, chopped

3 shallots, chopped

2 celery sticks, chopped

3 tablespoons olive oil

2 large garlic cloves, chopped

120g ham, ideally Bayonne, diced

1 First make the stock. Place the chopped vegetables in a large pan with the oil and garlic. Heat until sizzling, then sauté gently for about 10 minutes until softened. Stir in the ham and cook for a few minutes more. Add about 2 litres of water, bring to the boil, then turn down to a very gentle simmer and cook, uncovered, for about an hour until reduced by half. Strain into a jug: you should have around a litre. Discard the vegetables and ham.

2 Clean the saucepan and return the stock with the chestnuts. Bring back to the boil, then simmer gently for 20–30 minutes until the chestnuts are softened.

3 Whizz in a blender until smooth and creamy. Pass through a sieve into a clean pan, rubbing with the back of a ladle. Add some salt and peppers to taste, remembering that the ham will have already seasoned the stock. If the soup is a little thick then let down with boiling water to adjust.

4 Meanwhile, blend the cheese until softened, and mix in the truffle oil to taste.

5 Reheat the soup but do not boil, then divide between four warmed bowls. Top each with a *quenelle* of truffle cream if wanting to impress, or a dollop if feeling relaxed!

COOK'S NOTES
ÉCLADE

Éclade (*or, as the Charente locals say,* églade) *adds a Gascon touch. We smoke the chestnuts first over pine needles. This is simple to replicate at home. Put two to three fistfuls of dry pine needles in the base of a small barbecue or even a large wok.*

Loosely wrap cooked shelled chestnuts in foil. Set fire to the pine needles, place the chestnuts on top, drizzle a little olive or vegetable oil over the needles and clamp a lid on top of the barbecue or wok. Leave for 10 minutes then uncover and use the chestnuts.

LA *GARBURE*

This is a classic 'peasant' cabbage and duck soup from the Béarn area, around Pau, and is the ultimate winter comfort food, cherished by many in the South West and all over France. It is not a sophisticated dish, and to make it fresher and tastier, I add chopped herbs and a splash of spicy vinegar. Or, if you were having the juices first as soup (with the meats following), you could stir some wine into the last mouthful of soup before you drink it. This is a countryside tradition we call *'faire le chabrol'*, which is still popular amongst the elderly. It is considered to be a warming tonic.

Serves 4

INGREDIENTS

1 medium green cabbage, e.g. Savoy

2 medium potatoes, peeled

1 medium turnip

1 large carrot

1 ham knuckle

100g Tarbais beans, soaked in cold water

2 *confit* duck legs

sea salt and freshly ground black pepper

1   Quarter the cabbage, cut out the core and roughly chop the leaves. Chop the other vegetables into small chunks. Then place everything together – the vegetables, ham knuckle, beans and duck legs – in a large saucepan. Add 1.5 litres cold water plus some seasoning – not too much salt, though, as the ham knuckle may be salty.

2   Bring to the boil, then turn the heat to simmer and cook gently for up to 2 hours until the meat falls from the bones and the beans are soft.

3   Roughly chop the herbs and mix into the hot soup, along with the vinegar and some wine too, if liked.

TO SERVE INGREDIENTS

a nice handful of chopped herbs, e.g. parsley, dandelion, nettle tops and borage

1 tablespoon Xipister vinegar or sherry vinegar

about 80ml white wine (optional)

TARBAIS BEAN SOUP *with* MUSSELS

Tarbais beans (also known as pole beans because they are planted alongside corn and grow up the stalks) are the traditional large white beans grown originally around the village of Tarbes in the foothills of the Pyrenees. The Tarbais haricot was the first bean to be granted the prestigious Label Rouge and IGP (Indication of Protected Geographical Origin). The beans have an affinity with seafood, and here the juices from the mussels, cooked *à la marinière*, are used in the bean purée, giving them a hint of the ocean.

Serves 4

INGREDIENTS

300g dried Tarbais beans, soaked overnight in cold water

1kg fresh mussels

2 tablespoons olive oil

2 shallots, chopped

1 sprig fresh thyme

1 bay leaf

250ml white wine

100ml double cream

3 tablespoons milk

sea salt and freshly ground black pepper

1 Drain the soaked beans and place in a large saucepan. Cover with cold water, bring to the boil, then reduce to a simmer and cook for about 45 minutes until tender and creamy. Strain off the excess water. Place the beans in a blender and whizz until smooth and creamy. Leave in the blender.

2 Meanwhile, scrub the mussels if necessary in cold water and pull off the beards. Discard any that remain open when you tug the beards.

3 Heat another large pan until hot, add the olive oil and shallots along with the thyme and bay, and brown for about 5 minutes.

4 Then pour in the mussels and wine, cover with a lid and cook for around 5 minutes until the shells open. Strain off the liquor from the pan into a jug through a small sieve and set the mussels aside to cool.

5 Tip the mussel liquor into the blender with the Tarbais beans, and add the cream, milk and seasoning. Blend until smooth and creamy once more.

6 Take the mussels from the shells and divide between four large soup plates. Scoop out the bean purée into a saucepan and heat until boiling, checking the seasoning, then pour over the mussels (the heat of the soup will be enough to reheat the mussels), and serve immediately. If you like, you could blanch some sugar-snap peas to serve in the soup.

COOK'S NOTES

XIPSTER VINEGAR

The Americans have Tabsaco, the Portugese peri-peri and the Basques enjoy their bottles of spiced Xipister vinegar. Red or white wine vinegar is steeped with a little oil, whole garlic cloves, thyme, a few small whole chillies and aromatic Espellette pepper. Use it in dressings for salads, splashed over hot grills or as a basting sauce. It is delicious sprinkled over hot asparagus and eggs or used in pickles, like the grapes on page 17.

*foreground:
Xipister Vinegar,
Guindillas peppers
are behind*

PEPPERS

ESPELETTE & OTHER PEPPERS

The south west of France not only shares a border with
Spain it has a shared culture with the Basques and Catalans.
Nowhere is this manifest more than in the foods and
ingredients, especially when it comes to sweet peppers
and chilli peppers, both of which originated in the new
world of the Americas, after they were brought back to
Europe by Spanish explorers following the epic voyages
of Christopher Columbus. Columbus and his men had been
in search of a short route to the East Indies for fiery black
peppercorns but instead made landfall on the Bahamas and
other islands that he later dubbed the 'West' Indies.

He may not have found the black peppercorns he was seeking
but he did come across many unknown, plants – chilli peppers,
tomatoes, aubergines and tobacco, which quickly made their
way into the cuisine of southern Europe. Columbus was also
responsible for giving the misleading name of 'pepper' to
this new food find. When he tasted chilli pepper he believed
he had found a new type of peppercorn (*Piper nigrum*),
so because it was fiery it was named pimiento, the Spanish
for pepper.

It wasn't until the 17th century that chilli was classified
separately but even better the new pepper could be grown
as annuals in temperate climates. Over the next two
centuries many hybrids were created and capsaicin, the
compound that gives chillies their heat, was bred out of
peppers giving us the sweet or bell pepper, or capsicum.
We call it *piment doux* (sweet pepper) in France, but often
this refers to a particular pepper from Les Landes, which is
long and green. This is the one that is used most typically
in the pepper dish Piperade (page 39). These peppers are
used in abundance in Basque dishes, and they can almost
be thought of as a unifying element of the cuisine.

ESPELETTE

Piment d'Espelette, or Espelette pepper, comes from around
the French village of Espelette, Pyrénées-Atlantiques, in the
northern Basque country. It was said to have been introduced
to the area by an Espelette-born man, Gonzalo Percaztegi,
who sailed with Christopher Columbus on his second voyage
(also credited with the introduction of maize). The strain
of pepper that he brought back to Espelette flourished and
developed over the years. It was used medicinally at first, but
then played a role in preserving, and today it has virtually
taken over the role of black pepper. It is a cornerstone of
Basque cooking.

The Espelette pepper is not hot, but it has a unique, slightly
sweet and aromatic flavour with a background smoky tang.
The people of the area are so proud of their special pepper
that, in 2000, it gained the coveted AOC (Appellation
d'Origine Contrôlée) status. This was followed in 2002 by
the European PDO (Protected Designation of Origin).
This means that the seeds are protected, and can only be
grown within the confines of a tightly controlled region of
ten villages, with nearly sixty registered producers, in an
area of around 480 hectares. An annual two-day pepper fiesta
is held every October with parades and communal feasts with
eating, drinking, buying, selling and celebrating the peppers
displayed in every possible manifestation!

The peppers are grown in large fields from spring to summer,
then harvested by hand from August until the first frosts.
The small conical pepper is green at first – from 7–14cm long
– then ripens to a magnificent red, which is when it is picked.
The peppers are strung together into wonderful *cordes* or
festoons (on each string is written the week of harvest), which
are hung on the facades of houses, and from balconies and
windows, to dry in the sun. Many are dried in special drying

WATERCRESS & LETTUCE *VELOUTE* *with* OYSTERS

The oyster beds around the coast of south-west France – in Marennes and Arcachon – are huge, extending for many kilometres, so it is not surprising that there are many popular recipes from this area which use them to great effect. This is a light easy soup with a beautiful bright green colour, nice served lightly chilled with lemongrass skewers of oysters.

Serves 4

INGREDIENTS

4 large fresh oysters (*fines de claire*, size 1)

4 lemongrass stalks

⅓ iceberg lettuce, shredded

½ baby gem lettuce, shredded

olive oil

2 bunches watercress

a small handful of parsley sprigs

a knob of butter

sea salt and freshly ground black pepper

1 Put a steamer basket over a pan of boiling water and place in the oysters, flat-side up. Cover and steam for 1 minute then uncover and remove the basket. The oysters will have opened. Take care not to let any of the juices inside run out. Tip these into a cup and reserve. Then remove the oysters from their shells, and cool.

2 Cut the lemongrass sticks into thin skewers and pierce an oyster on each. Chill until ready to serve.

3 Now, gently sauté the lettuces with 2 tablespoons of the oil in a medium saucepan until softened but not coloured, stirring once or twice, about 5 minutes.

4 Bring another pan of water to the boil. Cut the stalks from the cress and parsley, and blanch these for 1 minute, then add the leaves and blanch for another 2 minutes. Drain in a colander and plunge the cress straight into a big bowl of iced water. Leave for 5 minutes then drain, pressing down on the leaves to extract the water.

5 Mix the lettuces and the wilted cress and parsley in a blender with the reserved oyster juices and the butter. Whizz to a very smooth purée, scraping down the sides once or twice.

6 Add seasoning to taste, then pour the *velouté* through a fine sieve into a bowl, rubbing through with the back of a ladle. Chill until ready to serve.

7 Heat a little more oil in a small frying pan and quickly sauté the skewered oysters for a few seconds on each side to just reheat and lightly colour.

8 Pour the chilled soup into four soup plates and serve with an oyster skewer balanced on the side of each plate.

FLEURS & *LEGUMES*

SALADE *LANDAISE*

This very typical, rustic salad from Les Landes, with a cold base of green beans and hot topping, has two 'must have' Gascon elements. One is *confit* duck gizzards and the other a walnut oil dressing. It is the 'poor' dish of the area, rather like paella in Spain.

The dish can be served as a starter with or without sliced *magret* of duck, or turned into a main meal with roasted fresh duck breasts. If you wish to turn this into a main meal then pan-fry two fresh duck *magrets*, first on the skin side (which should be scored with a razor-sharp knife) then, after 3–5 minutes, flip over and cook the underside for 3 minutes until medium rare. Remove from the pan and stand for 5 minutes, then slice thinly and scatter over the salad.

Serves 4

INGREDIENTS

500g fresh whole green beans, topped and tailed

sea salt and freshly ground black pepper

2 medium shallots, peeled and finely chopped

2 tablespoons walnut oil

25g pine nuts, ideally toasted

50g chopped walnuts

½ x 400g jar *confit* of gizzards, thinly sliced

100g smoked duck *magret* (optional), thinly sliced

1 Blanch the beans in a big saucepan of boiling salted water for 5 minutes, then drain in a colander. Refresh in cold running water and set aside to drain. Season and dress with the shallots, walnut oil, both nuts and some seasoning.

2 Tip some of the fat from the jar of gizzards into a pan. Remove half the gizzards, slice and shallow-fry until hot. Toss into the beans.

3 Serve, topped with the sliced smoked *magret*, if using.

COOK'S NOTES 1

GIZZARDS

These are popular street food throughout the world and highly prized in south-west France! The gizzard is officially classified as offal, and is the muscular wall of a specialised duck or chicken stomach (which grinds up food before reaching the digestive tract proper). We buy them already confitted in duck fat in jars to be reheated in a hot frying pan.

COOK'S NOTES 2

PINE NUTS

The best pine nuts in the world for flavour come from Les Landes – of course! Otherwise buy Chinese nuts as a substitute, which are three times cheaper. We always lightly toast them before use, which can be done in bulk, then stored in a screw-topped jar.

PRIMAVERA TULIPS

Yes, this *is* a recipe using tulip flowers and stems! But, please don't worry, I am not suggesting you pull up your prize bulbs, you will still have flowers for next spring. (And they must not have been sprayed with pesticide.) It was an idea that came to me once at New Covent Garden Market, where I was buying flowers and foliage (I do all the flowers in the restaurants myself). There are so many flowers and leaves you can eat, so why not tulips? The stems have an asparagus-like flavour and the flowers are herbal, grassy in taste. You stuff the latter as you would courgette flowers. You may also wonder about tapioca, but this is sometimes used as a thickener in France.

Serves 4

INGREDIENTS

4 tulip flowers, long stems attached

100g tapioca

sea salt and freshly ground black pepper

100g sugar-snap peas

3 spring onions

3 sprigs fresh dill

200g shelled fresh or frozen peas

3 tablespoons olive oil

50g button mushrooms (*I like to use* mousserons, *but they are difficult to find*)

50g Parmesan cheese, freshly grated

1   First nip out the stamens from the tulip flowers. Check the petals are clean.

2   Put about 500ml water on to boil then stir in the tapioca and a little salt. Return to the boil then stir, and simmer for 4–5 minutes until soft. Drain.

3   Meanwhile, finely chop the sugar-snap peas, spring onions and dill. Set aside.

4   Cook the peas in about 500ml lightly salted water until just soft, about 8 minutes for fresh peas, 5 for frozen, then drain, reserving some of the water. Whizz in a blender with a tablespoon of oil until a thick purée, adding a little extra reserved water if necessary.

5   Soak the mushrooms in boiling water just to cover, and leave until softened, about 2–3 minutes, then drain, pat dry and finely chop. (If you were using *mousserons*, plus a small knob of butter, they would produce a flavourful *jus* that would be perfect saved to sprinkle over the tulips at the end.) Heat the remaining oil in a frying pan and fry off the mushrooms for 2–3 minutes then season. Mix in the cooked tapioca and Parmesan followed by the chopped sugar-snap peas, onions and dill.

6   Leave to cool, then spoon the stuffing into the centre of the four tulip flowers. Re-shape the petals around the filling.

7   Put a pan on to boil with a steamer basket fitted above. You might like to place a disc of baking parchment on the base of the steaming basket. Place the stuffed tulips and their stems on top.

8   Steam for 30–40 seconds until the petals wilt, then carefully lift each stuffed flower and stem on to a plate. Reheat the mashed peas, if necessary, and serve alongside the tulips, garnished with a herby green salad.

CHARENTAIS MELON *with a GRANITA* OF WHITE *LILLET*

This is a recipe dedicated to Bordeaux, as Lillet is an aperitif from that great Gascon city (see page 25). There are two types of Charentais melon available: the yellow produced in the Vendée, which has a superb flavour and is sold as *'rouge-gorge'* (two days' shelf life); and the green from Morocco (seven days' shelf life), which is also very good. The dish is perfect dining for those elegant ladies who like to lunch – slivers of orange-coloured melon with a light water ice made with white Lillet and spiked with black pepper.

Serves 4

INGREDIENTS

140ml white Lillet

45g sugar

a little freshly ground black pepper

2 medium Charentais melons

a few fresh basil leaves, to serve

1   Boil the Lillet in a small saucepan until reduced by half, about 5 tablespoons.

2   Now make a syrup. Dissolve the sugar in 90ml boiling water in a small saucepan, then boil for a minute. Mix with the Lillet. Leave to cool in a shallow freezer-proof container, then freeze, scraping the mixture every half-hour, until you have a crushed slush, or granita.

3   Meanwhile, halve the melons, scoop out the seeds, and peel. Using a swivel vegetable peeler cut some wafer-thin slices of melon and lay them out on four cold serving plates. Spoon crushed *granita* in the centre and serve, garnished with basil leaves.

PIPERADE BASQUAISE

This classic dish from *les pays Basque* is the Gascon answer to Provence's *ratatouille*. It differs in two main ways: there is no aubergine or red pepper. Instead we use a long sweet green pepper called *piment doux* ('sweet pepper'), and it is flavoured with Espelette pepper, a substitute for which is paprika. It makes the most wonderful breakfast dish topped with fried egg and crispy bacon, which is how we sometimes serve it at Le Comptoir, as a *terroir* dish. Otherwise simply drizzle it with Xipister or sherry vinegar (see page 32).

Serves 4

INGREDIENTS

500g green peppers, ideally *piments doux,* seeded and thinly sliced

500g ripe tomatoes

2 medium onions, thinly sliced

4 tablespoons olive oil

1 large garlic clove

2–3 sprigs fresh thyme

2 bay leaves

1 tablespoon tomato purée

½ teaspoon Espelette pepper or paprika

2 teaspoons sugar

sea salt and freshly ground black pepper

1 Heat the oven to 180°C/Gas 4.

2 Halve the peppers, cut off the stalk tops and remove the seeds. Wrap in foil and cook for 15–20 minutes in the preheated oven until just softened. Cool, then peel off the skin and cut the flesh into 5cm lengths. Set aside.

3 Blanch the tomatoes in a bowl of boiling water for a minute or so, then remove and cool. Score out the stalk ends, peel off the skins then cut the tomatoes in quarters.

4 In a large heatproof pan, gently sauté the onions in the oil with the garlic, thyme and bay for about 15 minutes until softened. Stir in the tomato purée, cook for 2 minutes then add the pepper strips and tomatoes, Espelette or paprika, sugar and seasoning.

5 Bring to the boil, then lower to a gentle simmer and cook for about an hour until the vegetables are soft and tender. Cool and serve warm or chilled. If you slightly undercook it, it is still good to eat. It is wonderful reheated the next day.

ASPARAGUS *EMULSION with* BLACK TREACLE

This is one way of using Gascony's wonderful white asparagus, although black treacle is not very French! Plump, sweet and juicy white asparagus is served with a treacle-flavoured sauce and an aniseed foam. To emulate what we do at Club Gascon, you will need a gas siphon (see below) to create the foam. If you haven't got a siphon, omit the gelatine, simply spoon the asparagus cream on top of the treacly asparagus.

Serves 4

INGREDIENTS

500g white asparagus spears

3 tablespoons olive oil

1 medium parsnip, peeled and thinly sliced

sea salt and freshly ground black pepper

80ml double cream

2 gelatine leaves

1 large tablespoon black treacle

1 teaspoon pastis (e.g. Ricard)

1 Trim the wooden ends of the asparagus spears and peel the skin with a swivel vegetable peeler. Then cut off about 2–3cm of the tips and set these aside. Slice the stems finely.

2 Heat 2 tablespoons of the oil in a shallow pan and stir in the asparagus stems and parsnip. Cook for a minute or two then cover with about 250ml water and some seasoning. Bring to the boil, then lower to a simmer and cook for about 15 minutes until the vegetables are tender and the water is reduced right down. Strain off any excess water and tip the vegetables into a blender with the cream.

3 Whizz until very smooth and creamy then pour through a fine sieve, back into the saucepan, rubbing with the back of a ladle.

4 Meanwhile, cover the gelatine leaves in a bowl with cold water and leave for 5 minutes until softened, then drain off the water.

5 Reheat the vegetable cream gently until piping hot, remove from the heat and add the softened gelatine leaves, stirring until dissolved. Pour this mixture into the gas siphon (see below) and keep at 60°C.

6 Make the treacle sauce. Heat a large metal tablespoon in a jug of very hot water, then use to measure off the treacle into a small pan. Add the pastis and 100ml water. Bring to the boil and then simmer gently for about 10 minutes until the liquid reduces by half.

7 Cook the asparagus tips by sautéing in a shallow pan in the remaining oil for 3–5 minutes until just softened. Mix in the treacle sauce and divide between four shallow bowls or plates.

8 Press the sauce siphon over the top with the creamy emulsion and serve.

COOK'S NOTES
USING A GAS SIPHON

The Swiss Kisag and iSi make good siphons – often listed as 'cream whippers' – which are not too expensive to buy. The siphons are charged by gas. The body is only three-quarters filled with sauce or cream: you must leave space for the aeration to take place. And the sauce must be silky smooth, otherwise you will block the siphon.

ASPARAGUS *FRICASSEE* *with* TARAMASALATA CREAM

In this recipe I have managed to use a Greek ingredient – a pâté of fish roe – in a French context. I think it works very well, the saltiness of the pâté with the sweetness of asparagus. Early summer is white asparagus time in Gascony, when the spears are plump and juicy, and in this recipe we serve them with green asparagus spears (good colours together), topped with a light taramasalata cream and some sautéed samphire. The taramasalata cream we pass through a siphon to create a light emulsion foam, but you can serve it as it is.

Serves 4

INGREDIENTS

1 bunch (about 250g) white asparagus

1 bunch (about 250g) green asparagus

1 tablespoon sugar

sea salt and Espelette pepper

a little olive oil

a good handful of samphire, rinsed and patted dry

1. First, start the taramasalata cream. Heat the cream and milk in a small saucepan until on the point of boiling, and remove from the heat and cool.

2. If making an emulsion foam, stir in the softened gelatine leaf at this point until dissolved. Leave to cool. When the cream is cool mix in the taramasalata.

3. Peel the end stalks of both types of asparagus with a swivel vegetable peeler. Boil the white spears in 1.5 litres water with the sugar and a tablespoon of salt for about 10 minutes until just tender. Then drain and set aside.

4. Heat 500ml water in a frying pan with 1 tablespoon olive oil and 1 teaspoon salt until boiling. Add the green asparagus, bring to the boil then cook for 5 minutes. Drain and mix with the white asparagus.

5. Heat another tablespoon oil in a frying pan and cook the samphire for about 3 minutes until softened but still crunchy. Set aside.

6. When ready to serve, arrange both asparagus on four serving plates. Spoon over the taramasalata cream or spoon the cream with the gelatine into a siphon and press out as an emulsion foam over the spears. Sprinkle with the crisp samphire and serve.

TARAMASALATA CREAM INGREDIENTS

3 tablespoons double cream

3 tablespoons milk

1 gelatine leaf, soaked in cold water until softened (optional)

3 tablespoons good bought taramasalata

VEGETABLES *BAYALDI*

The aubergine purée here is mixed with an onion compote, then topped with courgettes and tomatoes cooked in layers. It has become a French modern classic, mostly associated with Biarritz and *les pays Basque*. Light, summery and full of flavour, it is perfect to serve as a starter with slices of baguette, or it can be an accompaniment (perfect with the lamb Gasconnade on page 146).

The compote of onions is best made in bulk, and as such is useful to store in the fridge for other dishes when required (see below).

Serves 4

INGREDIENTS

2 medium aubergines

sea salt and freshly ground black pepper

⅓ recipe onion compote (see right)

olive oil

3 medium courgettes, thinly sliced

4 medium vine-ripened tomatoes, thinly sliced

1 First, heat the oven to 200°C/Gas 6.

2 Wrap each aubergine in foil, place at the top of the preheated oven and cook for up to 1 hour until soft, when a thin skewer can be easily inserted through the foil. Cool, unwrap, halve and scoop out the flesh into a bowl. Mash with a fork to a pulp and season lightly.

3 Lower the oven temperature to 180°C/Gas 4.

4 Mix the aubergine with the measured onion compote and spread on the base of a medium, shallow ovenproof dish.

5 Heat 3–4 tablespoons olive oil in a large frying pan and sauté the courgettes over a high heat for about 3 minutes until just browned.

6 Dip the tomatoes into a pan of boiling water for about 10 seconds then lift out into a bowl of cold water for a few minutes. Remove, and using a small sharp knife, nick the skin and peel. Slice the tomatoes about 5mm thick.

7 Layer the courgettes and tomatoes on top of the onion and aubergine, seasoning in between. Then bake in the reduced-temperature oven for 20 minutes.

8 Remove and cool slightly before serving, although this dish is equally nice served at room temperature.

COOK'S NOTES
ONION COMPOTE.

Slice 1kg Spanish or sweet white onions thinly then place in a saucepan with 80ml olive oil, 100ml water, 3–4 lemon thyme sprigs, salt and pepper. Heat until bubbling, then lower the heat and cook gently for 30–40 minutes, stirring occasionally until soft and almost pulpy. Remove the lemon thyme stalks. This compote can be tipped into a large jar to be stored in the fridge, but reserve about a third for this dish. Shallots can be cooked in the same way as well, but there is another shallot compote recipe on page 185.

LES FRITES

Deep-fried potatoes is probably the most popular dish in France, and in Gascony we do it a little differently. *Time Out* magazine voted the chips from Comptoir Gascon the best in London in 2007. My secrets are cutting the chips larger, two fryings in duck fat (of which we have a lot in Gascony!), and a final sprinkling of *fleur de sel*, all of which produce big flavours.

Serves 4

INGREDIENTS

4 medium potatoes, about 200g each

2 x 400g cans duck fat

fleur de sel or crazy salt (Espelette and salt mix)

1 Peel the potatoes into nice even shapes, then cut in 1cm thick slices. Cut these slices into 1cm sticks. Rinse in cold water and drain well, patting dry with a clean tea-towel.

2 Heat the duck fat in a chip pan to 130°C and cook the chips (about 2 portions at a time) in a chip basket for up to 15 minutes until the flesh feels just tender.

3 Lift from the hot fat and raise the heat to 190°C. Return the chips for another 6–8 minutes until golden brown. Drain on paper towel and crush over some *fleur de sel*.

LE POTAGER

COCOTTE of GRILLED VEGETABLES

This is one of those adaptable vegetable dishes, which we serve at Club Gascon. It is a *mélange* of your favourite seasonal vegetables – here summery – served with a light buttery vegetable broth spiked with some Xipister vinegar. It can be a light diet dish on its own or a perfect accompaniment to roast meats or grills. It is important to cook to the correct texture, a little *al dente*.

Serves 4

INGREDIENTS

1kg selection of seasonal vegetables – e.g. carrot sticks, baby corn, broccoli and cauliflower florets, sugar-snap peas and asparagus tips

sea salt and freshly ground black pepper

100g large cherry tomatoes

50g butter

100ml Xipister vinegar (see page 32)

½ size bunches chervil, coriander and dill, chopped

2 tablespoons olive oil

1 Prepare and trim the vegetables into little bite-size pieces so you have around 750g prepared vegetables.

2 Blanch them in a saucepan with 500ml boiling salted water, starting with the carrots and baby corn and finishing with the asparagus according to the texture of the vegetable. They should all be *al dente*. Drain the cooking water into a jug and set the vegetables aside to cool.

3 Grill the tomatoes on a hot ridged pan until the skins blacken and the flesh softens slightly. Set aside.

4 Make the sauce. Put the saved vegetable water into a wide shallow pan and boil down by half, then whisk in the butter, Xipister and some seasoning and continue to boil for another 3–5 minutes. Remove from the heat and stir in the herbs. Tip into a blender and whizz, or blend in the pan using a stick blender until smooth.

5 Heat the oil in a large non-stick frying pan and cook the blanched vegetables, stirring once or twice until lightly browned, about 5 minutes.

6 Divide between four shallow bowls and scatter over the still warm grilled tomatoes.

7 Reheat the vegetable sauce, whizz until frothy with your stick blender, then pour over the vegetables. Serve immediately.

ROAST PUMPKIN *with* *ROSEMARY* DRESSING

I love to eat pumpkins and squashes, and this recipe is one of my favourite ways to serve either – in roasted rosemary-flavoured chunks drizzled with a walnut oil and sherry vinegar dressing.

Serves 4

INGREDIENTS

leaves from 4–5 stems fresh rosemary

1 small/medium pumpkin, about 800g

2–3 tablespoons olive oil

sea salt and freshly ground black pepper

40g sugar

60ml walnut oil

20ml sherry vinegar

about 100g watercress

1   Put the rosemary leaves into a small saucepan and cover with 3–4 tablespoons of boiling water. Leave to infuse for an hour.

2   Meanwhile, heat the oven to 180°C/Gas 4.

3   Cut the pumpkin into quarters then de-seed, peel and cut the flesh into chunks of roughly 2cm. Mix in a bowl with the olive oil and seasoning, then tip into a roasting pan. Roast in the preheated oven for about 20 minutes.

4   Strain the rosemary water into a small saucepan and add the sugar. Heat, stirring, until the sugar dissolves, then simmer for 5 minutes.

5   Remove the pumpkin from the oven, pour over the rosemary syrup, stirring to mix. Season with black pepper, then return to the oven for a further 10 minutes.

6   Whisk the walnut oil, vinegar and some seasoning in a small jug or bowl and toss with the watercress.

7   When the pumpkin is tender, remove from the oven and divide between four serving plates or shallow bowls. Top with the watercress salad and serve.

GRATIN *of* BUTTERNUT SQUASH *& CHESTNUT*

This is a winter dish, a perfect marriage of butternut squash, Gascon chestnuts and fennel. We serve this at Le Comptoir, and while it is not specifically Gascon, it is delicious as a main-meal vegetarian dish or an accompaniment for ham or lamb.

Serves 4

INGREDIENTS

1 butternut squash, 600–700g

1 large fennel bulb

3 fat garlic cloves, crushed

500ml double cream

1 teaspoon 5-spice powder

100g cooked and peeled or vacuum-packed chestnuts

sea salt and Espelette pepper

1   Preheat the oven to 180°C/Gas 4.

2   Slice the squash in half lengthways, remove the seeds and peel off the thick skin. Slice the flesh about 1cm thick.

3   Quarter the fennel and then chop the flesh into 1cm cubes.

4   Place the crushed garlic in a blender with the cream and 5-spice powder and whizz until smooth.

5   Arrange the squash slices and chopped fennel in a large gratin dish, sprinkling in between with the chestnuts and seasoning. Pour over the garlic cream.

6   Bake in the preheated oven for about 45 minutes to 1 hour until tender and bubbling and golden on top. Serve warm.

COQUILLETTES *GRAND'MERE* NENETTE

Serves 4

I grew up on this Gascon pasta dish. My mother worked hard while raising me on her own, and so I saw a lot of my maternal grandmother, Marguerite. This was her version of what the Brits call macaroni cheese. Simple and delicious, it is pasta cooked in fresh stock (often the liquor left over from a *pot-au-feu*, see page 151) mixed with cheese and flashed under a hot grill to make it crisp on top.

INGREDIENTS

200g *coquillettes* (small macaroni or pasta shells)

1.5 litres fresh chicken or duck stock (or perhaps from leftover *pot-au-feu*, see page 151)

50g butter

150g cheese, ideally the Gascon cheese Ossau Iraty (or use Gruyère or Doux de Montagne), grated

sea salt and Espelette pepper

1   Place the pasta in a large saucepan with the stock. Bring to the boil, stirring, then lower to a simmer and cook until the pasta is tender and almost all the stock has been absorbed. The mixture must be 'juicy'.

2   Remove from the heat, stir in the butter and when melted check the seasoning, adding Espelette pepper to taste.

3   Then mix in half the grated cheese and stir until melted. Tip all the mixture into a gratin dish and sprinkle over the rest of the cheese.

4   Heat a grill until hot, and brown the top of the gratin until bubbling. Cool for 5–10 minutes before serving. Warning, this dish is very addictive!

3

DISHES *from the* RIVER *&* OCEAN

RIVIERE ET *OCEAN*

Look at a map of the *Sud-Ouest* of France and you will see the whole vast area is cross-hatched with rivers, lakes and estuaries. Water, water everywhere trickling down from the Pyrenees, first as streams and then gathering speed to flow into the great rivers of the Lot, Leyre, Adour, Dordogne and Garonne and finally rushing into the great Gironde Estuary (with a branch to the left for the Arcachon basin) and out into the Atlantic. Small wonder the Romans named this region *Aquitania* (the modern Aquitaine) after the Latin word for water '*aqua*'.

Local fisherman Christophe by his boat Kiki after our visit to the oyster beds in the Archachon basin

RIVIERE ET OCEAN

And where there is water there will be fish and crustaceans: carp, pike, zander, sturgeon, salmon, trout, eels, lampreys, crayfish and oysters. Many of these swim free and wild but pollution, estuarial netting and other man-made works are affecting natural stocks, in some cases badly from oil spills and diseases. Increasingly, a number of species are now reared in fish farms, which helps towards restoring depleted stocks. Some of the farms hatch juveniles such as salmon and sturgeon, which are then released into the wild where hopefully they feed on a natural diet to give them the flavour of what we once remembered. The fast flowing rivers and clean waters from the Pyrenees teem with brown trout alongside their farmed rainbow trout 'cousins', plus eels and lampreys. Lampreys were once a feature of British rivers too, on which almost a thousand years ago Henry I, the Norman son of William the Conqueror, feasted his fill until he died (allegedly) of a gluttonous surfeit. We do occasionally include a dish of *lamproies à la Bordelaise* on our Club Gascon menu when supplies permit.

But back to the sea, where the Basques were famed for centuries as fearless fishermen braving terrifying weather in their small wooden sail boats. The Bay of Gascony (now renamed Biscay) saw fishermen set sail for the hunting grounds of North America and Greenland to catch teeming supplies of cod, mackerel and herring, which were then salted en route back to France to become such great staples of the French diet as *morue* and *stockfish*. Then, ever resourceful, when war between the British and French deprived them of the fishing grounds, the fishermen turned to anchovies, sardines, hake and more recently tuna. Oh, and barbecued freshly caught sardines are my idea of fishy heaven. Fortunately, when it comes to the pot or plate, fish adapt so readily to a great variety of flavours, textures and accompaniments, even smoking over pine needles or violet tea. It is coming from this tradition that forms my belief that one can often be more creative with fish than meat.

RIVIERE

EEL *CONFIT with* BEETROOT-DRESSED LENTILS

Fresh eels are popular in France and highly prized in certain British communities too. They do need to be cooked or cured soon after killing, though, which is why they are sold live. If you prefer, ask the fishmonger to kill your eel for you. We like to give them a light salting first to firm the flesh, then cook them slowly in duck fat for *confit*. Lentils are a perfect accompaniment for many fish dishes, and here they are a deep purple because they are cooked in beetroot juice. Nicest served at room temperature.

Serves 4-6

INGREDIENTS

1 fresh eel, about 1–1.5 kg

100g coarse sea salt

2 teaspoons sugar

1kg duck fat

1 punnet beet shoots or other cress-type shoots

a little grated fresh horseradish

1 Cut the eel into sections about 4cm thick. Stir the salt and sugar together in a large bowl, then mix in the eel pieces. Place in the fridge to marinate for about 12 hours.

2 Remove the eel, rinse under cold running water and leave in a bowl of cold water for 20 minutes, changing the water two to three times, then drain again. Dry.

3 Preheat the oven to 90°C/Gas ½, and heat the duck fat to 100°C.

4 Put the eel pieces in a medium roasting pan and pour over the duck fat; it should cover the pieces. Cook in the preheated oven for 2 hours.

5 Remove the pan from the oven and leave the eel to cool in the fat. Remove from the fat, drain and place on a long serving dish. (Strain the fat and use again for another fish dish.)

6 Meanwhile, make the lentil salad. Sauté the onion and carrot, thyme and bay in two-thirds of the oil for 5 minutes. Add the lentils and 580ml of the beet juice, season lightly, bring to the boil, and then simmer for about 20 minutes until the lentils are tender. Remove from the heat and gently stir in 2 tablespoons of the duck fat from the eel.

7 Boil the remaining beet juice in a small pan until reduced by half and cool. Then use it to make a vinaigrette with the remaining oil, balsamic vinegar and seasoning. Mix the dressing into the lentils and check the seasoning.

8 Divide the lentils between four plates and top with the eel pieces. Snip the shoots from the punnet with scissors, sprinkle over the eel along with the horseradish, and serve.

SALAD INGREDIENTS

½ onion, chopped

1 small carrot, chopped

2 sprigs fresh thyme

1 bay leaf

6 tablespoons olive oil

150g Puy lentils, no need to soak

700ml beetroot juice (see below)

sea salt and freshly ground black pepper

1½ tablespoons balsamic vinegar

COOK'S NOTES

FRESH JUICES
Where a recipe calls for vegetable juices, I like to use a juicing machine. Chop up freshly peeled vegetables and press through the juicer according to manufacturer's instructions.

RIVIERE ET OCEAN

FROGS' LEGS *with* OLIVADE *& AVOCADO*

Frogs are caught, eaten and much appreciated in Gascony. Their legs, which have a texture like snails, are served to be nibbled from the bone with a dip served alongside, in this case my refreshing *olivade* (a mixture of green olives, watercress, basil and avocado), which is a close relation of *tapenade*. This olive paste is good served on *croûtes* as a starter.

You should be able to buy fresh frogs' legs sold in pairs, ready skewered.

Serves 4

INGREDIENTS

28 frogs' legs on the bone, ideally fresh

1½ tablespoons olive oil

80g butter

sea salt, freshly ground black pepper and Espelette pepper

6 garlic cloves, chopped

1 bunch (20g) parsley, de-stalked and sprigs chopped

1 Pat dry the frogs' legs and set aside.

2 Make the *olivade*. Roughly chop the watercress and cook in the oil for 5–6 minutes until wilted and softened. Remove, cool and scoop out into a blender.

3 Add the olives, basil, lemon juice and some seasoning and whizz to a smooth purée, scraping down the sides once or twice. Scoop into a sieve set over a bowl and rub the pulp through with the back of a ladle.

4 Peel, stone and scoop out the avocado flesh into a bowl and mash with a fork. Combine with the *olivade* and spoon into a serving bowl.

5 When ready to serve, cook the frogs' legs. Heat the oil and butter in a frying pan and when hot sauté the frogs' legs to a golden brown, about 2 minutes. Then season, add the chopped garlic, and cook for another minute.

6 Toss in the parsley, and serve from the pan with the *olivade* on the side.

OLIVADE & AVOCADO INGREDIENTS

1 bunch watercress (about 100g)

1 tablespoon olive oil

100g pitted green olives

1 bunch (20g) basil, roughly chopped

juice of 1 lemon

2 ripe avocados

SPICED *MARINATED* TROUT *with* ROCKET *SORBET*

A simple recipe using fillets of trout marinated in a spiced salt and served *carpaccio*-style with a sorbet of rocket leaves. The latter has a deep clean flavour, and it is very refreshing.

Serves 4

INGREDIENTS

4 trout fillets

2 teaspoons juniper berries

2 star anise

2 teaspoons green cardamom pods

1 tablespoon coarse sea salt

rocket leaves, lemon juice and good olive oil, to serve

1   Check the fillets for pin bones and pull out any with your fingertips. Lay the fillets skin-side down in a shallow dish.

2   Place the whole spices in a small dry frying pan and roast over a medium heat for 1–2 minutes until they release their aroma, then tip into a spice grinder or crush in a pestle and mortar. Mix with the sea salt and sprinkle evenly over the trout. Cover and chill for 24 hours in the fridge.

3   Meanwhile, make the sorbet. Make a syrup with the sugar, 100ml water and 10 twists of the pepper mill in a large saucepan. When dissolved, add the rocket and simmer for 1 minute until wilted.

4   Remove and blend in a food processor to a smooth purée, then whizz in the oil. Tip into a shallow freezer container and cool. Then freeze, scraping the ice crystals every hour as they form. You should have a crunchy green water ice by the end.

5   Wash the spiced salt from the trout and pat dry. Cut the fillets across into strips.

6   Serve on plates, garnished with more rocket leaves (tossed with lemon juice and a little olive oil) and sorbet shavings on the side.

SORBET INGREDIENTS

50g caster sugar

freshly ground black pepper

500g rocket leaves (about 5 bags)

50ml walnut oil

GLAZED ZANDER *with* A *VERJUICE* SAUCE & CRUNCHY *GRAPES*

Zander is a river fish, closely related to perch, and in fact is often called pike-perch in English. It is popular in many parts of Europe, including Gascony. It suits a full-flavoured sauce like this sweet-sour one based on verjuice and maple syrup. In this dish I serve the pan-roasted fillets on a creamy Jerusalem artichoke base topped with crunchy grapes. You could also add some fresh pomegranate seeds for extra vibrant colour. The combination of flavours and colours in this dish also suit fillets of cod, haddock or halibut.

Serves 4

INGREDIENTS

4 x 150g zander fillets, skinned

sea salt and freshly ground black pepper

olive oil

some fresh pomegranate seeds, to garnish (optional)

about 100g crunchy grapes (see page 16), omitting the bacon

1 Trim the fillets to neaten, check for any pin bones with your fingertips and pull out if necessary. Sprinkle with 2 tablespoons of the salt and set aside in the fridge for 2 hours.

2 Meanwhile, make the verjuice sauce. Boil the lemon juice with the maple syrup for a minute then add the verjuice and simmer for about 10 minutes until reduced by half. Strain through a fine sieve into a small bowl and set aside.

3 Make the artichoke purée. Cut the artichokes into even-sized chunks and boil in lightly salted water with the lemon juice for 10–15 minutes until tender. Drain and return the artichokes to the pan with the cream, ground almonds, olive oil and some seasoning. Bring to the boil, simmer for 5 minutes, then pour the mixture into a food processor and whizz to a smooth purée. For extra smoothness, you can rub the purée through a sieve with the back of a ladle into a heatproof bowl. Keep warm.

4 When ready to cook and serve, preheat the oven to 180°C/Gas 4.

5 Remove the zander fillets from the fridge, wash off the salt and pat dry. Rub the zander fillets with some olive oil and place in a roasting pan, skin-side down. Pour over the verjuice sauce. Cook for about 10 minutes in total, glazing once or twice with the sauce until nicely glazed, and the flesh feels firm when pressed.

6 Reheat the artichoke purée and divide between four warm plates. Top with the zander fillets and surround with the crunchy grapes. Drizzle the remaining sauce around.

VERJUICE SAUCE INGREDIENTS

juice of 1 lemon

3 tablespoons maple syrup

200ml verjuice (see below)

ARTICHOKE PUREE INGREDIENTS

250g Jerusalem artichokes, thinly peeled

a good squeeze of fresh lemon juice

200ml double cream

2 tablespoons ground almonds

1 tablespoon olive oil

COOK'S NOTES

VERJUICE

From the French vert jus, *green juice, this is made from pressed unripe grapes, and is used to sharpen sauces. It has the tartness of lemon juice and the acidity of vinegar, but is less bitter than either.*

Previously popular throughout medieval Europe (made also from crab apples) it is still popular throughout the Middle East, where wine vinegar is not used for religious reasons.

RIVIERE ET OCEAN

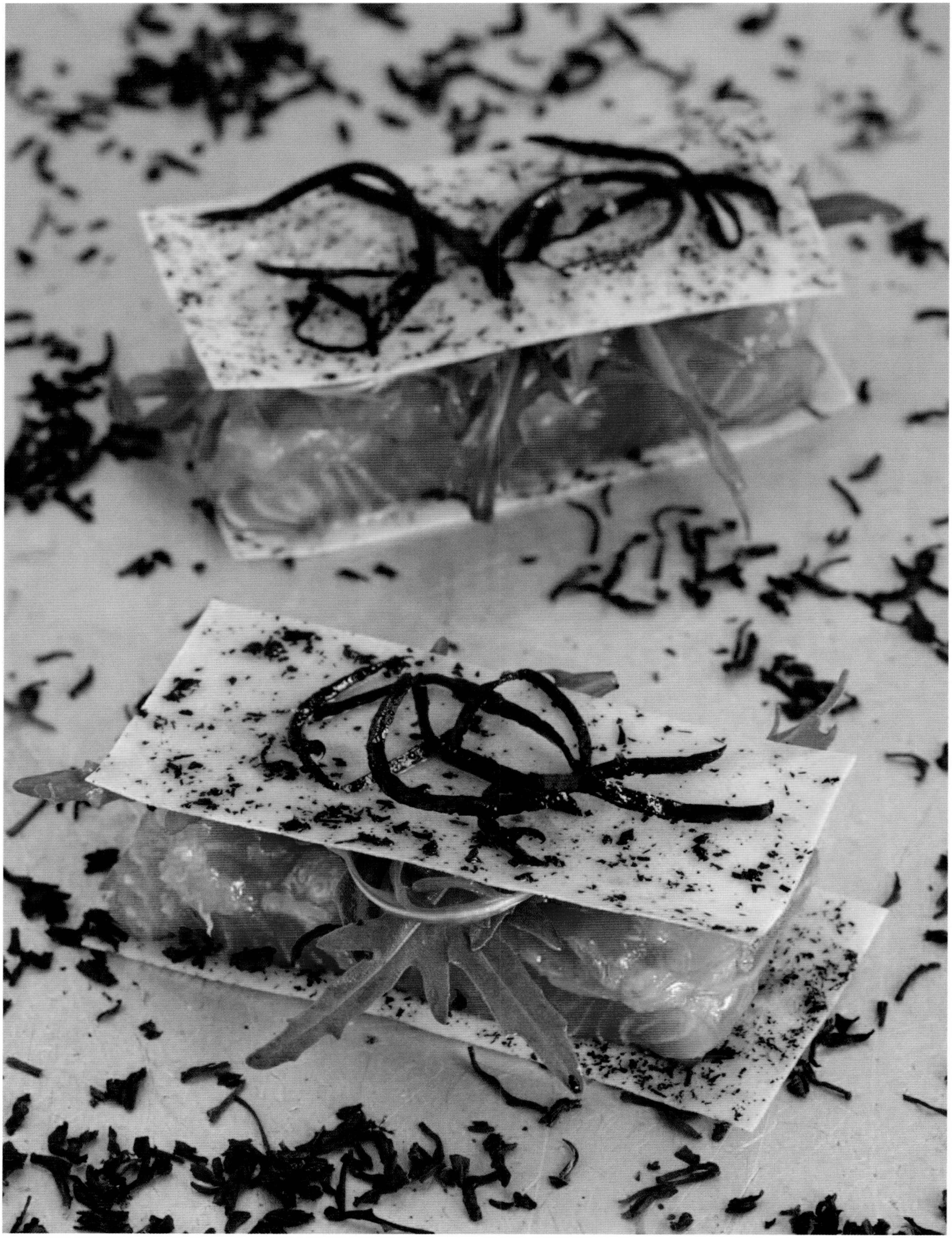

CONFIT OF SALMON with VIOLET TEA OIL, FILO & A CITRUS RELISH

The colours for this recipe are stunning. Bright pink salmon, with an orange relish sandwiched between crisp filo and topped with violet-coloured lemon julienne. Sounds wild – it is – and it's also quite delicious. The violet tea, a speciality of Toulouse, can be replaced by Lapsang.

Serves 4

INGREDIENTS

4 skinless salmon fillets, 100g each

100g coarse sea salt

5g violet tea leaves (see right) or Lapsang Souchong leaves

250ml sunflower oil

4 sheets filo pastry

2 lemons

2 teaspoons *Sirop à la Violette* (violet syrup) (see right)

sea salt and Espelette pepper

2 tablespoons citrus relish (see right)

a handful of rocket leaves

extra virgin olive oil

CITRUS RELISH

This relish is also good with cold meats.

10 clementines or 5 oranges

25g sugar

20ml olive oil

2 kumquats, halved, seeded and finely chopped

Espelette pepper

1 Lay the fillets in a shallow heatproof dish and cover liberally with the salt. Set aside for 15 minutes, then rinse off in cold water and pat dry. (This helps to firm and cure the flesh and does not make the fish taste over salty.) Wash and dry the dish then replace the fish fillets.

2 Meanwhile, grind the tea leaves in a pestle and mortar until fine and mix into the sunflower oil in a saucepan. Gently heat this oil to a temperature of 40°C: you can check this using a metal sugar or fat thermometer.

3 Pour the oil over the fish and set aside until the oil is cold, then remove the fish and pat off the oil with paper towel. This standing in oil is enough to cure it. It needs no further cooking. Save the oil.

4 Heat the oven to 150°C/Gas 3.

5 Brush a sheet of filo with the tea oil and lay another one on top then place both on a flat metal baking sheet lined with baking parchment. Top with another piece of baking parchment and another flat baking sheet.

6 Bake the filo in the preheated oven for 5 minutes. Remove the top, baking sheet and parchment; the filo should be pale golden. Cool on a board and repeat the whole process with the remaining two filo sheets. Cut the cooked filo sheets into eight rectangles slightly bigger than the salmon fillets.

7 Finally, make the violet-lemon julienne. Using a swivel vegetable peeler, remove strips of lemon zest from the lemons, making sure there is no pith attached. Cut these strips into very fine julienne strips. Place in a small saucepan, cover with water, bring to the boil then drain the water. Refill with more water and repeat the boiling and draining. Change the water twice more. This will soften and tenderise the lemon zest.

8 Pat the zest strips dry with paper towel, then place in a small bowl and spoon over violet syrup to cover. Season with a little salt, then add a squeeze of lemon juice. Store at room temperature for about an hour until you are ready to serve.

9 Now, place one rectangle of filo on a plate. Spoon over some citrus relish, top with a *confit* salmon fillet and some rocket, a trickle of olive oil and then top with another filo rectangle. Do the same with the other three portions. Divide the violet-lemon strips on top of all four filo parcels, and serve.

COOK'S NOTES 1

VIOLETS

These pretty flowers have been the emblem of Toulouse since about the 16th century, and there is a festival held there every year in the spring. Every windowbox gleams purple, and numerous violet products are on offer: violet perfumes, soaps, candied violets (a particular speciality of the city), chocolate-covered violets, bread, cakes and biscuits flavoured with violets. Violet teas and violet-flavoured syrups are sold in many good delis and health food shops, but are available at our own on-line shop: www.gasconline.com

COOK'S NOTES 2

CITRUS RELISH

Cut the peel and pith from the clementines or oranges and chop the flesh roughly. Place the flesh in a saucepan with the sugar and about 5 tablespoons of water. Bring to a gentle boil then simmer until it forms a compôte, that is a slightly chunky purée.

Remove from the heat, mix in the olive oil and chopped kumquats, and season with Espelette pepper. Store in the fridge until required. Will keep for a week or so.

PAN-FRIED SALMON with BRAISED LEEKS & IZARRA

A simple salmon dish served with creamy leeks and a rich shallot and butter sauce flavoured with the Bayonne liqueur Izarra. You need the green version here, but you could replace it with Manzana Verde, a wild apple liqueur made in the Basque country. Both, however, can be found on line, if you search.

Serves 4

INGREDIENTS

4 x 50g salmon steaks, skin on

a splash of olive oil

a small knob of butter

sea salt and freshly ground black pepper

about 4 sprigs fresh tarragon

1 First, make the sauce. Simmer the shallots in the wine until softened and the liquid is reduced right down, about 10 minutes. Then whisk in the butter and stir in the Izarra. Set aside.

2 For the leeks, trim off the roots and green parts then cut the leeks on the diagonal into small batons, about 3cm long. Put into a pan, cover with cold water, season lightly, add the butter, then bring to the boil and simmer for about 10 minutes until very soft and the liquid has been absorbed.

3 To cook the salmon, heat a little oil in a non-stick frying pan with the butter. Cook the salmon skin-side down first, lightly seasoned on the flesh side, for 3 minutes until the skin is crisp. Then carefully turn over and cook for another 2–3 minutes. The flesh should feel lightly springy when pressed. Do not overcook.

4 To serve, reheat the leeks if necessary and divide between four warm large shallow bowls. Spoon over the Izarra sauce and top with a salmon steak. Garnish with the tarragon and serve.

SAUCE INGREDIENTS

2 shallots, thinly sliced

250ml dry white wine

100g chilled butter, diced

3 tablespoons green Izarra liqueur

BRAISED LEEKS INGREDIENTS

4 medium leeks

50g butter, softened

ROAST STURGEON *with* BRAISED CELERY & *SEAWEED* BUTTER

Sturgeon is farmed in the estuary of the Gironde (see page 22). It is a fearsome, primeval fish with a tough skin, so buy it ready filleted. The flesh, though, is firm with a delicious full flavour. For the seaweed butter you will need some Atlantic dulse (*Palmaria palmata*), a seaweed, which can be bought fresh from fishmongers, depending on the season or, failing that, dried from health-food shops.

Serves 4

INGREDIENTS

1 small head celery, with leaves

sea salt and freshly ground black pepper

50g butter, softened

25g fresh dulse or 15g dried (soaked in hot water then drained)

1 shallot, thinly sliced

4 x 150g sturgeon fillets

grated zest of 1 lime, ideally a Combava (Thai kaffir) lime, (freeze the squeezed juice for another recipe)

1   Remove the leaves from the celery and set aside. Trim the roots and separate the long stalks. Using a vegetable peeler, peel off the thick ribs of the outside stalks, but reserve the peelings. No need to peel the inner softer stalks.

2   Cut all the stalks into batons about 5cm long. Boil in salted water until tender, about 20 minutes, then set aside in the water to keep warm.

3   Place the peelings in a pan with half the celery leaves and strain in 250ml of the reserved cooking water. Bring to the boil and simmer for about 10 minutes, then tip everything into a blender and whizz until smooth. Return to the pan, straining through a sieve and rubbing with the back of a ladle.

4   Chop the celery leaves and whisk in 25g butter. Stir in the dulse and shallot and keep warm.

5   Heat a large non-stick frying pan until hot, melt the remaining butter and cook the sturgeon fillets for about 3–4 minutes each side until just firm. Season to taste.

6   Strain the celery sticks from the pan, then mix with the seaweed butter to glaze. Spoon on to four warmed plates, scatter with the grated lime zest and top with a sturgeon fillet.

GATEFOLD 2: OYSTERS

OYSTERS

France is Europe's biggest oyster producer. Most oysters are farmed in *parcs* (up wooden poles) and one of the biggest areas is found along the Atlantic coast of south-west France.

These oyster *parcs* or beds stretch from the estuary of the Charente in the north, across the Ile d'Oléron, down south to Marennes and the estuary of the Gironde, an area known as Marennes-Oléron of just over 6,000 hectares. Further on down the Atlantic coast lie the oyster beds of the Bassin d'Arcachon, a large bay, almost an inland sea, filled twice daily by the tide.

KNOW YOUR OYSTER

Names can be very confusing so here is a brief guide. There are three major types of oyster found in France. The European flat oyster or *huître plate*, are known as 'natives' in England but in south west France Marennes, and the gravettes d'Arcachon. Then we have farmed oysters, the Portuguese or rock oyster, the *huître creuse* and the Pacific or Japanese oyster, the *huître creuse du Pacifique*. This is the largest and most successful of all the three, and has been becoming more important over the years.

Over the centuries the cultivation of oysters in the south-west fluctuated according to fishing controls and government encouragement, but the industry was given an unexpected boost quite by accident. In 1868, *Le Morlaisin*, a ship carrying live Portuguese oysters destined for sale in England, was hit by a massive storm. The captain took refuge in the slightly calmer waters of the Gironde estuary and was forced to dump his cargo. Those still alive produced offspring in the already established beds at Marennes-Oléron, and these became the first generation of Portuguese oysters in France. They thrived until gill disease led to its decline and eventual extinction in the early 1970s. It was then that the Pacific oysters were introduced from Japan, which now form the main harvest.

SPICY MACKEREL *with* TOMATO, PAPRIKA & WINE *COMPOTE*

Fresh mackerel fillets make excellent eating and they are a very popular fish in south-west France. As a rich oily fish, it is well complemented by a hot cooked tomato compote, which is spooned on to the raw fillets and lightly cooks them, for a sort of *escabeche*. It's very easy to do at home, and you could keep the marinated fillets for a day or so in the fridge.

Serves 4

INGREDIENTS

4 fresh mackerel fillets, about 125g each (skin on)

fine sea salt and freshly ground black pepper

¼ teaspoon ground paprika

1 Lay the mackerel fillets, skin-side down, on a dish with slightly raised sides. Mix 1 teaspoon of the salt and the paprika together in a small sieve and shake over the mackerel flesh. Set aside whilst you make the compote.

2 Blanch the tomatoes for a few seconds in a pan of boiling water, then remove and plunge into a bowl of ice-cold water for a few minutes. Remove the skins and, using the tip of a small knife, score out the stalk ends and then cut each tomato into quarters. Scoop out the seeds and cut the flesh into small dice, *à brunoise*.

3 In a medium saucepan, gently sauté the chopped onions in the oil for about 10 minutes until softened but not over browned. Stir in the tomato purée and paprika. Cook gently for another 5 minutes, then stir in the wine and tomato dice.

4 Raise the heat and cook for 10 minutes, stirring occasionally until slightly pulpy. Season with black pepper and mix in the coriander.

5 Spoon the mixture immediately on to the mackerel fillets, to cover the flesh, and leave until cold. The heat from the piping-hot compote is enough to cook the fish. Serve the dish lightly chilled.

TOMATO, PAPRIKA & WINE COMPOTE INGREDIENTS

6 tomatoes

2 onions, chopped

3 tablespoons olive oil

2 teaspoons tomato purée

2 teaspoons ground paprika

½ x 750ml bottle (325ml) dry white wine

a small fistful of fresh coriander leaves, roughly chopped

SARDINES *with* COCO BEANS & LAVENDER VINAIGRETTE

Coco beans are dainty-sized haricots, very much part of summer cooking in the south-west of France. They are around at the same time as lavender is flowering, which is why we like to dress them in a lavender infusion. You could use any other haricot-type bean, dried or fresh.

Serves 4

INGREDIENTS

120g dried coco beans

1 fat garlic clove, roughly crushed

1 sprig fresh thyme

1 bay leaf

2 tablespoons lavender vinegar (see below)

75ml olive oil

sea salt and freshly ground black pepper

2 tomatoes

1 large sprig fresh dill, chopped

4 large sardines, gutted

1   Soak the beans overnight in cold water. Next day, drain, cover with fresh cold water then add the garlic, thyme and bay leaf. Bring to the boil, lower to a simmer and cook for 30 minutes until just tender.

2   Meanwhile, make a dressing with the lavender vinegar, olive oil, salt and pepper. When the beans are cooked, drain and toss in the dressing and leave until cold.

3   Dip the tomatoes in a pan of boiling water for a few seconds, then remove, skin, halve and de-seed. Slice or chop the flesh, season and mix in the dill, then stir into the beans.

4   Season and grill or barbecue the sardines, about 5 minutes, and serve with the coco bean salad.

COOK'S NOTES

LAVENDER VINEGAR

Gently heat about 200ml of red wine vinegar and stir in 1 tablespoon dried lavender flowers (or a good handful of unsprayed fresh). Leave until cool – at least an hour – then strain into a bottle or jug. You can use it to add an acidic and flowery freshness to sauces, mayonnaise, vinaigrette. You could steep the lavender for longer, for a more intense flavour.

HADDOCK *with* BASIL MASH *&* SAUCE VIERGE

A nice homely dish, this is basically fish and mash, with a sunny Mediterranean twist of basil and tomato sauce. Any white fish will do, but haddock makes a nice change. In the restaurant, we make a velvety smooth potato purée incorporating as much olive oil, butter and cream as the potato will hold, but you may like to use less.

Serves 4

INGREDIENTS

4 x 150g haddock fillets, skin on

150ml olive oil

50g fresh basil (2 bunches)

800g potatoes, peeled

sea salt and freshly ground black pepper

50–100g butter

50–100ml double cream

1 large tomato

juice of 1 lemon

1 Check the fish fillets for any pin bones and pull them out with your fingertips. Set aside.

2 Make an infused basil oil. Heat the olive oil in a pan and add about three-quarters of the basil leaves. Heat for about 10 seconds, then remove and cool. Strain off about 3 tablespoons of the oil and set aside. Place the remaining oil and all the infused leaves into a blender and whizz to a purée.

3 Cut the potatoes into even-sized chunks, then boil in salted water for 12–15 minutes until tender. Drain and mash until smooth and creamy, then beat in as much of the butter and cream as you like, as well as the basil purée. Season to taste and keep warm.

4 Make the *sauce vierge*. Put the tomato into a pan of boiling water for a few seconds, remove and cool, then peel off the skin. Halve, de-seed and chop the flesh into small cubes. Mix it with the remaining infused basil oil and the lemon juice. Season with salt, then add the remaining basil leaves, shredded.

5 Cook the fish. Heat a knob of butter in a frying pan and sauté the fish skin-side down until the flesh feels just firm and turns white. Season in the pan. There should be no need to turn it.

6 Reheat the basil mash and divide between four warmed plates. Place a fish fillet on top and surround with the *sauce vierge*.

TURBOT with CAULIFLOWER & BROCCOLI in GRAPEFRUIT & CAMPARI SAUCE

Steamed turbot fillets are served with an unusual salad of cauliflower and broccoli florets dressed with a Campari and grapefruit dressing. (You could also use sea bass, sea bream or monkfish instead of the turbot.) Nice served with some *millas* fritters (see page 150) and a few green olives.

Serves 4

INGREDIENTS

4 x 150g turbot fillets

sea salt and freshly ground black pepper

a little extra virgin olive oil

a knob of butter (optional)

SALAD INGREDIENTS

½ cauliflower

½ head broccoli

100ml fresh pink grapefruit juice

60ml Campari

100ml fresh carrot juice (made with a juicer)

Espelette pepper (optional)

juice of 1 lemon

2 kumquats, cut into small dice

1   Cut the cauliflower and broccoli into florets, then slice thinly in a mandolin or Japanese slicer or with a razor-sharp knife.

2   Make the dressing. Put the grapefruit juice, Campari and carrot juice into a pan with a little Espelette pepper if using, and boil down until reduced by half. Mix into the cauliflower and broccoli, toss with the lemon juice and season. Then mix in the small kumquat dice.

3   Check the fish for any pin bones with your fingertips and pull out any you find. Pat the skin dry with paper towel. Heat a non-stick frying pan (ideally with ovenproof handles) until hot and sprinkle in sea salt to a fine even layer.

4   Place the fillets, skin-side down, on top. Leave for about a minute and check how it is cooking by lifting the fillet. Tip a little olive oil and a knob of butter into the pan and continue cooking for a further 3 minutes or so. There is no need to turn the fish. If the fillets are thick, you can flash the pan to finish cooking (if it has ovenproof handles) into a hot oven preheated to 200°C/Gas 6.

5   When the fish is cooked, set it aside. Divide the cauliflower and broccoli salad between four dinner plates and sit the fish on top.

RED *MULLET &* GOLDEN *QUINOA* RISOTTO

Red mullet or *rougets* are landed along the coastlines of Gascony, and are delicious. I serve them with quinoa, a grain which comes from South America. Pronounced 'keen-wah', it is known as the 'super grain of the Incas' because it is so healthy. It is similar in texture to millet, and doesn't need much cooking. I have also added mussels and baby squid to my risotto, so this is a truly great fishy treat of a dish.

Serves 4

INGREDIENTS

4 medium red mullets, filleted

1kg fresh mussels, washed and de-bearded

4 tablespoons olive oil

100ml dry white wine

2 bay leaves

2 sprigs fresh thyme

1 large fennel bulb

juice of 1 lemon

2 tablespoons chopped fresh dill

sea salt and freshly ground black pepper

a knob of butter

QUINOA RISOTTO INGREDIENTS

50g baby squid (optional)

2 tablespoons olive oil

a good pinch of Espelette pepper (optional)

120g quinoa

1 shallot, chopped

½ teaspoon saffron (or spigol, see below)

1 small chorizo sausage, finely chopped

1 Check the mullets for pin bones and remove them with your finger-tips. Trim the edges to neaten the fillets. Set aside in the fridge.

2 Cook the mussels. Heat a tablespoon of olive oil in a large saucepan and when hot tip in the prepared mussels. Pour in the wine, add the bay and thyme, and cover with a lid. Cook on a medium heat for about 5 minutes then uncover. The mussels should all have opened. Those that haven't should be discarded. Strain off the cooking liquor into a bowl through a fine sieve.

3 Cool the mussels and remove them all from the shells. Set aside.

4 Prepare the fennel. Halve lengthways, cut out the base core and slice thinly. Place in a bowl with 2 tablespoons oil, the lemon juice and half the dill. Season and allow to marinate.

5 If using, wash the squid, cut into small dice, and marinate in 1 table-spoon oil with a pinch of Espelette pepper.

6 Now cook the quinoa. Using a large pan heat the remaining oil and stir in the quinoa and shallot. Cook for 2–3 minutes then add the saffron (or spigol) and cook another minute or so. Pour in the mussel liquor, stir and bring to the boil, then cover and turn the heat down. Cook for about 10 minutes, then uncover, stir in the diced squid, chopped chorizo and remaining dill. Season and keep warm.

7 Finally, cook the mullet fillets. Heat the last of the oil in a non-stick frying pan and cook the fillets, skin-side down. They should take no more than 2–3 minutes. Stir in the butter and heat until it sizzles and browns the fish. Remove from the heat.

8 Toss the mussels into the pan and cook on a high heat until browned. Serve the fish with the quinoa risotto, mussels and fennel.

COOK'S NOTES 2

SPIGOL

This blend of spices is a saffron substitute, popular in Spanish and Catalan-style dishes for colouring and flavouring, principally paellas and other rice dishes. It is sold in sachets.

COOK'S NOTES 1

SAUCE OF RED MULLET PASTE

The image shows the mullet served with this paste which is an ideal accompaniment to the recipe.

Use the heads from the mullets to make a simple sauce. Heat 3 tablespoons olive oil in a frying pan and brown the heads over a high heat. Add 2 table-spoons chopped fennel and sauté on a medium heat for 5 minutes then deglaze the pan with a tablespoon of pastis (Pernod or Ricard). Stir in about 700ml water plus some sea salt and pepper. Bring to the boil then turn down to a gentle simmer and cook for 3 minutes until reduced by half. Tip the heads and liquid into a food processor or blender and whizz until smooth and creamy. Pass through a sieve into a saucepan, pressing down with the back of a ladle. Check the seasoning and reheat gently to serve.

RIVIERE ET OCEAN

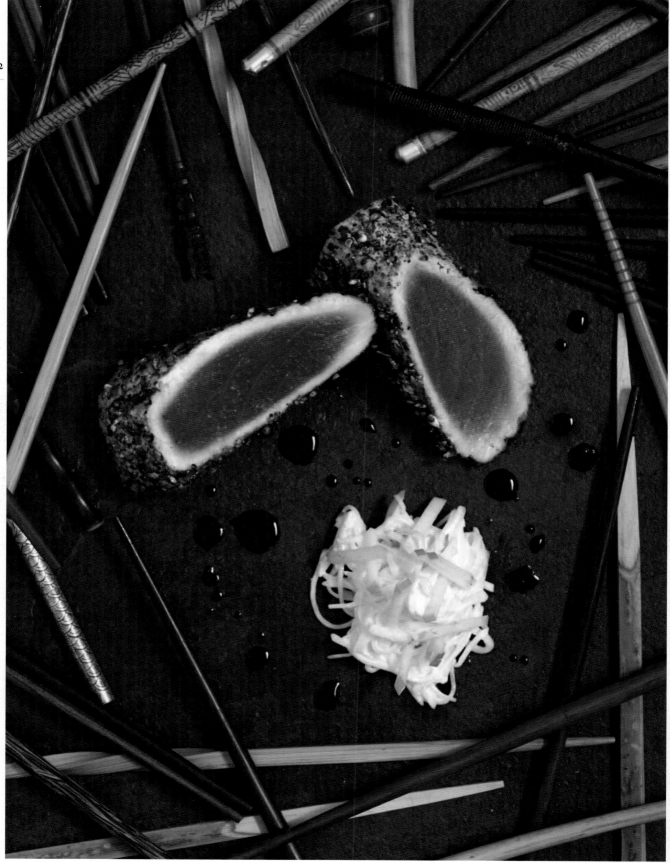

PEPPERED TUNA *with* *RÉMOULADE &* *PASTIS* SAUCE

As a meaty fish, tuna can take some robust accompanying flavours such as pastis, balsamic vinegar and crushed black pepper. I have given extra flavour and texture to the traditional celeriac *rémoulade* by adding *julienne* of Granny Smith apple. The dish is served cold, and you must take care not to overcook the tuna. It should really be cut like sushi. (You could adapt the dish to use four tuna steaks.)

Serves 4

INGREDIENTS

400g fresh yellowfin tuna loin, in the piece

30g coarse sea salt

a little olive oil

20g coarsely ground black pepper

1 medium celeriac

juice of 1 lemon

100g mayonnaise, ideally home-made

1 Granny Smith apple

sea salt and freshly ground black pepper

1 Place the tuna in a shallow dish and sprinkle all over with the salt, turning it, then leave to sit for half an hour. Rinse and pat dry. Brush the loin with some olive oil, then sprinkle on all sides with the crushed pepper, wrap in clingfilm and chill for an hour.

2 Meanwhile, make the *rémoulade*. Peel the celeriac and cut first in thick slices, about 5mm, then cut into thin julienne sticks. Fill a bowl of cold water and add the lemon juice, then drop in the celeriac. Leave for 5 minutes, then drain and pat dry. Mix with seasoning and then the mayonnaise.

3 For the sauce, put the Martini, pastis, balsamic vinegar, cardamoms and sugar into a small saucepan and boil down until reduced by two-thirds to a light syrup. Set aside.

4 Heat a non-stick frying pan until hot, unwrap the tuna and cook quickly on all sides for about 1–5 minutes, depending on how you like tuna, rare or medium. Remove from the heat and leave to stand for a few minutes.

5 Finally, quarter the apple, peel, core and cut into fine *julienne* sticks. Stir these gently into the *rémoulade*.

6 Cut the loin into nice thin pieces, and arrange on a plate with the *rémoulade*. Drizzle the strained sauce around and serve.

SAUCE INGREDIENTS

2 teaspoons Martini Rosso

20ml pastis (e.g. Pernod or Ricard)

80ml balsamic vinegar

2 whole green cardamoms

2 teaspoons sugar

PRAWN & MUSHROOM *VELOUTE*

You may by now be recognising our way of cooking mushrooms: we always blanch them first which gives us lightly cooked mushrooms and a nice clear broth with a light mushroom flavour. This broth should always be saved to use as stock for soups or sauces. Here it is the basis of a *velouté*, perfumed with prawns as well, which is served with sautéed mushrooms, and a prawn, mushroom and radish toast on the side.

Serves 4

INGREDIENTS

500g brown/Paris mushrooms, cleaned

100g butter, softened

200g prawns, patted dry and peeled

a pinch of plain flour

sea salt, Espelette pepper and freshly ground black pepper

3 tablespoons duck fat

juice of 1 lemon

4 slices brown country bread

8 radishes, trimmed and thinly sliced

1   Make the *velouté* first. Put the mushrooms into a large saucepan with 600ml water. Bring to the boil then simmer for 2 minutes. Drain the mushrooms in a colander and reserve the water. Set the mushrooms aside. Return the water to the pan and boil down to 400ml.

2   Blend 50g butter, half the prawns and the flour in a food processor to a paste, then whisk into the hot mushroom broth. Season to taste and pour through a sieve into a bowl and set aside. Discard the prawns in the sieve. Chop the remaining prawns.

3   Heat the duck fat in a frying pan and sauté the blanched mushrooms for about 5 minutes, stirring, until lightly browned. Remove a quarter of the mushrooms and crush with a fork. Stir in half the lemon juice, season and set aside.

4   Blend the remaining butter with some salt, two peppers, and the remaining lemon juice.

5   Toast the bread and spread with the seasoned butter, then top with the crushed mushrooms, remaining chopped prawns and the radishes.

6   Divide the remaining mushrooms between four warmed soup bowls. Reheat the *velouté* to boiling, and pour into the bowls. Serve with the toasts on the side.

RIVIERE ET OCEAN

GIANT PRAWNS *with* COCONUT MILK & *LILLET* DRESSING

This is a delicious variation of stir-fry prawns, where East meets (south-)West with coconut milk from Asia and white Lillet from Gascony. Ideally, you will use milk and flesh from a fresh coconut, cracked open with a hammer.

Serves 4

INGREDIENTS

28 large raw shelled prawns or langoustines

2 baby gem lettuces, roughly chopped

2 tablespoons ready-made vinaigrette

2 tablespoons olive oil

leaves from 4 sprigs fresh tarragon

100g coconut flesh, fresh grated or dried shavings (those you buy for muesli)

1 First make the sauce. Boil the Lillet down to about 75 ml (5 table-spoons) then set aside.

2 If using a fresh coconut, hammer in two holes through the 'eyes' using a heavy skewer and drain off the milk. Reserve 4 tablespoons and mix with the Lillet, balsamic vinegar and olive oil. Season lightly and mix half of this into the prawns. Leave to marinate for 30 minutes.

3 Separate out the baby gem leaves and toss with the vinaigrette. Divide between four plates.

4 Heat the oil in a non-stick frying pan and stir-fry the prawns for about 5 minutes until cooked. Toss in the tarragon along with the remaining coconut sauce.

5 Spoon on top of the lettuce and sprinkle lightly with the grated coconut.

SAUCE INGREDIENTS

200ml white Lillet (see page 25)

4 tablespoons coconut milk, ideally fresh but canned is acceptable

2 tablespoons white balsamic vinegar

2 tablespoons olive oil

sea salt and freshly ground black pepper

CARPACCIO SCALLOPS *with STRAWBERRIES, PIQUILLOS & WATERMELON GRANITA*

Thin slices of scallop are served *carpaccio*-style with a beautifully coloured strawberry and sweet red pepper coulis and topped with a vibrant watermelon water ice. How summery can you get? But you must ensure the scallops are very fresh. The spirit – either a red sake (made from red rice) or a lemon vodka – slightly cooks them.

Serves 4

INGREDIENTS

12 large very fresh scallops

5 tablespoons very good quality olive oil

½ ripe watermelon, seeded

100g caster sugar

juice of ½ lemon

a little Espelette pepper

2 large strawberries

100g piquillo peppers

4 teaspoons red sake or lemon vodka (optional)

sea salt and freshly ground black pepper

1 Remove the scallops from the shells, take out and discard the orange roes, and pull off the small nugget of muscle from the side. Wash in cold water then pat dry. Slice each scallop as thinly as possible across for *carpaccio* slices. Brush lightly with some of the olive oil, place in a container and chill whilst you make the *granita* and sauce.

2 Scoop out about 12 small balls from the watermelon and set aside in the fridge.

3 Scoop out the remaining flesh from the watermelon into a blender, you should have around 500g. Add the sugar, lemon juice and some Espelette pepper. Whizz to a purée then pour into a shallow freezer-proof container and freeze.
As the mixture freezes, break it up with a fork into crunchy *granita* or water ice.

4 Then make the sauce, which is just as easy. Simply whizz the strawberries and piquillos into a sauce using a hand-held blender or food processor.

5 Using a pastry brush, cover the base of four chilled plates with the sauce, then arrange the scallop slices on top in rows or a circle (*rosace*). Scoop the *granita* in the centre and garnish with the melon balls. Finally, drizzle with the last of the oil and season with salt and black pepper.

ROAST *SCALLOPS with* POLENTA *&* *SQUID INK* SAUCE

Polenta, or *millas* in Gascony, is excellent served with pan-fried scallops, and I've made it very Mediterranean using squid ink, and adding a sauce of the scallop roes. You can serve this dish in one of two ways, depending on whether you have a gas siphon to make a foam (see below). If you use the squid ink in the polenta, you will have the white discs of scallop displayed on a black background. You could also use squid instead of the scallops.

Serves 4

INGREDIENTS

8 large scallops

1 tablespoon olive oil

sea salt and freshly ground black pepper

30g squid ink (buy from a good fishmonger)

½ teaspoon Espelette pepper

25g butter

a good handful of rocket leaves, to serve

1 Remove the scallops from the shells (or ask the fishmonger to do this for you), and save the orange roes. Pull off the little nuggets of muscle from the sides. Wash the scallops, pat dry and store in the fridge.

2 Heat about a teaspoon of the olive oil in a small pan and sauté the scallop roes and muscle nuggets, with some salt and pepper, for 3–5 minutes. Then cover with about 250ml water, and simmer for about 10 minutes. Strain the liquid into a small bowl, pressing down with the back of a spoon to extract all the juices, and discard the trimmings. Squeeze in the squid ink, the remaining olive oil and the Espelette pepper, and whisk together. Keep warm.

3 Make the polenta. Heat the milk in a large non-stick saucepan and add the garlic. Add the olive oil and Espelette pepper. Then when the milk is just on the boil, turn the heat to medium and pour in the polenta in a steady stream, stirring briskly with a long-handled wooden spoon. The mixture will thicken and begin to plop and splutter, which is normal. Partly cover the pan and turn the heat to low. Cook for 10 minutes. Remove and let it stand whilst you cook the scallops.

4 Heat the butter in a small non-stick frying pan and fry the scallops for about a minute on each side. Season in the pan.

5 Spoon the polenta on to four warm shallow bowls, top with the scallops and then the sauce. Garnish with the rocket leaves and serve hot.

POLENTA INGREDIENTS

50g instant polenta

500ml milk

4 garlic cloves, crushed

2 tablespoons olive oil

½ teaspoon Espelette pepper

COOK'S NOTES
SQUID INK
POLENTA FOAM

In our restaurants, we like to make a foam of squid ink polenta for this dish, in which case, omit the squid ink from the sauce and mix it into the polenta which can then be passed through a siphon as a foam (see page 40).

CAPPUCCINO of BLACK PUDDING with LOBSTER & ASPARAGUS

This recipe is a symphony of colour. Pink and green from the lobster and asparagus, topped with a frothy black pudding sauce and a dab of whipped frothy hot milk, just like a cappuccino coffee! It is not particularly traditional, but the combination of surf and turf is very Gascon in feel. You must, however, buy a very good black pudding, not one made with breadcrumbs: a French version would be best.

Serves 2

INGREDIENTS

1 carrot, chopped

1 medium onion, chopped

1 celery stick, chopped

¼ teaspoon black peppercorns

sea salt and freshly ground black pepper

1 live lobster, Canadian or native

250g French *boudin noir* or smooth UK black pudding, peeled if necessary

300g fresh asparagus spears, bases peeled

50g butter

3 tablespoons milk (optional)

1   Make a *court-bouillon* first. Put 2 litres of water into a saucepan with the carrot, onion, celery and peppercorns. Add a little salt, bring to the boil, then simmer for 20 minutes.

2   Plunge the lobster into the simmering water, cover and cook for 5 minutes to blanch it, then remove the lobster from the pan and cool on a board.

3   Remove the claws and cut the body shell in half down the centre. Pull out the tail meat in one piece and cut it into 2cm cubes. Crack the claws and peel off the shell, then cut up the meat also. Set the meat aside. (Don't waste the shells or head – pop into a food bag and freeze to make stock for another time, or lobster oil, see page 82.)

4   Measure out 250ml *court-bouillon* into a pan and add the black pudding. Simmer for 4 minutes, stirring, then either blitz with a hand-held blender or tip into a blender and whizz on a fast speed until very smooth and creamy.

5   Pour this blended mixture through a fine sieve placed over a small saucepan, and rub through with the back of a ladle.

6   Blanch the asparagus in a pan of boiling salted water for about 1 minute until just tender. Drain and reserve.

7   Melt the butter in a sauté pan and cook the lobster pieces until nicely browned all over. Season to taste. Place the lobster on two warm plates or shallow bowls. Arrange the asparagus around the side of the plates.

8   Reheat the black pudding sauce until piping hot and using a hand-held blender, whizz it, moving the wand up and down to create a foam. Spoon the foam over the lobster.

9   At the same time, if using, froth up the milk in a small pan using a small whisk and spoon the white froth on top of the black froth. Serve immediately.

COOKS NOTES

For a quicker more simple version of this recipe, use whole small lobster tails instead of shelling a larger lobster and slicing the flesh.

RIVIERE ET OCEAN

LOBSTER *with* CHESTNUT *VELOUTE* & *FOIE GRAS*

This may look an unlikely recipe – seafood, chestnuts and *foie gras* – but it brings together three prime elements of Gascon cuisine: the sea, the woods and the farm. It is a celebratory soup, I think, expensively combining lobster and *foie gras*, and would be perfect for the start of a Christmas meal.

Serves 4

INGREDIENTS

2 lobsters,
about 600g each

½ x recipe lobster oil
(see below)

100g cooked chestnuts,
vacuum-packed or
canned, unsweetened

400ml milk

100ml chicken stock

1 teaspoon bouillon
powder

sea salt and freshly
ground black pepper

200g duck *foie gras*

1   Prepare the lobster as the recipe on (see page 80). You should have the body and claw meat, plus the shells and head for stock and flavoured oil.

2   Make the oil (see below) and set aside.

3   Put the chestnuts and milk into a pan, bring to the boil, then simmer for 5 minutes. Remove and whizz in a blender or food processor. Add the chicken stock with bouillon powder. Season to taste, then return to the pan.

4   Meanwhile, slice the *foie gras* into eight neat pieces. Heat a non-stick frying pan until hot and cook the foie gras for 2–3 minutes, browning on each side (without extra fat), then remove. Add the lobster pieces and cook for 3 minutes, turning once or twice.

5   Reheat the chestnut *velouté* and pour into four shallow soup bowls. Add the lobster and foie gras pieces and finally drizzle over the lobster oil.

LOBSTER OIL

INGREDIENTS

the lobster heads and
all the shells

12 sprigs fresh thyme

2 bay leaves

2 whole garlic bulbs, cut
in half

200ml vegetable oil, e.g.
sunflower or rapeseed

You will only need half of this quantity in the above recipe. Store the rest in the fridge for another time. The oil would be good over pasta, or grilled chicken or fish.

1   Heat the oven to 180°C/Gas 4. Scatter the head and shells of the lobsters on a roasting pan and roast for 5 minutes. Remove and crush up the head and shells with a rolling pin. Put into a medium saucepan with the herbs, garlic and oil. Add about 500ml water. Bring to the boil, then turn the heat right down, cover the pan and cook for about 1 hour. You should then have some wonderfully flavoured oily *jus*. Strain this and set aside to cool.

BABY SQUID *with* *ESCABECHE* & A FENNEL *HERB* SALAD

Baby squid are increasingly seen in fish markets all over Europe, and they are easily available from many British fishmongers these days, including the fish counters of top-end supermarkets. The *escabeche* sauce is refreshing and summery, a Gascon *terroir* flavour that I associate with the Basque town of St Jean de Luz.

Serves 4

INGREDIENTS

800g baby squid, cleaned

olive oil, for cooking

2 garlic cloves, crushed

1 teaspoon Espelette pepper

sea salt

1 medium fennel bulb, halved, cored and thinly sliced

some small handfuls of fresh parsley, dill, oregano and savory or thyme, all chopped

1   Wash the squid in cold water, then drain and pat dry with paper towel. Mix with a little olive oil, half the crushed garlic, Espelette pepper and some salt. Set aside.

2   Soak the thinly sliced fennel in iced water for about an hour, then drain and pat dry or spin in a salad spinner.

3   Make the *jus*. Boil the vinegar and sugar until reduced by half, then stir in the oil, wine, garlic, bay leaf, thyme and Espelette pepper. Bring to the boil for a few seconds, then remove and add the balsamic.

4   Pour about 2 tablespoons of this *jus* over the sultanas in a bowl and leave until cold and the raisins have plumped up. Add the carrot and shallot to the remainder of the *jus*.

5   Cook the squid briefly in a hot frying pan until white and just firm. Do not overcook. Then divide between four large shallow soup plates and pour over the *escabeche jus* (pick out the bay and thyme first).

6   Make the salad by tossing together the fennel, chopped fresh herbs and seasoning. Mix in the plumped raisins and place on top of the squid.

ESCABECHE JUS INGREDIENTS

100ml white wine vinegar

1½ teaspoons sugar

2 teaspoons olive oil

4 tablespoons dry white wine

1 fat garlic clove, crushed

1 bay leaf

1 sprig fresh thyme

½ teaspoon Espelette pepper

4 tablespoons balsamic vinegar

50g sultanas

30g carrot, finely diced

30g shallots, finely diced

BABY *SQUID with* TOMATO SAUCE *&* *CHORIZO* FOAM

Gascony borders Basque and Catalonian Spain, and so there is bound to be some influence in food terms which, in this case, means spicy chorizo. This is a lovely simple dish, which you can top with a sophisticated foamy sauce.

Serves 4

INGREDIENTS

800g baby squid, cleaned

150ml olive oil

5 fat garlic cloves, crushed

sea salt and Espelette pepper

1   Wash the baby squid, then drain and pat dry. Place in a bowl, drizzle with a third of the oil and mix in the garlic and about ½ teaspoon Espelette pepper. Set aside.

2   Make the compote. Blanch the tomatoes in a bowl of boiling water for a few seconds, then drain, cool and peel off the skins. Remove the stalk ends, then roughly chop the flesh and crush with a large fork. Heat a third of the remaining oil and fry two-thirds of the chorizo and all the red onion for about 5 minutes, stirring once or twice. Stir in the tomato purée, chopped fresh tomatoes, garlic, thyme, bay leaves and seasoning. Bring to the boil, then turn down and simmer for 20–25 minutes, stirring occasionally, until you have a pulpy sauce. Remove the thyme and bay leaves, and keep warm.

3   Now prepare the sauce. Heat the remaining chorizo in a saucepan and add 100ml of water, the last of the olive oil and the Xipister. Simmer for 5 minutes, then tip into a blender and whizz to a purée. Pour through a sieve over a pan or bowl, rubbing with the back of a ladle, then return the sauce to the pan and reheat gently. Whisk in the butter until smooth and set aside.

4   Sauté the marinated squid, stirring until just pale and firm, then season and remove. The flesh should be just firm, do not overcook. Spoon over the compote. Using a hand-held blender (like a Bamix) whizz the sauce until you have a good foam. Divide this foam between the dishes and serve immediately.

TOMATO & CHORIZO COMPOTE & SAUCE INGREDIENTS

500g tomatoes

150g chorizo sausage, diced

2 red onions, thinly sliced

2 teaspoons tomato purée

6 garlic cloves, chopped

1 sprig fresh thyme

2 bay leaves

3 tablespoons Xipister vinegar (see page 32)

25g butter, chilled and diced

ATLANTIC
'BARLEYSOTTO'

Much of the Gascon coast faces the Atlantic, so the seafood in this recipe reflects this – cold-water mussels, scallops and squid, although you could use any other shellfish such as prawns or clams. We use barley in this cross between a risotto and a paella, which has been a great success at both Club Gascon and Cellar Gascon. Barley takes longer to cook than rice but it is more amenable to being reheated, even overcooked.
The barley would be a wonderful dish for a party; you could prepare it all virtually in advance, and then just grill some fish when your guests are ready. (If using a fish like sea bass, for instance, you could make a stock with the fish bones and use this to cook the barley.)

Serves 4

INGREDIENTS

1kg fresh mussels

200g baby squid, cleaned

8 large scallops, cleaned (see page 77, roes optional)

90ml olive oil

150ml dry white wine

2 bay leaves

2 sprigs fresh thyme

2 shallots, thinly sliced

200g pearl barley

1 x 400g can fish soup, e.g. lobster bisque

3 tablespoons mascarpone cheese

50g Parmesan, freshly grated

2 sprigs fresh dill, chopped

sea salt and freshly ground black pepper

1   Wash the mussels in cold water, then drain. (Discard any mussels that are still open when you tap them as this shows they are not alive.) Marinate the squid and scallops in a third of the oil and set aside.

2   Heat a large saucepan until hot then add another third of the remaining oil and tip in all the mussels plus the wine, bay leaves and thyme. Cover and cook for 5 minutes, when the mussels should have opened. (Again, discard any that are firmly closed as they may not be safe to eat.)

3   Strain the cooking liquor into a bowl and reserve (you should have around 150ml). Cool the mussels then pull them from their shells and set aside.

4   Wash out the mussel pan, return to the hob and heat the last of the oil. Gently sauté the squid and scallops for about 5 minutes until tender, then scoop out with a slotted spoon. Stir in the shallots and cook for another 5 minutes until softened but not browned.

5   Stir in the barley, then add the mussel liquor and the fish soup. Return to the boil then reduce to a simmer and cook for about 40 minutes, stirring occasionally until the grains are *al dente* and softened.

6   Remove from the heat and mix in the mascarpone, Parmesan, dill, squid, scallops and mussels. Check the seasoning, reheat until hot and serve.

4

DISHES *from the* FIELDS *&* PASTURES

PRES *ET* PATURAGES

I like to categorise my menus in terms of landscapes. Meat, poultry and game feature strongly in Gascon cuisine, as one might expect in a land of smallholders and farmers nurtured in tradition and a respect for the landscape. So this chapter is sub-divided into Foie Gras (Ducks and Geese), Plumes Et Poils (Feather and Fur) and Cuir Et Abats (Leather, Innards and Sausage Meat) to reflect the region in France most associated with ducks, geese, pork and game reared on the lush river plains, pine-forested sand dunes, valleys or grassy foothills that stretch up to the foothills of the Pyrenees.

PRES ET PATURAGES

Like all animal farming, beasts and birds destined for the table become what they are fed. Maize (or corn) is the principal grain of the region and large stretches of Gascony gleam green and gold in the summer with it. Corn is fed not only to chickens and pigs, it also forms the main diet for ducks and geese. During the *gavage* – the three week fattening period for *foie gras*, traditionally reared ducks and geese are fed with true corn, not a mash. The Label Rouge programme started during the 1960s with *Poulet jaune des Landes* traditional corn feeding. The birds are slow growing and free to range in the forests of Les Landes, where they rootle for grubs and plants in addition to the daily corn allowance. Housed in portable sheds called '*marensines*', they can be moved from cornfield to woods depending on seasons and food availability. This gives their flesh a flavour and firmer texture.

Where older traditions survive, the mistress of the house will still rear birds in her farm yard (the *basse-cour*) and might also have *a pigeonnier* or dovecote, all of whom would share in the table and vegetable garden scraps. And corn is popular too with us humans in the form of *millas* or cornmeal, which we serve like polenta, soft and creamy or set, cut and fried.

Pigs, reared in commercial numbers in farms or singly in the *basse-cour*, are salted or air-dried, mostly for hams or sausages. The best known, Toulouse sausage, must consist of a quarter fat to flesh, be hand-chopped not machine-minced, and coiled like a serpent to qualify for the respected name. Truly delicious in *cassoulet* (my family version is on page 120) or grilled and served with a Prune and Mustard Sauce (page 165). Gascon butchers really do use all parts of the pig, including the ears (see my recipe on page 21); even the blood is saved for *boudin noir*, or black pudding.

Now to red meat, where again the landscape affects flavour and quality. Whilst we do use a lot of excellent British beef in our London restaurants, cooks in Gascony might choose Chalosse cattle, grazed on the plans of Les Landes, a cross between Limousin and Blonde d'Aquitaine. South-west lambs have a distinctive flavour depending on their final grazing. We use both *agneau des Pyrenees* and *agneau de Pauillac* in our London restaurants, depending on the season. The latter, from the heart of the Gironde, is sometimes labelled *pre-sale* to emphasis the salty tang of the sea breezes.

And this section finishes with one of my favourite meat courses, innards! It is a celebration of offal and 'off-cuts' with livers, hearts, kidneys and sweetbreads. You will also find a big section on *foie gras*, a food that I, like many of my countrymen and food lovers around the world, greatly enjoy but which continues to suffer a bad press, mostly from ignorance of country traditions. We only use *foie gras* from traditional suppliers, not factory-farmed versions. I hope you will take time to read about the country methods of our suppliers (see *foie gras* on gatefold following page 96).

The famous black pig.
This rare bread pig is
what makes the world
famous jambon de Noir
de Bigorre.

BAYONNE HAM

The cured ham which has become so famous world-wide may take the name of the Basque port of Bayonne, from where it is shipped but it actually comes from the valley of the River Adour. To qualify as a genuine *jambon de Bayonne* (which now holds the EU staus of IPG – Indication Géographique Protégée), the pigs have to be one of eight clearly defined breeds reared in an area ranging from Deux Sèvres in the north to Aveyron and the Aude in the east. After curing, and before the ham leaves the factory, its skin is stamped with a Basque cross and the word 'Bayonne'.

The best hams come from the traditional Basque pig (*Pie Noir du Pays Basque*) or the Bayonne white. In recent year the *Noir de Bigorre* (a Gascon black pig) has also been given the Bayonne ham treatment. Outdoor reared, the pigs forage for acorns, chestnuts and roots on wooded hillsides, with a daily treat of grain or veg- etables to persuade them not to stray too far.

Cured and air dried the quality of the salt is paramount. It must come from the salt pans of the Adour estuary or those near Béarn. After hanging inside for several months, the hams undergo '*pannage*', where a mixture of pork fat and flour are used to seal the cut end of the joint (to prevent the interior drying out). Many producers then rub the whole ham with Espelette pepper, which gives a spicy tang and bright red colour to the skin. Drying follows, and the hams, which began their curing process in late October/early November, are ready for the market by the end of the following July.

For the best tasting texture, I think it should be cut into thin, almost transparent slices (like Parma ham), but it is also delicious cut slightly more thickly and eaten by itself, for me the ultimate piggy treat (see page 20) . I highly recommend a visit to Bayonne at Easter, for the Ham Fair, a tradition that goes back over 500 years.

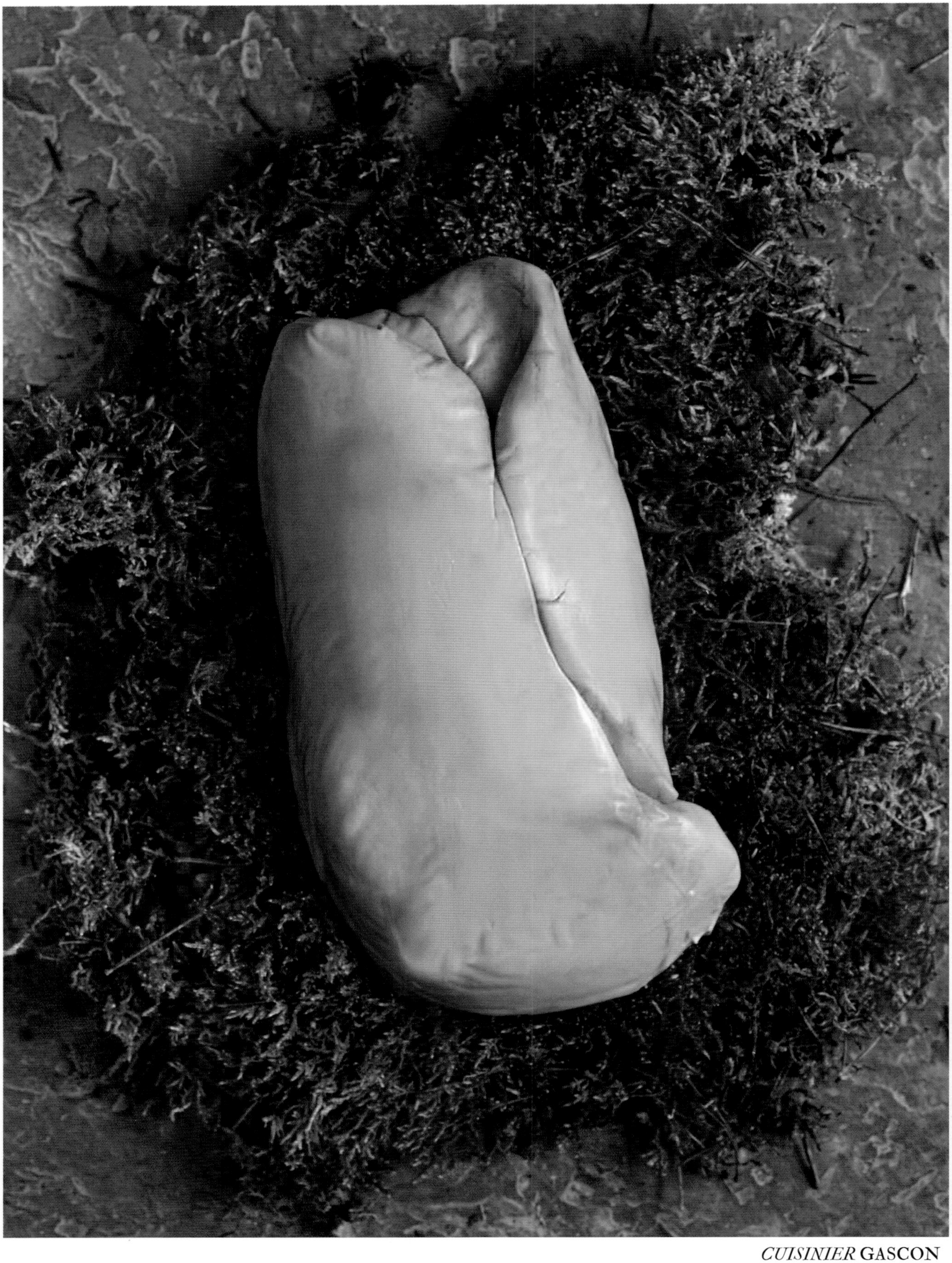

FOIE GRAS

CLASSIC FOIE GRAS *SAUTERNES*

This is the simplest and most classic way of preparing good *foie gras*. It is known as *'foie gras en torchon'*, cooking in a cloth. (You could use the less traditional foil as well.) You will need to use a sweet dessert wine – the classic Sauternes, or the slightly cheaper Monbazillac – plus at least a kilogram of duck fat.

Serves 4

INGREDIENTS

400g fresh duck *foie gras* (the large lobe only)

sea salt and freshly ground black pepper

200ml Sauternes or Monbazillac wine

1kg duck fat

1 Prepare the lobe as described on the *foie gras* gatefold facing page 96, making sure to clean all the nerves etc. Sprinkle with 1 teaspoon of sea salt and some freshly ground black pepper. Re-shape the lobe.

2 Pour the wine into a small pan and flambé until the flames die down then cool. Pour over the *foie gras* in a small dish, cover and chill for 24 hours. Then roll the *foie gras* in a muslin cloth, tie at both ends, and fit inside a terrine, about 1kg size.

3 Preheat the oven to just under 100°C/Gas ½. Melt and heat the duck fat heat in a pan to the same temperature. Pour the fat into the terrine and bake in the preheated oven for 20 minutes. Remove from the oven, cool and chill.

4 When ready to serve, remove the *foie gras* package from the fat (this can be used again and again, with its wonderful *foie gras* flavour). Unwrap the cloth and slice the *foie gras* thinly with a sharp knife dipped in hot water. Perfect with thinly sliced toast.

Genevieve with one of her ducks. Her family farm in Aubaron is one of the small suppliers to Maison Biraben (see suppliers page 256).

GATEFOLD 3: FOIE GRAS

FOIE GRAS

Foie gras is one of the culinary treasures of France's south-west, and many by-roads in the region are lined with signs for '*produits regionaux*' (which could be duck or goose *foie gras* or *confit*) or '*dégustation*' (taste before you buy).

'*Foie gras*' translates literally as 'fat liver'. To attain a fat liver, you must have a fat goose (*oie*) or duck (*canard*), which entails fattening or over-feeding the bird, a process known in French as *gavage*. The process is not new – paintings in the tombs of some Ancient Egyptians show farmers holding geese by the throat feeding them with balls of grain. It is thought they served the fattened creamy livers sweetened. And there are many apparent references in Greek and Roman literature to fattened livers served at sumptuous banquets, the geese fed a diet of figs. It was a technique applied to other animals too, fattening them before slaughter and it is interesting to note that wild ducks and geese will overfeed themselves before migrating. Maybe the Romans introduced the technique to the local Basque tribes in their province of Aquitania and the tradition continued for centuries in France, receiving a boost in the 17th century, when maize arrived from the New World, via Spain. *Foie gras* ducks and geese have been fed on maize ever since.

France is the world's primary producer of *foie gras*, the majority coming from Gascony, Les Landes and the Dordogne, where duck is the prime bird used; the other major *foie gras* area of France, Alsace, tends to specialise more in goose.

Foie gras used to be a seasonal product. As geese do not breed more than once a year, birds born in the spring and fattened in the autumn would be ready in early winter, coinciding with Christmas demand. Duck, however, are more prolific breeders, and can be bred for meat all year round and a by-product of the *gavage* are plump duck breasts, or *magrets*.

BUYING FOIE GRAS

In perhaps no other area of food 'manufacture' is the finished quality so dependent on how the product has been produced. Happy ducks and geese will deliver the best *foie gras* – it would be counter-productive for the farmer to maltreat his birds – and to be certain you have a proper liver, one that will not dissolve into a puddle of fat when in contact with your hot pan, you need to have a fair idea of its provenance.

In our restaurants, we buy duck livers from selected small and traditional suppliers in the south-west of France, and we look for livers of around 500g, which are usually firmer-textured. When buying raw livers, the two lobes (one slightly larger than the other) should be intact, a pale pink to beige in colour, without any visible defects on the surface, and so smooth as to be almost waxy in appearance. They should smell pleasant, not too strong.

You can buy duck *foie gras* throughout the year, while that of goose is best in November and January. Even with ducks, the summer is difficult; when the weather is too warm, the ducks are not that keen on eating -maybe they are happier swimming in cool water.

PREPARING FRESH FOIE GRAS

A *foie gras* lobe comes as a pair of lobes with one side slightly larger than the other. Otherwise they are treated in the same way, that is gently and with care.

First, if the *foie gras* is to be eaten lightly cooked or pressed (rather than simply sliced and fried see right) it needs to be brought to room temperature, around 20-30 minutes so the two halves can be gently pulled apart and then de-veined.

You will need a chopping board, a sheet of non-stick baking parchment paper, some hand sanitiser or thin sanitised gloves and a dessert or soup spoon with a rounded end to ease out the veins without breaking the flesh.

Foie gras is and always has been considered a luxury, and in France its consumption is usually associated with celebrations. For instance, because of its one-time seasonality, it used to be bought in the greatest quantity at Christmas time. Oddly enough, the Egyptians are said to have eaten *foie gras* as a pudding, and indeed until quite recently, it was eaten in France at the end of a meal, presumably when the sweeter wines were served.

Nowadays it has become an introduction to a meal, but still with a sweet white wine such as Sauternes. I also like to serve it marinated in a particular spirit, with a shot glass of that same spirit. Otherwise, a good Champagne or port would be ideal accompaniments. To try *foie gras* as a dessert see page 115, just like the Ancient Egyptians.

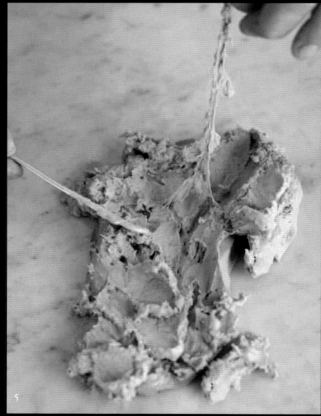

3 Locate the main veins at the centre of the larger lobe and using the tip of the handle of the spoon work the end under the main part of the nerve to expose it without cutting through it. Use a gentle scraping action to scrape away the flesh whilst you pull up the main nerve with your fingers then work your way along the oblique side or secondary nerves, again pulling them up gently with one hand as you scrape underneath with the spoon end.

4 Scrape gently and pull until you have exposed the length of all the nerves. When you have reached the end of the lobes, snip off the nerves with a sharp knife or small scissors.

5 Repeat the process with the smaller lobe. Then gently reassemble by pressing the two lobe sides together, wrap in cling film if liked and store, upside down, in the fridge.

PREPARING & COOKING FOIE GRAS

I serve *foie gras* in many ways in my restaurants: salted, smoked, sautéed, baked and steamed. It can also be eaten raw and chilled, like a *carpaccio* (see page 110). The simplest way of cooking a lobe of *foie gras* is by sautéing. Season the liver well, and preheat a good non-stick pan (no oil). When the pan is hot and starts smoking, add the *foie gras*: do not crowd the pan. Sear for about 40 seconds, then turn over and cook for a further 40 or so seconds (but this will depend on size). The pieces should have browned nicely. Remove from the pan, and if cooking other pieces, get rid of any burned fat.

I often marinate *foie gras* before cooking it. Armagnac is traditionally used in Gascony, but Sauternes (or the cheaper Monbazillac or sweet Jurançon) are also well known. Over the years I have explored other marinade alcohols such as Sangria, saké, ouzo or Baileys. See the step-by-step instruction on preparing a lobe above and inspirational ways of cooking it on page overleaf.

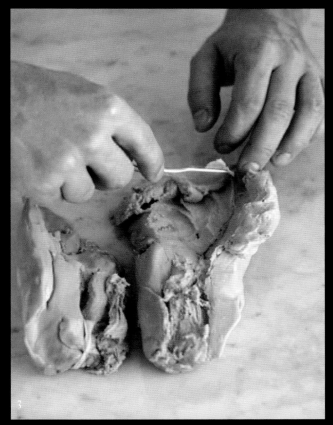

To slice and fry fresh *foie gras* – there is no need to devein. Just cut slices about 1.5cm thick and spread out on non-stick baking parchment ready for cooking. Or, the slices can be individually wrapped in cling film and frozen. These slices can then be thawed for about 30 minutes and then fried as normal.

1 Remove the *foie gras* lobes from the fridge at least 20-30 minutes before de-veining to ensure the smooth soft flesh is not broken and you can easily pull out the nerves.

2 Lightly oil the worktop or chopping board and lay a non-stick parchment sheet on top. Place the lobe on the sheet, large lobe down. Open both lobes very gently apart to expose the central nerves. The nerve positions are very similar in both lobes (one is always a little larger than the other).

Foie gras is quite delicious cooked lightly on a barbecue over smouldering pine branches or needles. Either – place it straight on top of a griddle with smouldering pine branches underneath to just sear the outside, about 2 minutes, then remove (see picture right/below). Or, cook it wrapped in foil (see above) to retain the delicious cooking juices similar to the eclade style, see page 29. You'll have a beautifully aromatic *foie gras* with pine flavoured fat to die for.

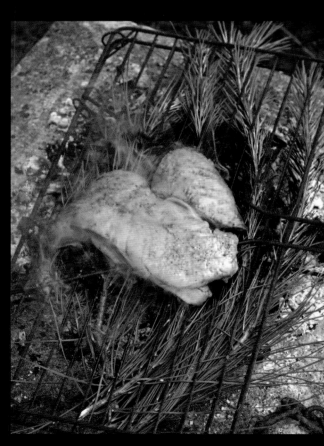

1 Tear off a large sheet of foil, place on a barbecue grill and top with several handfuls of dried pine needles.

2 Tear another sheet of foil at least double the size of a lobe of *foie gras*. Fold this in two; place the *foie gras* in the middle, season with salt and Espelette pepper and wrap up the foil into a parcel sealing the ends.

3 Light the pine needles and when light and flaming, place the *foie gras* parcel on top, join sides up.

4 Cook for 2 minutes then remove and carefully unwrap, saving the delicious aromatic fat and juices inside.

FOIE GRAS
MAURESQUE

How many of you try to recreate memories of Greek holidays, stuffing a bottle of ouzo in your return luggage only to find it languishes in the kitchen cupboard for months afterwards? Well, I have a solution for that – use it as a marinade for *foie gras*. Ouzo is basically a pastis, a spirit with an aniseed flavour. We serve this simply pan-fried with toasted brioche and an *orgeat* (almond) jelly. The flavours are those of Mauresque ('Moorish'), a popular cocktail in southern France, of *orgeat* syrup, pastis and iced water, and you could drink this with your *foie gras*!

Serves 4

INGREDIENTS

400g fresh duck *foie gras* (the large lobe only), de-veined (see *foie gras* gatefold facing p96)

200ml ouzo or pastis

50g granulated sugar

fine sea salt and freshly ground black pepper

1 tablespoon *orgeat* syrup (see right)

1 teaspoon agar-agar flakes

4 slices brioche

1   Marinate the *foie gras* in the ouzo for up to 24 hours in the fridge, then drain off the ouzo into a small bowl. Roll the *foie gras* tightly in clingfilm like a sausage.

2   Add enough ouzo to the sugar to moisten it, then leave to dry out at room temperature. Grind it to a fine powder with a pestle and mortar and mix with a little salt for an aromatic, anise-flavoured powder.

3   Put a large pan of water on to boil and fit a steamer basket inside. Place the rolled *foie gras* in the basket, then cover and steam for 10 minutes. Remove the *foie gras* carefully, cool and chill.

4   Meanwhile, make the *orgeat* jelly. Boil the *orgeat* syrup with 100ml water, add some freshly ground black pepper and stir in the agar-agar flakes until dissolved. Simmer for 1 minute and pour into a small container to cool, then chill until set.

5   To serve, unmould the *orgeat* jelly and chop into small cubes. Toast the brioche slices. Unwrap the *foie gras* and cut into slightly larger cubes, then toss lightly in the ground sugar. Serve the *foie gras* – which looks like Turkish Delight! – with the toast and *orgeat* jelly cubes.

COOK'S NOTES
ORGEAT SYRUP

This is a sweet syrup made from freshly ground almonds, sugar and rosewater or orange-flower water. It can be made at home (there are recipes on the net), or bought in good delicatessens. It is most famously used in the Mai Tai cocktail.

FOIE GRAS *on the ROCKS!*

The 'on the rocks' of the title comes from some large pebbles I picked up in Gascony, wanting to use them as platters on which to serve *foie gras*, which I have since done at Club Gascon. There is a double meaning though, as the liquid used to marinate the *foie gras* – here gender divided – is served as a shot on the side, again on the rocks (this time ice). The *foie gras* for *les monsieurs* is marinated in Armagnac and the shot is *Floc de Gascogne*; the *foie gras* for *mesdames* is marinated in elderflower cordial, while the shot is a glass of the same cordial topped up with Champagne.

Serves 4

INGREDIENTS

400g fresh duck *foie gras* (the large lobe only), de-veined (see *foie gras* gatefold facing page 96)

sea salt and freshly ground black pepper

100ml elderflower cordial

2 tablespoons Armagnac

INGREDIENTS TO SERVE

1 *pain d'épices* (see right)

2 tablespoons pomegranate seeds

3 tablespoons blueberries

a few dandelion leaves, washed

some baby cress, washed

1   Divide the *foie gras* in two, season with salt and peppers then marinate one half in the elderflower cordial and the other in Armagnac. Cover and set both aside in the fridge for 6 hours.

2   Meanwhile, cut some wafer-thin slices of *pain d'épice* and dry out in a low oven until crisp, about 1–2 hours. Reserve in an airtight tin.

3   Remove the *foie gras* from the marinades, drain and pat dry. (Save both marinades to sprinkle as *jus*.) Wrap each tightly in clingfilm as a sausage.

4   Prepare a pan and steaming basket and cook the *foie gras* rolls in the steamer basket for 10 minutes. Remove and cool then chill.

5   Unwrap each *foie gras* roll in turn and slice thinly with a knife dipped in very hot water. Serve on plates, two plates for ladies and two for men, sprinkled with the appropriate marinades and garnished with the pomegranate seeds, blueberries, leaves and gingerbread toasts. If the men and the ladies insist on trying each other's foie gras, then that is perfectly acceptable!

COOK'S NOTES PAIN D'ÉPICES

This is a rich spiced French cake, literally 'spice bread', not to be confused with British gingerbread.

PRES ET PATURAGES

FOIE GRAS *SANGRIA*

A variation of the *foie gras* with ouzo on page 97, except this time you make a jelly with a Sangria. One is Greek or Turkish, this one is definitely Spanish – but then Spain is very close to Gascony, and there are many ingredients and ideas which are shared. Sangria is something we drink in the summer, so this dish is very summery, I feel.

Serves 4

INGREDIENTS

400g fresh duck *foie gras* (the large lobe only), de-veined (see *foie gras* gatefold facing page 96)

sea salt

1 To make the Sangria, put the red wine into a medium saucepan with the Cassis, Lillet, sugar and spices. Bring to the boil, then simmer for 20 minutes until reduced by about three-quarters to 250ml. Remove from the heat and cool.

2 Place the *foie gras* in a shallow dish and pour over the cooled Sangria. Leave to marinate for 4 hours.

3 Remove the *foie gras* from the Sangria (which you retain), and roll in clingfilm as a sausage. Put a large pan of water on to boil and fit a steamer basket inside. Place the rolled *foie gras* in the basket, then cover and steam for 10 minutes. Remove the *foie gras* carefully, cool and chill.

4 Meanwhile, make the jelly. Reheat the Sangria until almost boiling, stir in the soaked gelatine, stir until dissolved, then pour into a shallow dish. Leave to cool and then chill until set. Unmould on to a chopping board and chop into small cubes.

5 To serve, slice the *foie gras* thinly and serve on plates with the chopped jelly alongside.

SANGRIA JELLY INGREDIENTS

1 x 75cl bottle Spanish red wine

100ml crème de Cassis

5 tablespoons red Lillet

100g sugar

a pinch each of ground cinnamon, 5-spice powder and freshly ground black pepper

1½ gelatine leaves, soaked in cold water

ROLLED FOIE GRAS PIQUILLO PEPPERS

Foie gras is very easy to shape and we like to do this in clingfilm at the restaurant with a filling of smoky piquillo peppers. Steam the rolls lightly to cook, then chill and slice.

Serves 4

INGREDIENTS

400g fresh duck *foie gras* (the large lobe only)

100g piquillo peppers, drained

sea salt and Espelette pepper

1 De-vein the *foie gras* (see *foie gras* gatefold facing page 96), divide it into two long pieces and season with salt and Espelette pepper.

2 Place one half of *foie gras* lengthways on a sheet of clingfilm then lay the piquillos on top, trimmed to fit. Top with the rest of the *foie gras* and roll up in the clingfilm, twisting the ends like a sausage.

3 Put a large pan of water on to boil. Lay the clingfilmed sausage in a steamer basket and steam for about 10 minutes over a medium heat.

4 Then remove the roll, cool on a plate and pierce through the clingfilm a few times to release the fatty juices. These you should gather into a small jug.

5 Chill the roll until firm, then unwrap and serve in slices with the reserved juices brushed over each slice.

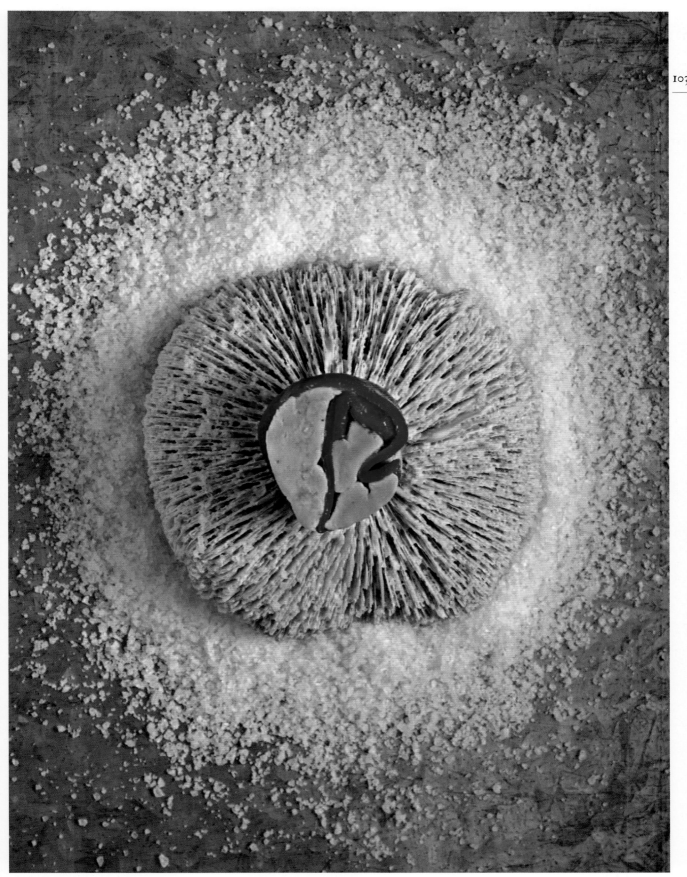

PRES ET PATURAGES

FOIE GRAS & CRAB *TERRINE with PIPÉRADE*

The surf and turf element of this recipe is something I really like. It is not particularly Gascon, although with the *pipérade* it could be Basque. The layering effect of this terrine is particularly attractive. Serve it in slices with more *pipérade* on the side and a *tranche* of good toast. You could also roast some crab claws to echo the crab-meat content, which you serve warm, to be eaten in the hand.

Serves 4

INGREDIENTS

400g fresh duck *foie gras* (the large lobe only)

sea salt and Espelette pepper

100g *pipérade* (see page 39), plus extra to serve

100g fresh white crab meat

crab claws to serve (optional)

1   Prepare and de-vein the *foie gras* (see *foie gras* gatefold facing page 96). Season with salt and Espelette pepper.

2   Heat the oven to 100°C/Gas ½. Lightly oil and line the base of a small (500ml size) terrine.

3   Place a third of the *foie gras* on the base of the terrine. Then mix the *pipérade* into the crab meat and spread half this on top of the *foie gras*. Press another third of *foie gras* on top, then the remainder of the crab and *pipérade*. Finally top with the last of the *foie gras*.

4   Place the terrine in a small roasting pan and pour enough boiling water into the pan to come halfway up the sides of the terrine dish (a *bain-marie* or water bath), then cook for about 45 minutes.

5   Check the centre temperature with a probe; it should register at least 60°C. Remove the terrine from the oven and cool, weighted down lightly on top to press the mixture as it cools.

6   Chill, then serve in slices with more *pipérade*, and crab claws on the side if liked.

TERRINE OF *FOIE GRAS, RABBIT* & LETTUCE

An unusual and delicious coarse-cut terrine to be served in slices as a starter. You don't have to use the best *foie gras*, simply any spare or leftover that you don't know how to use! It's set in the fridge, but remains fairly soft, with its *foie gras* 'sauce'. It's nice served with a green salad dressed with a vinaigrette made with *Moût de Raisin* mustard (see below).

Serves 6-8

INGREDIENTS

4 rabbit legs

1 small onion, sliced

1 large sprig fresh thyme

2 bay leaves

1 fat garlic clove

6 gelatine leaves, soaked in cold water

1 tablespoon duck fat or olive oil

sea salt and freshly ground black pepper

300ml Sangria Jelly (see page 101)

2 baby gem lettuces

300g fresh duck *foie gras*, at room temperature

1   Bone the rabbit legs, and dice the flesh into small 1cm cubes. Place the bones in a small pan, with the onion, thyme, bay leaves and garlic clove, and cover with cold water to about 2cm above the bones. Bring to the boil, then cover and simmer on a low heat for 30 minutes. Strain the stock into a bowl and set aside. Stir in the soaked gelatine leaves until dissolved, and cool.

2   Sauté the diced rabbit meat in a pan with the duck fat or oil for 3 minutes. Season and mix in the Sangria jelly. Cool and set aside.

3   Separate out the baby gem leaves and cut into strips about 3cm wide.

4   Cut the *foie gras* into small 1cm cubes, mix with the rabbit stock and whizz in a blender until smooth.

5   Line a 1kg terrine with clingfilm. Pour in half the *foie gras* mixture and then add half the baby gem leaves, then half the diced rabbit and Sangria jelly. Repeat the layers once more, using all the ingredients, then chill until firm and set.

6   Unmould the terrine and slice thinly with a sharp knife dipped into boiling water.

COOK'S NOTES

MOUT DE RAISIN

Moût de Raisin is a strong and sweet mustard, sometimes called Moutarde Violette *(because of its colour), made from the leftover grape must in wine making. Use it instead of other mustards in your vinaigrettes.*

FOIE GRAS
BORDELAISE

Foie gras is traditionally complemented with sweet dessert wines, and is good too with port. These little baked custards – what I would call 'flans' – are served at room temperature with a reduced port sauce. They resemble crème brûlées, and can actually be caramelised on top with some brown sugar. To balance the sweetness, you could then sprinkle some salt and some nut and seed muesli (see page 16) on top.

Serves 4

INGREDIENTS

150ml milk

110g fresh duck *foie gras*, diced

2 free-range eggs, beaten

sea salt

300ml ruby port

3 tablespoons reduced duck or chicken stock

1 Heat the oven to 100°C/Gas ¼. Lightly grease four medium small ramekins, about 100ml capacity and place in a small roasting pan.

2 Scald the milk until about to boil. Place the *foie gras* cubes and eggs into a food processor or blender and whizz to a purée whilst you pour in the hot milk through the spout on the lid. Add a little salt.

3 Strain through a sieve into the ramekins. Pour enough boiling water into the roasting pan to come halfway up the sides of the dishes.

4 Bake in the preheated oven for 10 minutes until the top starts to skin, then remove immediately from the oven to cool.

5 Meanwhile, boil the port down in a shallow saucepan until reduced by two-thirds to around 100ml, then mix in the stock and a little salt. Remove from the heat and cool.

6 When ready to serve, pour some sauce on top of each ramekin and serve.

FOIE GRAS POPCORN

This is probably the most fancy – and the most exciting – of my *foie gras* recipes. As is well known, geese and duck are fed on corn before they are ready for slaughter, so the flesh is already imbued with a sweet corn flavour. We enhance this further by smoking the *foie gras* lightly over denuded corn cobs and spooning a corn sauce on the side. To top this, I also like to caramelise fresh corn kernels to scatter around the plate. You don't need to do all this at home, you could just use one of the suggested garnishes.

Serves 4

INGREDIENTS

400g fresh duck *foie gras* (the large lobe only)

olive oil

sea salt and freshly ground black pepper

3 fresh corn cobs

1 garlic clove

2 teaspoons mascarpone cheese

2 tablespoons caster sugar

8 baby corns, slit in half

1   De-vein the *foie gras* (see *foie gras* gatefold facing page 96). Then drizzle lightly with some olive oil and season lightly. Wrap in foil and chill until ready to serve.

2   Strip the kernels off the three fresh cobs and set them aside. Keep the denuded cobs, and dry them in a low oven for about an hour.

3   Make the corn sauce. Put 150ml water into a saucepan with a third of the sweetcorn kernels, 2 tablespoons olive oil, the garlic and some salt and pepper. Simmer for about 8 minutes then remove from the heat and tip into a blender. Whizz until smooth.

4   Pour the mixture into a sieve placed over a bowl and rub the mixture through with the back of a ladle. Return the mixture to the pan, mix in the mascarpone and check the seasoning. Keep warm.

5   Now place the dried corn cobs in the base of a wok or over barbecue coals and heat until they start to smoke.

6   Put the foil parcels of *foie gras* on a rack on top of the wok or barbecue, cover and cook for 10 minutes. Set aside for 10 minutes to cool, still in the foil.

7   In the meantime, heat a large frying pan until hot and scatter in the remaining corn kernels. Sprinkle with the sugar and, shaking the pan over a medium heat, cook the kernels until they are coated in the sugar and beginning to caramelise. Tip out into a bowl to cool.

8   Unwrap the *foie gras* then cut in thick slices. Pan-fry in another hot non-stick frying pan for about 2 minutes until lightly golden on each side. Keep warm whilst you quickly toss in the baby corn to heat in the same pan fat.

9   Serve the *foie gras* with the warmed sauce, small baby corns and caramelised 'popcorn' alongside.

CARPACCIO OF FOIE GRAS *with* FIGS & WALNUT

Foie gras that has been reared in a wholesome, natural state (see *foie gras* gatefold G4:1) is so good it can be eaten raw, simply cut in wafer-thin slices and sprinkled lightly with what I like to call 'crazy salt' – sea salt mixed with Espelette pepper. You can also add a drizzle of Xipister vinegar or a light brushing of Sauternes wine. We serve this shaped as roses on a bed of a *carpaccio* of figs accompanied by chopped fresh walnuts. It is also extremely good served with a glass of fine port.

Serves 4

INGREDIENTS

400g fresh duck *foie gras* (the large lobe only)

8 fresh black figs

1 Prepare the *foie gras* (see *foie gras* gatefold facing page 96). Keep chilled until almost ready to serve.

2 Snip the tops off the figs and cut each in half lengthways. Lay a sheet of non-stick baking parchment paper out on a large board and press each fig half cut-side down, then cover with another non-stick sheet. Using a large rolling pin roll the fig halves as thin as you can, 3mm thick or less, (like a £1 coin).

3 Then lift the figs still in the paper on to a flat sheet and freeze until solid. (Sometimes, we then use a metal round cutter and cut out neat rounds of frozen fig.)

4 When ready to serve, cut the *foie gras* in wafer-thin slices. We obviously use a slicer, but you could use a Japanese mandolin or a very sharp knife dipped in hot water between each slice.

5 Lay some frozen figs on a plate, then top with the *foie gras* slices, which you can fold in a *rosace* or circular rose pattern. (You could do this slightly in advance, but you must clingfilm each plate, and leave in the fridge.)

6 Mix together the salt and Espelette pepper, my crazy salt. Sprinkle over the *foie gras*, then drizzle or carefully brush over the vinegar or Sauternes and walnut oil.

7 Scatter walnuts around and serve with toasted brioche slices.

INGREDIENTS TO SERVE

2 teaspoons *fleur de sel*

¼ teaspoon Espelette pepper

Xipister vinegar (see page 32) or Sauternes wine

a little walnut oil

a few fresh shelled walnuts

4–8 slices country bread or brioche, toasted

PRES ET PATURAGES

CLUB GASCON FOIE GRAS SANDWICHES with BABY CORN PICKLE

The ultimate snack is a brioche bap sliced and filled with *foie gras*, a tomato compote and a side pickle of baby corns.

Serves 4

INGREDIENTS

400g fresh duck *foie gras* (the large lobe only)

sea salt

4 small to medium brioche buns (or rich soft baps)

1 baby gem lettuce, leaves separated

BABY CORN PICKLE INGREDIENTS

100ml sherry vinegar

100ml olive oil

½–1 teaspoon Espelette pepper

40g sugar

8 baby corn

1. First, make the pickle. Put the sherry vinegar, oil, 100ml water, Espelette pepper (to taste), sugar and a little salt into a saucepan. Bring to the boil, stirring until the sugar dissolves, then add the baby corns. Simmer for 5 minutes, then remove from the heat and cool.

2. For the compote, strip the kernels from the cobs by cutting down with a sharp knife. Dip the tomatoes into a pan of just-boiled water, then skin and dice the flesh. Simmer the tomatoes until they become juice, then add the sliced onion and cook gently in a pan for about 30 minutes. Mix in the corn with the garlic and bay and cook for another 15 minutes. Stir in the balsamic, Xipister and sugar and cook for 2 minutes more. Season and cool.

3. Cut the *foie gras* into four thick slices. Heat a non-stick frying pan and cook the *foie gras* just enough to sear on both sides, about 30 seconds, then remove.

4. Slice the buns in half and place them to heat in the fat remaining in the pan.

5. Sandwich the *foie gras* in the buns with a spoonful of compote and some lettuce leaves in between. Serve the pickle on the side.

TOMATO AND CORN COMPOTE INGREDIENTS

2 corn on the cobs

2 beef tomatoes

1 small onion, sliced

2 garlic cloves, crushed

2 bay leaves

2 teaspoons balsamic vinegar

2 teaspoon Xipister vinegar (see page 32)

1 teaspoon sugar

TASTOU

This dish is perhaps the ultimate toasted sandwich –
bread spread with *foie gras*-flavoured fat (left over from
cooking *foie gras*), filled with truffle and lightly grilled.

Serves 4

INGREDIENTS

1 fat garlic clove,
sliced in half

8 medium slices country
bread

4 tablespoons duck *foie
gras* fat

50g black truffle

crazy salt (2 teaspoons
fleur de sel mixed with
½ teaspoon Espelette
pepper)

1   Rub the cut side of the garlic halves over one side of each of the bread
    slices and spread these with the *foie gras* fat.

2   Slice the truffle as thinly as you can and arrange over four of the
    fat-spread slices, then sandwich together with the other bread slices,
    fat-side down. Wrap each sandwich in clingfilm and chill overnight.

3   The next day, preheat the oven to 200°C/Gas 6.

4   Remove the clingfilm, and place the sandwiches on a baking sheet.
    Bake in the preheated oven for about 10 minutes until crisp and
    golden.

5   Sprinkle with crazy salt, cut into quarters and serve immediately.

TURRON FOIE GRAS

Foie gras, surprisingly enough, can be served as a dessert, and this recipe is often on offer in Club Gascon. The *foie gras* is first marinated in Baileys Irish Cream then, after cooking, is cut in squares and pressed into a mould with chunks of *turrón*, a soft Spanish nougat, and walnuts. The finished dish is served with a passionfruit sauce. The idea is quite a challenge for many customers, but the tastes are amazing.

Serves 4–6

INGREDIENTS

350g fresh duck *foie gras*

3 tablespoons Baileys Irish Cream

2 teaspoons caster sugar

65g *turrón* nougat, cut in small cubes

50g fresh walnut halves

6 passionfruits

1 tablespoon lemon juice

10g cocoa powder

some small crisp meringues, to serve

1   De-vein the *foie gras* (see *foie gras* gatefold facing page 96), then lay in a dish and sprinkle over the Baileys and sugar. Cover and leave for 5 hours in the fridge, turning once or twice.

2   Preheat the oven to around 75°C/Gas ¼.

3   Place the *foie gras* in a heatproof dish, cover and bake for 20 minutes. Remove and cool, then drain off the pan juices.

4   Re-shape the *foie gras* in a mould (like a small loaf tin), pressing in the cubes of nougat and walnut halves, like a chess board. Cover the top with clingfilm and weigh lightly down as you chill the mould until firm.

5   Meanwhile, make the passionfruit sauce. Halve and scoop out the flesh and seeds from all the fruits. Put two-thirds of this in a small saucepan with the lemon juice. Boil for about 2 minutes, then strain into a cup through a tea strainer to catch the seeds. Return the juice to the pan and scoop in the remaining fruits.

6   When ready to serve, unmould the *foie gras* mixture, then cut into bite-sized cubes, using a hot knife. Lightly dust each cube with cocoa powder by sifting through a fine sieve.

7   Serve with the passionfruit sauce spooned around, and pieces of meringue.

PLUMES
& POILS

The rôtie in one of Gascony's
crown jewels – probably the
world's most famous bistro –
and certainly the original:
La Tupina, Bordeaux.

PRES ET PATURAGES

GASCONY PIE

This is a great favourite at our bistro, Le Comptoir. It actually has nothing to do with traditional Gascony, although it uses very familiar Gascon ingredients (mushrooms and duck). We invented it some seven years ago, and is one of my favourite recipes in the book. The name suggests pastry, of course, but it is really a little baked pâté which looks, when turned out, as if encased in pastry. It's easy to make, and delicious to eat.

Serves 4

INGREDIENTS

2 large duck *magrets* (about 400g total weight)

2 free-range egg whites

fine sea salt and freshly ground black pepper

300ml double cream, chilled

100g *chanterelle* or brown chestnut mushrooms, finely chopped

20g butter, plus a little extra, melted

1 First, remove the skin from the *magrets* (use in duck scratchings, see page 15), then check for any sinews in the flesh and cut out. Then chop the flesh roughly and place in a food processor with the egg whites plus 1 teaspoon salt and ½ teaspoon pepper. Whizz on full speed for about 3 minutes, stopping the machine twice and scraping down the sides. (In the restaurant, we would then rub this purée through a fine sieve for the ultimate smooth velvety texture.)

2 Preheat the oven to 180°C/Gas 4.

3 Scrape the mixture into a large bowl and mix in 250ml of the double cream, using a whisk. Chill whilst you make the mushroom filling.

4 If using *chanterelles*, wash in tepid water then pat dry. Sauté in 20g of butter over a medium high heat until softened, about 3 minutes, then season lightly.

5 Drain the cooking juices off into a cup and tip the mushrooms on to a plate. Return the juices to the pan and add the remaining cream. Bring to the boil and cook for a minute or so until reduced by half, then return the mushrooms. Remove from the heat, tip out on to a plate and cool.

6 Brush the insides of six ramekins (medium 120ml size) with the melted butter.

7 Spoon about two-thirds of the creamy duck purée into the ramekins, making a well in the centre with the back of a teaspoon. Divide the mushrooms between them, then top with the remaining duck purée and smooth flat with the back of a teaspoon.

8 Place the ramekins in a small roasting pan. Pour boiling water into the roasting pan to come to within 1 cm of the top of the ramekins, then cover the whole pan with a sheet of foil. Bake in the centre of the preheated oven for 18–20 minutes until the tops of the 'little pies' are just firm when pressed. Remove from the oven and peel off the foil.

9 Stand the ramekins for 5 minutes, then run a table knife around the sides and invert each 'pie' on to a serving plate. Serve garnished with a nice green salad with bacon lardons and hazelnuts.

LE *FAMEUX* *CASSOULET*

You may well know that there is not one ultimate *cassoulet* recipe but dozens, and each town in the South-west will claim theirs is the original. As I don't want to stir up this hornets' nest, I give you my mother's own personal favourite, which does not have a crust of breadcrumbs (my family likes the *cassoulet* moist and saucy). One thing that you must bear in mind is always to cook a large *cassoulet* at least a day ahead, which enhances the flavour, then you can reheat it as required. It is the perfect party dish.

Serves 10-12

INGREDIENTS

600g dried Tarbais or Lingot beans, soaked overnight in cold water

2 onions, chopped

2 carrots, chopped

200g air-dried ham, e.g. Bayonne, chopped

200g pork fat (*couenne*) or unsmoked fatty bacon, chopped

1 ham bone, chopped into 3–4 chunks

1 litre duck or chicken stock, or water

cloves from 1 head garlic, about 10, crushed

sea salt and freshly ground black pepper

4 ripe tomatoes, finely chopped or crushed in a mouli

5 Toulouse sausages, halved

5 *confit* duck legs, halved

a little extra virgin olive oil or some duck fat, to serve

1 Drain the soaked beans and place in a large saucepan covered with water, bring to the boil, then simmer for about 5 minutes and drain.

2 In a large ovenproof saucepan (like a Le Creuset), sauté the chopped vegetables with the chopped ham and pork fat for about 10 minutes until softened. There is no need to add any oil or duck fat as the pork fat will render down.

3 Preheat the oven to 150°C/Gas 2.

4 Add the beans, ham bone pieces, stock (or water) and garlic to the vegetables and ham. Season lightly and bring to a gentle boil. Then tip the crushed tomatoes on top, cover and place in the preheated oven for 1 hour.

5 Uncover after the hour and add the sausages and duck pieces, re-cover and return the *cassoulet* to the oven for another 30–60 minutes, or until the beans are tender. The dish should still be quite 'juicy'. Remove the ham bones, pull off any tender meat and add to the *cassoulet*.

6 Ideally, cool the *cassoulet* and store in the fridge for at least a day, so that the flavours mature. Then reheat gently until hot and bubbling and mix in some olive oil or duck fat to enrich. If you really do like a crusty top, heat the *cassoulet* under a hot grill for a few minutes. If you need anything else – the *cassoulet* is filling! – a green salad would be good.

COOK'S NOTES

A true Gascon would choose the thin-skinned Tarbais beans for the ultimate cassoulet. They are grown around the village of Tarbes, and traditionally planted with corn so the pole acts as a prop for the vine to cling to as it grows. The vine and beans become entangled and so must be harvested by hand. The beans are bigger than haricots, and their main advantage is that when stewed for a long time, they retain their shape.

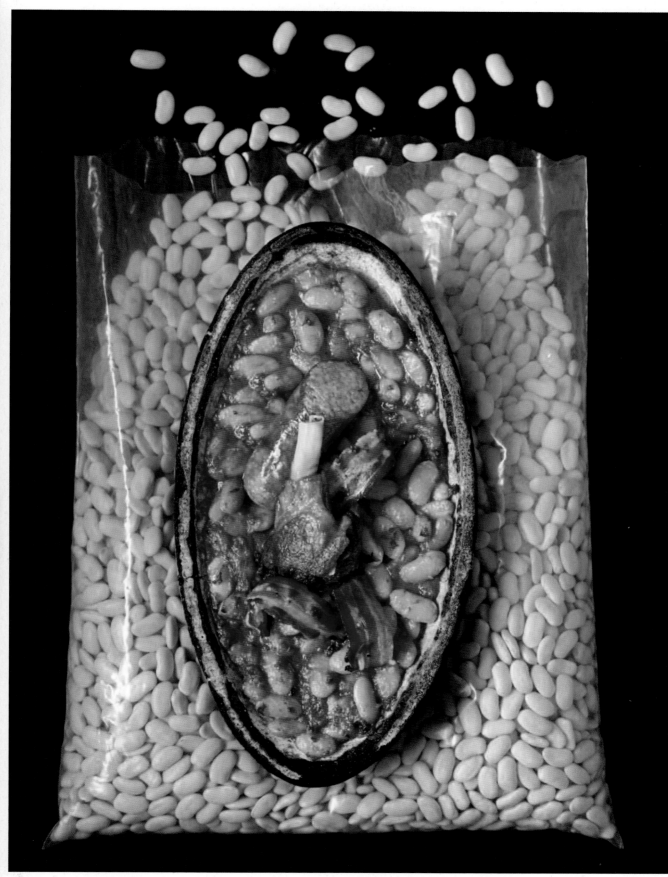

PRES ET PATURAGES

DUCK *CONFIT* with *CREME* FORTE

Duck *confit* is one of the most important dishes of Gascony. For success, you must buy some fat duck legs, you can't use normal duck legs. The thickness of the skin will give you a clue as to the quality of the duck; it should have a lot of fat, like ham. Basically, with a *confit*, what you are doing is preserving. After the duck has been cooked in its fat, it can be cooled and then stored covered with its fat. It will keep for weeks in the fridge.

If the *confit* duck legs are unmistakeably Gascon, the sauce is an invention of mine. To complete the south-western effect, you could serve the *confit* with some *pommes sarladaise* (from Sarlat, in the Dordogne, a bit further north). They are potatoes fried with garlic in duck or goose fat. But after that combination, you wouldn't be able to work, and would have to relax for the rest of the afternoon.

Serves 4

INGREDIENTS

4 large duck legs

about 100g coarse sea salt

about 1 litre duck fat

2 large sprigs fresh rosemary

2 large shallots, thinly sliced

150ml double cream

3 tablespoons white wine vinegar

freshly ground black pepper

1 Place the legs in a shallow dish and sprinkle over the salt, rubbing into the skin. Leave for 24 hours, then remove the legs and brush away as much salt as possible. Place the legs in a thick-based saucepan side by side. Pour over the fat and add the rosemary sprigs.

2 Heat for a few minutes, then lower the heat to very low and cook for 2–3 hours until the tip of a knife pushed into the centre of a leg indicates it is very tender. Remove from the heat and carefully lift out the legs with a slotted spoon on to kitchen paper to drain and cool. (Don't discard the fat. Strain it through a fine sieve into a large container, cool and chill in the fridge for many other uses.)

3 In the meantime, make the sauce. Put the shallots, cream, vinegar and some pepper into a medium saucepan and heat slowly until it starts to thicken. Simmer for about 5 minutes, then set aside.

4 When ready to serve, heat a little of the saved duck fat in a large frying pan and reheat the legs on the skin-side only until crisp and browned. Don't be tempted to turn them or the skin will not crisp. If the flesh is not completely hot after the skin is well browned, then remove them to a medium oven to continue to heat through.

5 Serve the legs, browned-skin-side up, with the sauce on the side.

DUCK & *CARROTS* *A L'ORANGE*

This is the way we like to serve a great French classic in the Club Gascon style. The orange dressing is best made in a large batch, and the remainder stored in the fridge to be used as a general (but delicious and unusual) salad dressing. Muscatel vinegar is made from the white Muscatel grape; it is smooth, bitter-sweet and golden in colour, great with strawberries.

Serves 4

INGREDIENTS

1 whole duck, about 4–5kg

sea salt, freshly ground black pepper and Espelette pepper

500g baby carrots, trimmed and halved lengthways if necessary

ORANGE SAUCE INGREDIENTS

500ml duck stock (made from carcass and flavourings, see method)

50g sugar

3 tablespoons Muscatel vinegar

2 tablespoons sherry vinegar

grated zest and juice of 3 oranges

5 tablespoons Curaçao

2 fat garlic cloves, roughly chopped

juice of ½ lemon

ORANGE DRESSING INGREDIENTS

12 sugar cubes

2 oranges

1 free-range egg yolk

1 tablespoon sherry vinegar

200ml grapeseed oil

1   Cut the duck into portions. Pull the legs out from the body and, using a very sharp knife, cut them where the thigh joins the body. Then, using the same knife, slice off the breasts from the carcass, making sure the tip of the knife is always in contact with the rib cage so you keep all the flesh on the fillet.

2   To make the stock for the sauce, using strong poultry shears, cut the carcass into four chunks and place in a large saucepan. Cover with about 1.5 litres cold water plus some onion, bay leaf, thyme sprigs and a little seasoning. Bring to the boil, then simmer until reduced down to about 500ml. Strain the stock off and reserve. Discard the bones etc.

3   To make the orange sauce, put the sugar and two vinegars into a medium saucepan, and bring to the boil, stirring. Cook until reduced by half. Then add the orange zest and juice, the Curaçao, garlic, lemon juice and some seasoning. Again cook until reduced by half. Then add 500ml stock and boil until reduced down by two-thirds to a syrupy sauce. Strain through a sieve and set aside in a smaller saucepan.

4   To make the orange dressing, rub the sugar cubes over the skins of the oranges to extract the zest. Then juice the oranges. Place the sugar and juice in a medium bowl with the egg yolk and vinegar. Whisk with a balloon whisk or hand-beater until smooth, then gradually trickle in the oil as if making mayonnaise, adding a little seasoning to help it all emulsify. Set aside.

5   Blanch the carrots in boiling water for about 2 minutes, then drain and rinse in cold water to cool down. Drain again and set aside.

6   Now you are ready to cook the duck. Heat a large non-stick pan and when hot add the duck legs, pressing them to the hot pan to help brown. Turn as necessary. Season and cook on a medium heat for about 30 minutes, turning, until tender. Remove the legs and keep warm. Then raise the heat.

7   Slash the duck breast skins in a criss-cross pattern with a sharp-bladed knife, and press the breasts skin-side down into the pan. Cook for 5 minutes (draining off any fat that drains out) on each side until the breast meat feels just firm. Remove from the pan and rest for 5 minutes.

8   Return the legs and breast to the pan and pour over the orange sauce. Bring to the boil and simmer for about 2 minutes to slightly reduce the sauce.

9   Reheat the carrots in a third of the dressing over a low heat (keep the rest for later). Then to serve the duck, cut through the leg and thigh to separate. Slice the breasts on the diagonal and divide the slices and the leg pieces and their sauce between four warmed dinner plates. Spoon the carrots and dressing alongside the duck. Nice with baby new potatoes and a green vegetable like beans, shredded cabbage or a salad. You could sprinkle some muesli on top for added crunch if you like (see page 16).

PRES ET PATURAGES

DUCK *CAKE*

Gascons excel at wholesome 'gutsy' dishes, like this potato cake topped with shredded *confit* of duck mixed with a garlicky *persillade*. It's not traditional, more playing on the theme of the English fishcake, but with Gascon ingredients! Serve with a well-seasoned rocket salad.

Serves 4

INGREDIENTS

2 *confit* duck legs from an 800g jar

600g potatoes

sea salt and freshly ground black pepper

100g butter, chilled and cut into small cubes

10 garlic cloves, finely chopped

leaves from 1 bunch (about 30g) flat-leaf parsley, finely chopped

1 Remove the duck *confit* from the jar and pat dry, then shred the duck flesh finely, discarding the bones. Save some of the fat for heating the duck shreds, and save the rest for another time.

2 Steam the potatoes until just tender, then remove and cool. Peel off the skins, roughly chop the flesh and crush in a large bowl with a fork. Season nice and gently, then stir in the cubes of butter.

3 Heat a large non-stick frying pan until hot and place four metal cutters, about 7cm in diameter, on to the pan base.

4 Spoon in the crushed potato, pressing down to firm, and cook until golden brown on each side. Do not touch the pancakes for at least 2–3 minutes to allow the potato cakes to get a nice crispy skin.

5 In another frying pan, heat a little duck fat and when hot stir-fry the shredded duck until golden and hot. Season and mix in the garlic and parsley. Spoon the hot duck on top of the crisp potato cakes to serve.

TERRINE OF SMOKED DUCK & TROMPETTE MUSHROOMS

Duck and *foie gras* are used in many terrines in Gascon cooking. This one, however, is unusual, and very easy (once you find your ingredients). You will need a jar of cooked duck gizzards and smoked duck *magret*. It makes a roll which is merely chilled, no fussing around with a *bain-marie*, then served in slices as a starter, garnished with dressed trompette mushrooms.

Serves 6

INGREDIENTS

1 kg potatoes

100g butter

100g pine nuts, toasted

sea salt and freshly ground black pepper

300g *confit* duck gizzards

2 smoked duck *magrets*

1 Boil the potatoes in their skins until just tender, about 15 minutes, then drain and cool. Peel the skins off, then mash the flesh until smooth with the butter. When creamy, add the pine nuts. Check the seasoning.

2 Drain the gizzards of any *confit* fat and pat dry, then slice thinly. Remove the skin from the *magrets* and cut the flesh into small dice, about 1cm thick. Mix the gizzards and *magret* into the potato and chill until firm.

3 Lay a large sheet of clingfilm on a board and spoon the mixture down the centre. Shape into a long smooth roll with your hands. Wrap in clingfilm, seal well and chill for at least 6 hours or until firm.

4 Meanwhile, wash the mushrooms in cold water, then drain well and pat dry. Plunge the mushrooms into a pan of boiling water for a few seconds, then drain and pat dry again. Cool, then dress with the hazelnut oil, chives and some seasoning.

5 Unwrap the terrine and cut into twelve slices. Arrange two on each plate and spoon the mushrooms on top or alongside.

TROMPETTE MUSHROOMS INGREDIENTS

300g fresh trompette mushrooms, or 100g dried and soaked

20ml hazelnut oil

1 bunch fresh chives, chopped

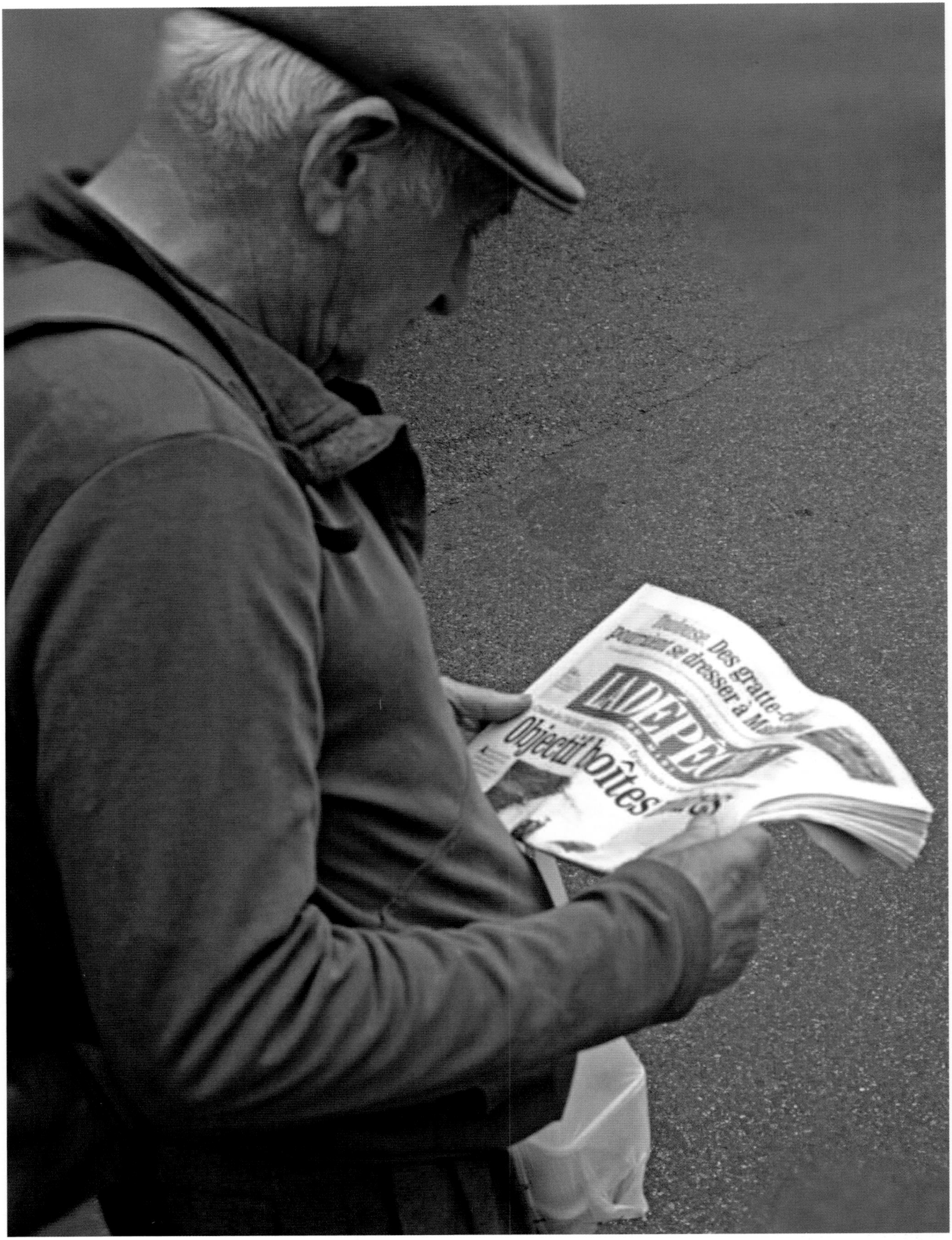
Objectif boîtes

DUCK *MAGRET* *CARPACCIO* with DILL & PEAS

You will need a large duck *magret* for this recipe which is rolled, half frozen then sliced as thin as the Italian *carpaccio*. The Japanese peas coated with *wasabi* (which you buy in a packet, like crisps) add good flavour and texture, allied with the fresh peas and the light dill vinaigrette. It's very herby and spring-like, retaining the flavour of the meat.

Serves 4

INGREDIENTS

1 large duck *magret*

40g Japanese dried crispy peas flavoured with *wasabi*

100g podded green peas, fresh or frozen

2 tablespoons olive oil

fleur de sel (see below)

DILL FROTH INGREDIENTS

2 tablespoons white balsamic vinegar

good pinch fennel seeds

1 star anise

3–4 sprigs fresh dill, finely chopped

1 teaspoon egg white

1   Skin the *magret* (save the skin in the freezer to cook as duck scratchings for later, see page 15). Cut the *magret* in half lengthways, then turn one half round and press next to the other so they make an even roll, like a *boudin* sausage. Wrap tightly in clingfilm and place in the freezer.

2   Meanwhile, make a dill froth by placing the vinegar, fennel, star anise, dill and 5 tablespoons water into a small saucepan. Bring to the boil, then set aside to cool.

3   Crush the dried Japanese peas roughly to a chunky powdery texture.

4   Lightly cook the fresh or frozen peas, then drain and set aside.

5   Remove the half-frozen duck *magret* and, using a very sharp freezer knife, slice very thinly into rounds. Arrange these on four chilled plates in a round or rosace. Brush the duck with some olive oil and sprinkle with *fleur de sel*. Then cover with the Japanese pea mix.

6   Strain the dill froth juice into a small bowl, add the egg white, and using a hand-held blender, whizz to a froth. Spoon this immediately over the duck. Scatter around the fresh peas and serve.

COOK'S NOTES 1

EXTRA DECORATION

Some of the fresh peas can be removed with a slotted spoon, crushed to a purée, then mixed with an egg yolk and some wasabi *paste to flavour, then used as dots on the plates.*

COOK'S NOTES 2

FLEUR DE SEL

This is a French salt that is harvested by hand: workers on the salt pans scrape off the top layer of salt before it sinks to the bottom. It is often quite grey in colour due to its mineral content. It is expensive, and comes slightly damp. Use it as you would herbs, sprinkling over just before serving.

POULET *GRAND'MERE*

Like me, many people must have fond memories of their grandmother's roast stuffed chicken. This is mine, wonderful French comfort food, especially when made with a large yellow Landes bird. Failing that, any quality corn-fed chicken will do.

Serves 4–6

INGREDIENTS

1 large corn-fed roasting chicken, around 1.8–2kg (with giblets)

1 large ripe tomato

50g duck fat or olive oil

100g day-old good country bread, cut into small 1cm cubes

the heart and liver of the bird, chopped

100g pitted green olives, chopped

10 large garlic cloves, chopped

3–4 sprigs fresh thyme

2 teaspoons *fleur de sel*

freshly ground black pepper

40g butter

1 Heat the oven to 180°C/Gas 4. Pull out any pads of fat at the entrance to the body cavity. Wash the bird inside and out, then pat dry.

2 Dip the tomato into a small pan of boiling water for a few seconds, then remove, cool slightly, peel and chop or crush.

3 Heat the duck fat or oil in a large frying pan and toss in the bread cubes, stirring until lightly browned. Remove with a slotted spoon to a medium mixing bowl. Sauté the heart and liver for 3–5 minutes in the same fat, stirring until lightly browned, and mix with the bread cubes in the bowl, along with the olives, garlic, leaves from the thyme sprigs, a little of the salt, and pepper to taste.

4 Cool the stuffing until tepid, then spoon into the chicken's body cavity, pressing down lightly with the back of the spoon. Tie the legs up together with kitchen string, which will help hold the stuffing in the cavity.

5 Heat the butter in the same frying pan and brown the bird all over in it, holding down on all sides, protecting your hands with a clean tea-towel.

6 Place in a roasting pan and scatter with the remaining salt and more pepper. Roast for 1¼–1½ hours, spooning over any pan juices and fat that drain out. The flesh is cooked if, when you pierce the flesh between the thigh and breast, clear juices run out. Roast until this is achieved.

7 Remove the bird from the oven and stand for 10–15 minutes to rest. Carve, allowing some breast and leg meat per portion, and spooning out the cooked stuffing from inside. There should be enough pan *jus* for you to drizzle over each serving.

LA *POULE* AU *POT*

When the dashing Gascon King Henri IV of Navarre assumed the crown of France at the beginning of the seventeenth century (changing religions from Protestant to Catholic on the basis that 'Paris was worth a mass'), he also expressed a desire that every French peasant would be able to afford to put a chicken into a pot (as they did in his native Gascony). And since then the dish of poached chicken in broth with vegetables has been a great French favourite. The broth is served to start the meal, with a handful or two of vermicelli simmered in it to add bulk, and then the meat carved and served with the stuffing and simmered vegetables. What could be more wholesome and tasty?

Serves 6

INGREDIENTS

1 large free-range roasting chicken, about 2 kg

2 onions, studded with 3–4 cloves each

3 carrots, roughly chopped

2 turnips, roughly chopped

2 celery sticks, chopped

2 leeks, washed and chopped

sea salt and Espelette pepper

1–2 fistfuls small soup pasta or vermicelli

1. Prepare the bird by removing the giblets of liver, heart and neck. You may be lucky and also get the gizzard, if available. Wash the body cavity and pat dry with paper towel.
2. Make the stuffing. Chop the chicken breast meat, liver, heart and gizzard if you have them. Save the neck to cook in the broth.
3. Soak the bread in the milk, then break up into pieces. Put the 200g chicken meat, chopped giblets, soaked bread, garlic, nutmeg, Armagnac and eggs into a food processor or blender. Whizz to a purée, then scoop out into a bowl and mix in seasoning and the diced ham. Thrust into the body cavity of the bird and, using thin kitchen string, stitch up the entrance to the body.
4. Put the bird into a large pot with the onions, carrots, turnips, celery, leeks and bony neck. Cover with cold water. Season, bring to the boil, then lower the heat and simmer for 2–2½ hours until the bird is very tender when pierced between the breast and thigh.
5. Remove the cooked bird from the pot and keep warm on a platter. Lift out the vegetables with a slotted spoon and keep warm.
6. Stir the pasta into the broth, and return the broth to the boil. Simmer for 5–10 minutes until the pasta is tender. This is your starter.
7. Carve or pull the bird into chunky portions and serve with the vegetables. Ideally accompany with gherkins, mustard (e.g. grainy *moutarde de Meaux* or Espelette mustard), and hot new potatoes.

STUFFING INGREDIENTS

200g chicken breast meat

the liver, heart and gizzard of the bird

150g good country bread

100ml milk

4 fat garlic cloves, chopped

½ teaspoon freshly ground nutmeg

100ml Armagnac

3 free-range eggs, beaten

300g Bayonne ham, finely diced

CHRISTMAS GOOSE STUFFED with HAY

Goose is, not surprisingly, a popular meat in Gascony, and never more so than around Christmas. This is my suggestion for a French-style Christmas feast, cooking the 'stuffing' separately and filling the body of the goose to be roasted with fresh, clean hay. This imparts a delicious grassy flavour to the meat. You can buy hay from all good pet shops.

Serves 6

INGREDIENTS

1 oven-ready goose, around 6–7kg, with heart and liver

3–4 fistfuls fresh hay, about 150g

50g duck or goose fat

sea salt and freshly ground black pepper

1 Preheat the oven to 180°C/Gas 4.

2 Stuff the body cavity with as much hay as it will hold. Place in a large roasting pan with the duck or goose fat, season well and roast for 40 minutes, then lower the heat to 160–70°C/Gas 3 and cook for 30 minutes a kilogram, pouring off the cooking fat once or twice. When the bird is cooked, remove it to a warm platter, and leave to rest.

3 Pour off the fat from the pan until you have just meat juices left. Put the pan on the hob on a medium heat and stir in 150ml water, scraping up the meaty deposits to deglaze. Bubble for a few minutes then strain the *jus* into a jug and set aside.

4 Meanwhile, make the stuffing. Using a large sauté pan, sauté the chopped heart and liver, chicken livers and mushrooms in some of the saved roasting fat for about 5 minutes, then add the Armagnac and stir for a minute or two.

5 Add the *jus*, shallot compôte and the sausagemeat. Stir and cook for another 5 minutes until the sausagemeat is cooked.

6 Mix in the prunes, bread pieces and chestnuts, reheat until piping hot and cook for a further 5 minutes. Then stir in the *foie gras* and check the seasoning.

7 Carve the goose, remembering the breasts are quite shallow. Give each guest a portion of leg and breast meat each and a good spoonful of stuffing.

STUFFING INGREDIENTS

the heart and liver of the goose, finely chopped

100g chicken livers

200g button mushrooms, chopped

3 tablespoons Armagnac

150g shallot compôte (see page 185)

125g good sausagemeat, broken up

100g Agen prunes, stoned and chopped

100g day-old rustic bread, torn into small pieces

125g vacuum-packed chestnuts, chopped

100g *foie gras*, cut into cubes

COOK'S NOTES

USING HAY

I like the idea of using unusual ingredients in my cooking. You could also make a stock with hay, which produces a wonderful grassy flavour, ideal for cooking potatoes for a purée, say. Put some clean fresh hay in a saucepan, and set it alight. Pour on some water to cover well, and simmer for an hour or so.

PRES ET PATURAGES

ROAST GROUSE *with* CROUSTOUS & CHICORY *CONFIT*

Game birds are popular in our restaurants when we have them on the menu, and we always look forward to the start of the grouse season. We like to serve our grouse with a French twist, along with a creamy *millas* (polenta) sauce. And, instead of cooking the birds whole, we bone out the breasts and legs and use the carcass for a stock for a sauce. The livers and hearts are spread on crispy toasts which we call by their Gascon name, *croustous*.

Serves 4

INGREDIENTS

4 oven-ready grouse, with giblets if possible

150g butter, chilled

3 shallots, chopped

1 teaspoon freshly ground black pepper

30g polenta

½ x 75cl bottle dry white wine

4 tablespoons Armagnac

4 neat slices good country bread, for toast

sea salt and freshly ground black pepper

CHICORY CONFIT INGREDIENTS

4 heads chicory

juice of 2 oranges

50g sugar

50g butter

20g pine nuts

1 Preheat the oven to 100°C/Gas ½.

2 Make the chicory *confit* first. Remove the outside leaves and set aside. Halve the chicory lengthways and place cut-side down neatly in a shallow ovenproof dish to fit snugly. Pour over the juice of 1 orange, sprinkle with the sugar and butter, and add water to just cover. Bake in the preheated oven for up to an hour until tender, the liquid has evaporated and the chicory is caramelised.

3 Next, prepare the birds (see right) to give you chopped leg meat, whole breasts, a carcass and leg bones. Check the insides of the birds for the hearts and livers, and set these aside in the fridge.

4 Start the sauce. Melt 50g of the butter in a large saucepan and add the bones, frying until they are browned, then add the shallots and pepper. Cook for 5 minutes, then stir in the polenta and cook for 10 minutes on a medium heat, stirring once or twice until coloured.

5 Deglaze with the wine and simmer until almost all the wine has reduced. Stir in 500ml cold water, bring to the boil, and simmer another 10 minutes. Tip everything from the pan into a powerful blender, bones and all, and whizz until smooth, then strain through a sieve into another pan, rubbing with the back of a ladle. Set aside until ready to serve.

6 Chop the grouse livers and hearts finely and brown in a small pan with a knob of the remaining butter, half the Armagnac and some seasoning. Add a ladle of the sauce and simmer very gently for 10–15 minutes until reduced down. Set aside to cool.

7 Use another knob of butter and brown the diced leg meat for 1–2 minutes, seasoning and stirring, then mix into the chicory along with the remaining orange juice and pine nuts. Slice up the reserved outer chicory leaves and stir those in too.

8 When you are ready to serve, finish the sauce. Reheat and add the last of the Armagnac and whisk in half of the remaining chilled butter in small chunks. Reheat the chicory *confit*.

9 Heat the final amount of butter in a sauté pan and fry the breasts lightly on each side, seasoning to taste, until they are just pink inside. Toast the bread and spread with the liver mix. Divide the chicory between four warmed plates, top with two breasts each, spoon the sauce around and garnish with the toasts.

COOK'S NOTES

PREPARING GAME BIRDS

When you buy them, we are presuming that they have been hung as appropriate, plucked and drawn, so are oven-ready. For small birds, we like to do a bit of advance preparation, separating legs and breasts from the carcass frame (using the carcass for stock). Remove the legs from the birds where the thigh joins the body. Cut the meat from the legs and chop into small pieces. Then, using a small very sharp knife, remove the breast fillets in whole neat pieces, leaving the skin on. Chill the boned meats.

ROAST *PHEASANT* *with* *ALE* & LIME

I like the flavour of pheasant, but the meat can often be very dry. So I tend to tenderise the breasts first, here in a yoghurt marinade. I like to serve pheasant with fresh flavours, which you get here with the citrus juices, which make for a fairly unusual sauce. The cabbage compote, though, is more traditional, using the Gascon ingredients of duck fat and chestnuts, although I have added some dates...

Serves 4

INGREDIENTS

2 oven-ready pheasants

2 garlic cloves, crushed

3 tablespoons milk

200g Greek yoghurt

1 teaspoon Dijon mustard

finely grated zest and juice of 1 lime

some Espelette pepper

a knob of butter

1 tablespoon vegetable oil

1 litre brown ale

sea salt and freshly ground black pepper

juice of 1 pink grapefruit

a little sugar or honey

1 First, prepare the birds as on page 132, leaving you with breast fillets, diced leg meat, the bones and carcass.

2 Make the yoghurt marinade. Simmer the garlic in the milk for a minute or so and cool. (This can be done in the microwave in a cup on a medium setting.) Mix this garlic milk with the yoghurt, mustard, lime zest and Espelette pepper. Spoon on to a dinner plate and press the breast fillets, flesh-side down, on top. Do not cover the skin with marinade, just cover loosely with clingfilm and chill for 24 hours.

3 Make the sauce. Crush the carcass bones roughly and brown in a large saucepan with the butter and oil, then stir in the ale, lime juice and seasoning. Simmer for about 1–1½ hours until the liquid is reduced down. Add the grapefruit juice, and simmer again for about 5 minutes then taste: if a bit bitter, add sugar or honey to balance the flavour. Strain into another pan and set aside.

4 Meanwhile, make the cabbage compote. Quarter, cut out the cores and shred the cabbage thinly. Heat a tablespoon of duck fat in a large saucepan and brown the diced leg meat, seasoning to taste. Cook for about 5 minutes, then remove with a slotted spoon. Set aside.

5 Add and heat the remaining duck fat in the pan, and stir in the shredded cabbage until wilted. Cover and cook for 5 minutes until tender. Return the browned leg meat, and stir in with the chestnuts, dates, preserved lemon and pine nuts. Season, cook for 2–3 minutes and keep warm.

6 To serve, preheat the oven to 180°C/Gas 4. Remove the breasts from the marinade, wipe it off and place the breasts skin-side up on a non-stick baking dish. Bake in the preheated oven for 5–10 minutes until the flesh feels slightly bouncy when pressed, indicating it is cooked to just pink. You may like to check by piercing with a skewer. Set aside whilst you reheat the sauce and cabbage.

7 Divide the cabbage between four warmed plates, top with the breasts and spoon the sauce around.

CABBAGE AND CHESTNUT COMPOTE INGREDIENTS

1 small Savoy cabbage

4 tablespoons duck fat

4 vacuum-packed or canned chestnuts, chopped or crushed

2 stoned dates, chopped

1 tablespoon preserved lemon (see page 15)

1 tablespoon pine nuts, toasted

GREY-LEGGED PARTRIDGE *with* WINE-GLAZED CHICORY

I may be French but I prefer to serve the English grey-legged partridge at my tables, roasted whole and garnished with celery leaves. Again bitter-sweet chicory is the best accompaniment to this game bird.

Serves 4

INGREDIENTS

4 oven-ready grey-legged partridges

a little butter

a little vegetable oil

1 celery stick, cut in thin sticks or batons

celery salt, sea salt and freshly ground black pepper

1 Cook the chicory first. Put the wine into a large shallow sauté pan or saucepan and heat. Flambé, if you want to, by putting a lighted match or taper to the wine so it catches fire. The flames soon die down as the alcohol burns off. Then add the *Cassis*, sugar and sherry and heat to boiling.

2 Meanwhile, halve the chicory heads lengthways and place cut-side down in the pan. Simmer until the heads are tender when pierced with the tip of a knife, about 1 hour. Remove the heads using a slotted spoon and set aside. Boil the pan liquid down until reduced by half until quite syrupy. Keep warm.

3 When ready to cook the partridge, heat the oven to 180°C/Gas 4.

4 Put the birds into a shallow roasting dish with knobs of butter inside and the breasts brushed with oil and seasoned with celery salt, sea salt and pepper. Roast for 20–25 minutes, then remove and rest for 15 minutes.

5 Reheat the chicory and mix in half the syrupy sauce. Divide between four warm dinner plates. Place the birds on top and spoon the remaining sauce over the birds. Garnish with the celery batons and serve.

WINE-GLAZED CHICORY INGREDIENTS

½ x 75cl bottle red wine

2 teaspoons *crème de Cassis*

100g sugar

180ml sherry

6 chicory heads

BUTTERFLIED QUAILS
with A CABBAGE *&* *SULTANA* COMPOTE

Little quails may look cute but they are quite tricky to eat unless partly boned. Fortunately, you can now buy birds with the body carcass boned out, leaving the breasts and legs attached. Opening them up to 'butterfly' them makes them easier to cook as well. I also sometimes serve these quails cold, with a *piquillo* sorbet and a salad seasoned with lavender; very summery.

Serves 4

INGREDIENTS

4 part-boned oven-ready quails, butterflied

a little vegetable oil

butter

sea salt and freshly ground black pepper

100ml white balsamic vinegar

1 Make the compote first. Quarter the cabbage, cut out the cores then slice the leaves finely. Melt the butter in a large saucepan and add the cabbage and sultanas. Pour in the wine and sugar. Season and bring to the boil, then cover and reduce the heat to a simmer. Cook for about an hour until very tender and reduced. Add the chicory leaves, silver-skin onions and chives.

2 Preheat the oven to 180°C/Gas 4.

3 Heat a little oil and butter in a large frying pan and when hot press in the quails, skin-side down, to brown. Remove to a small roasting pan, reshape into a bird shape and season. Roast in the preheated oven for about 10–15 minutes until the flesh feels just firm when pressed but still a little springy. Remove from the oven and allow to rest whilst you deglaze the pan.

4 Return the pan and roasting juices to the hob and bubble up for a minute. Pour in the vinegar and simmer, scraping up the pan juices, then simmer for 2–3 minutes.

5 Divide the cabbage between four warmed plates, top with the quails, and strain the pan *jus* over the top.

CABBAGE COMPOTE INGREDIENTS

1 small white cabbage

30g butter

50g sultanas

300ml dry white wine

2 teaspoons sugar

about 8 large chicory leaves, sliced

3–4 pickled silverskin onions, cut in strips

about 2 tablespoons chopped chives

SQUAB PIGEON with SPRING ONION MILK & ELDERFLOWER SAUCE

For those who find wood pigeon a little on the gamey side, then the domestically reared squab pigeon would be a lighter choice. We serve them separated into legs and breasts, with the carcasses used to make a light flowery sauce, then topped with an optional light frothy foam of oniony milk.

Serves 4

INGREDIENTS

4 squab pigeons, about 500g each

about 4 tablespoons olive oil

300g baby carrots, halved lengthways

sea salt and freshly ground black pepper

500g broad beans, podded

300g green asparagus, trimmed

50g white asparagus, trimmed

1 bunch spring onions (about 6–8), whites trimmed and set aside, green parts chopped

100ml milk

1. Cut the legs from the pigeons where the thighs meet the breasts. Using a sharp knife, cut the breast fillets off the breastbones as whole and neatly as possible. Set both aside in the fridge.

2. For the sauce, heat 2 tablespoons oil in a large saucepan and then brown the carcasses for 5–10 minutes. Stir in the chopped vegetables, garlic and herbs. Cook for 5 minutes.

3. Pour in the wine, and simmer for 5 minutes, then add the elderflower cordial. Boil gently until reduced by two-thirds. Add some seasoning, then strain into a small pan and set aside.

4. Prepare and cook the vegetables. Heat a little of the oil in a heavy-based frying pan and open-roast the carrot halves over a high heat until lightly browned. Season in the pan and set aside.

5. Blanch the podded beans for about 3 minutes then drain, refresh in a sieve under a cold running tap, then pop or slip the beans out of their skins. Set them aside.

6. Blanch the green asparagus in boiling water for 2–3 minutes, then drain and rinse in cold running water. Set aside with the carrots.

7. Heat a little more oil in another frying pan and gently sauté the white asparagus spears and whites of spring onion until just tender. Keep the vegetables warm whilst you finish cooking the meat.

8. Heat 2 tablespoons oil in a large frying pan, then sauté the squab legs, seasoning in the pan, for about 10 minutes, turning once or twice.

9. Remove the legs from the pan and add the breasts skin-side down and cook, without turning, for 4–5 minutes until still springy and juicy when pressed with the back of a fork. Return the legs to the pan and pour in a small ladle of sauce, stirring to coat the legs and breasts well. Heat until bubbling and hot.

10. Finally, make the spring onion milk. Simmer the green parts of the onions with the milk in a small saucepan for about 5 minutes. Whizz the onions and milk in a blender or food processor until smooth and frothy.

11. Serve the squab portions divided between four warmed dinner plates with the vegetables, and the frothy milk sauce spooned over.

SAUCE INGREDIENTS

2 tablespoons olive oil

100g mixture chopped carrot, leek and onion

1 garlic clove, roughly chopped

2–3 sprigs fresh thyme

1 bay leaf

350ml (½ bottle) red wine

100ml elderflower cordial

WOOD PIGEON *with* JERUSALEM ARTICHOKE GRATIN

There are four elements to this dish – a traditional creamy gratin of Jerusalem artichokes, a rich red wine *civet* sauce, and the *palombe* or wood pigeon garnished with balsamic pears. *Civet* sauce is perfect for many game meats, traditional with hare, so use it again in suitable dishes.

Serves 4

INGREDIENTS

4 oven-ready wood pigeons, hearts and livers saved

80g fatty ham or bacon

a little vegetable oil

2 tablespoons Armagnac

2 just-ripe pears

3 tablespoons balsamic vinegar

sea salt and freshly ground black pepper

JERUSALEM ARTICHOKE GRATIN INGREDIENTS

600g Jerusalem artichokes, scrubbed and thinly sliced

5 garlic cloves, chopped

2–3 tablespoons chopped fresh parsley

freshly ground nutmeg

150ml double cream

1 Prepare the birds as on page 136, separating breasts, legs and carcasses. Keep aside the livers and hearts too.

2 Make the sauce. In a large saucepan, heat the bacon until the fat starts to run. Add the pigeon carcasses, hearts and liver plus the chopped carrot, onion and leek. Sauté until nicely browned, then deglaze with the wine and boil for about 5 minutes. Add the pig's trotter, halved garlic, the thyme and bay. Pour in about 1.5 litres water, bring to the boil and simmer gently for 2 hours until reduced down by two-thirds, skimming regularly if liked. Strain the sauce into a bowl and set aside.

3 Preheat the oven to 180°C/Gas 4.

4 For the gratin, layer the artichokes in a gratin dish with the garlic, parsley, seasoning and some pinches of nutmeg. Pour over the cream, mixing lightly with a fork. Bake in the preheated oven for 15 minutes then lower the heat to 160–170°C/Gas 3 and cook for a further 45 minutes until the artichokes are tender when pierced. Keep warm.

5 Cook the pigeon legs. Heat the fatty bacon in a frying pan and when the fat starts to run add the legs, turning until they brown nicely. Stir in the Armagnac and cook until the alcohol evaporates. Pour in the *civet* sauce and simmer for about an hour or until the legs are tender. Then remove from the heat and keep warm.

6 For the pears, peel, quarter and core and pan-fry in a frying pan with a little hot oil until lightly browned, about 10 minutes. Deglaze with the balsamic for about 2 minutes and season with black pepper only. Keep warm.

7 Now, cook the pigeon breasts. Heat a little more oil in a frying pan and cook the breasts on the skin-side only for about 5–7 minutes until they are browned and just firm but still lightly springy. Season in the pan and remove from the heat.

8 Divide the hot gratin between four warmed plates. Reheat the legs in *civet* sauce and stir in the chopped parsley, sliced shallots and chopped garlic. Spoon over the gratin and top with the breasts and balsamic pears.

CIVET SAUCE INGREDIENTS

100g fatty streaky bacon, chopped

1 carrot, chopped

1 onion, chopped

1 leek, chopped

350ml red wine

1 pig's trotter, cut in half lengthways (optional)

2 garlic cloves, one halved, one chopped

2 sprigs fresh thyme

2 bay leaves

2 shallots, thinly sliced

5 sprigs fresh parsley, chopped

RABBIT LEGS *with* *SQUID* & CHORIZO

The popular Gascon surf and turf flavour combination of squid and chorizo also suits rabbit for a punchy bistro-style dish. Excellent with a bowl of my award-winning French fries on the side (see page 46).

Serves 4

INGREDIENTS

4 rabbit legs

2 tablespoons sunflower oil

20g butter

sea salt and freshly ground black pepper

1   Preheat the oven to 200°C/Gas 6.

2   Heat the oil and butter in a sauté pan and brown the rabbit legs all over, then season. If necessary, transfer to a shallow roasting pan and cook in the preheated oven for 20 minutes until done. Remove and set aside to cool.

3   Meanwhile, make the accompaniment. Take a third of the squids and cut into squares. Cut the remainder lengthways in half.

4   Sauté the chorizo in a large saucepan and when the fat starts to run, stir in the shallots, mushrooms and figs. Cook for 2–3 minutes, then pour in the port, stock and thyme. Simmer for 10 minutes, then stir in the squares of squid and cook for 3–5 minutes more. Finally add salt to taste, plus some Espelette and the chives.

5   Heat a little oil in another frying pan and stir-fry the remaining baby squids until nicely browned, season with salt and some more Espelette.

6   Spoon the chorizo sauce on to four warmed plates, put a rabbit leg in the centre of each and scatter around the sautéed squid.

CHORIZO AND SQUID INGREDIENTS

300g baby squids, washed and patted dry

100g cooking chorizo, cubed

4 shallots, sliced

100g button brown/Paris mushrooms, chopped

4 dried figs, tops snipped then chopped

100ml port

100ml veal or chicken stock

2 sprigs fresh thyme

a little Espelette pepper, to taste

a small bunch of fresh chives, chopped

a little olive oil

RABBIT *with* BUTTERNUT SQUASH & PAPAYA

This is a simplified version of a dish we have on our menus from time to time. It uses rabbit legs and fillets of the saddle, and we serve them with a purée of squash and papaya and a sauce made with the bones, heart and liver.

Serves 4

INGREDIENTS

1 whole rabbit

4 tablespoons olive oil

1 butternut squash

1 ripe papaya (paw-paw)

a few pinches of spigol (see page 70) or saffron

sea salt and freshly ground black pepper

1   Remove the front and back legs from the rabbit. Then using a thin-bladed sharp knife, cut off the loin fillets in two whole pieces from the saddle. Set aside in the fridge.

2   For the sauce, crush the bones with a rolling pin and brown in the oil in a large preheated saucepan with the liver and heart, roughly chopped. Deglaze with the wine and simmer until reduced, then add the Armagnac and cook until that evaporates also.

3   Add the leek, carrot, onion and garlic and cook for 10 minutes until softened, then pour in 1.5 litres water plus some seasoning and the herbs. Bring to the boil, then simmer gently for an hour or so until reduced down by half. Add the prune and carrot juices and boil down gently again until reduced by half. Strain the sauce into another saucepan and set aside.

4   Preheat the oven to 200 °C/Gas 6.

5   Brown the rabbit legs in a large frying pan in 1 tablespoon hot olive oil, then transfer to a roasting pan, season and roast in the preheated oven for about 20 minutes. Whilst they are cooking, cook the squash.

6   Peel, de-seed and cut the squash into small cubes. Do the same with the papaya. Sauté the squash in a large saucepan with 2–3 tablespoons more olive oil for about 5 minutes, then add the papaya cubes and cook 5–10 more minutes until softened, adding seasoning and some spigol to taste. When soft, whizz to a thick purée in a blender and scoop back into the saucepan to keep warm.

7   Sauté the rabbit fillets in another small frying pan in the last of the oil until just tender, about 5 minutes. Season.

8   When the legs are just tender, remove from the oven and set aside for 5 minutes to relax. Reheat the squash pulp and divide between four warmed plates. Put a leg on top of each. Slice the fillets on the diagonal into medallions and divide between the plates. Reheat the sauce until bubbling and spoon around.

SAUCE INGREDIENTS

the rabbit bones, heart and liver

2 tablespoons olive oil

175–200ml dry white wine

2 tablespoons Armagnac

1 leek, chopped

1 carrot, chopped

1 onion, chopped

3 garlic cloves, chopped

3 sprigs fresh thyme

1 bay leaf

500ml prune juice

100ml carrot juice

1 tablespoon sugar

HARE *with* BANYULS *SAUCE*, RED ONION *&* BEETROOT *PUREE*

Those who enjoy rich game meat will find this dish a delicious variation on jugged hare. The hare should ideally be supplied with a cup of blood that has drained as it hung. This is then used to thicken and enrich the red wine and Banyuls sauce, which is finished with a chunk of dark chocolate. Banyuls is a delicious sweet red wine from the Pyrenees; it is made from the Grenache grape, and tastes somewhat like a tawny port. A purée of beetroot and onion completes the warmth and richness of the dish. The latter is purple in colour, quite sweet in taste, and is an ideal accompaniment for any game dish.

Serves 4

INGREDIENTS

1 hare, about 2kg, skinned, with its blood

sea salt and freshly ground black pepper

2 tablespoons juniper berries, crushed

1 x 75cl bottle red wine

1 carrot, chopped

1 onion, chopped

1 garlic clove, chopped

2–3 sprigs fresh thyme

2 bay leaves

3–4 tablespoons olive oil

2 tablespoons plain flour

1 tablespoon tomato purée

½ x 75cl bottle Banyuls wine

a dash of sherry vinegar

20g dark chocolate, ideally 60% cocoa solids

PUREE INGREDIENTS

1 large red onion, thinly sliced

200g beetroot, thinly sliced

50g butter

about 600ml vegetable stock

1   Remove the leg and shoulder joints from the hare, then divide each in two. Next, using a long thin sharp knife, fillet out the two loins in whole neat sections. Crush up the carcass bones.

2   Rub some black pepper and the juniper berries into the loins, cover in clingfilm and chill. Place the eight leg joints into a bowl and pour over the red wine. Add the carrot, onion, garlic, thyme and bay leaves, mixing well together. Cover and chill for 24 hours.

3   Next day, drain the joints and pat lightly dry. Heat a large cast-iron casserole and add 2 tablespoons of oil. Dust the joints lightly with a little flour, shake off the excess, then sear them in the hot oil to brown, adding extra oil if necessary.

4   Drain the vegetables and herbs from the marinade with a slotted spoon and add these to the casserole along with the tomato purée and stir well to coat in the oil. Heat for about 5 minutes, then pour in the red wine and bring to the boil, stirring the base well to deglaze. Then add the Banyuls wine and return to the boil. Season, lower the heat, and simmer very gently for about 2 hours until the joints are very tender.

5   Meanwhile, make the purée. Layer the onion and beet slices in a heavy-based saucepan, dotting with the butter and season in between, then pour in the stock. Bring to a gentle simmer, cover and cook slowly until very tender, about 1 hour. Remove from the heat and cool slightly, then tip into a blender or food processor and whizz to a silky smooth purée that is quite soft and not too thick.

6   Remove the joints from the casserole and keep warm. Strain the liquid through a fine sieve into a large saucepan and boil until reduced by half.

7   Mix the blood with a dash of vinegar (this stops it coagulating) and a tablespoon of flour in a bowl, then gradually whisk in the wine sauce. Return to a low heat, stirring until thickened and smooth. Remove from the heat and stir in the chocolate until melted. Keep warm.

8   Finally, heat another tablespoon of olive oil in a frying pan. Remove the crushed juniper and pepper from the loin fillets, then roast them in the pan, turning occasionally for about 5 minutes until just cooked and still a little pink inside. Set aside to rest for 5 minutes, then slice into eight medallions.

9   Serve the purée in the centre of four warmed plates, with two joints and two medallions per serving on top. Coat the meat with a little of the sauce and spoon the rest around.

CUIR & *ABATS*

PRES ET PATURAGES

SEVEN-HOUR BRAISED LAMB *SHANKS*

Some years ago butchers couldn't give away the tasty lower legs of lamb called shanks. Now they are all the rage and the dish is popular throughout gastro pubs, which has had the effect of raising the price. Sorry, I can't help redress this situation, but shanks do make good eating, and here is my way of cooking them. It's not particularly Gascon, but very tasty. Serve with creamy, freshly cooked polenta or mash.

Serves 4

INGREDIENTS

4 lamb shanks, about 400g each

a little olive oil

1 x 75cl bottle red wine

1 onion, stuck with 3 cloves

1 large carrot, sliced

1 large leek, trimmed and sliced

2 bay leaves

3 sprigs fresh thyme

1 whole garlic bulb, sliced through the middle

sea salt and freshly ground black pepper

1 Heat the oven to 120°C/Gas 1.

2 Heat a large frying pan with a little oil and brown the lamb shanks on all sides.

3 At the same time, in a large cast-iron casserole pan, boil the wine for 2–3 minutes, then add the onion, carrots, leek, herbs and the halved garlic bulb.

4 When the lamb is browned, pick out the shanks with tongs and nestle them into the simmering wine and vegetables, adding extra water if necessary to ensure the shanks are submerged.

5 Season well and cover with a lid or foil, then braise in the oven for 7 hours, uncovering and turning the shanks two or three times. Remove from the heat when the meat is meltingly tender.

GASCONNADE

This roast leg of lamb studded with anchovies and garlic may look familiar, but the Gascons thought of it first! In Gascony milk-fed lamb (a speciality of the Pyrenees with lambs around six weeks) is the preferred choice, but it is not readily available outside the restaurant trade, so I would suggest you track down a young new-season's weaned lamb that will feed four. The lamb is really nice served with the vegetable Bayaldi on page 43.

Serves 4

INGREDIENTS

1 x 50g can anchovies in oil, drained

3 fat fresh garlic cloves

2 tablespoons olive oil

2 sprigs fresh thyme

1 leg of young lamb, about 1.5kg

sea salt and freshly ground black pepper

1   Pat the anchovies with paper towel and cut the fillets lengthways. Cut the garlic cloves lengthways also, then into slices.

2   Heat the oil in a small pan with the thyme sprigs for about a minute, then remove.

3   Using a sharp pointed thin-bladed knife make several stabs over the leg. Push an anchovy fillet and garlic shred into each hole, then place the leg in a small heatproof ovenproof dish. Wrap loosely with foil on top and chill for about 12 hours.

4   When ready to cook, heat the oven to 190°C/Gas 5.

5   Pour the thyme oil around the leg and draw up the foil to seal. Cook in the preheated oven for 45 minutes to 1 hour, uncovering two or three times and spooning the cooking juices over. Check the meat is just cooked by piercing with a thin-bladed knife. Lightly pink juices should run out; if the juices are quite bloody, then allow another 10–15 minutes.

6   When cooked, remove the pan of lamb from the oven and allow to stand for 15 minutes. Place the lamb on a warmed platter and carve.

7   Put the pan with the roasting juices back on the hob and stir in 2–3 tablespoons water. Heat until bubbling, scraping up the pan bottom with a wooden spoon to deglaze. Bubble for 2–3 minutes and season lightly then strain into a small jug. Pour over the lamb.

PRES ET PATURAGES

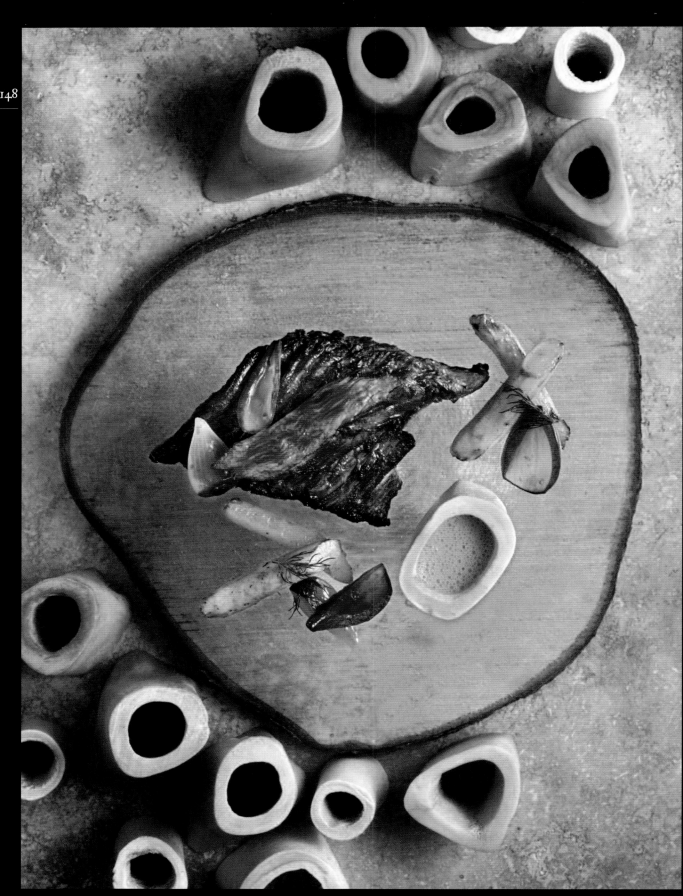

BEEF FILLET *with MARROW BONES*, OYSTER SABAYON *& GIROLLE MUSHROOMS*

Many cuisines associate beef and oysters (the British steak and kidney pie with added oysters, the Australian carpetbag steak), but this recipe is quintessentially French. The oysters are blended to make a hollandaise-type *sabayon*. The marrow bones are optional but assuming your butcher can get them the marrow is used to enrich the *girolles*. Serve with mashed potato.

Serves 4

INGREDIENTS

4 beef marrow bones, centre cut

sea salt and freshly ground black pepper

500g *girolle* mushrooms

2–3 tablespoons olive oil

2 sprigs fresh tarragon, leaves stripped and chopped

4 x 120–150g beef fillet steaks or onglet steaks

OYSTER SABAYON INGREDIENTS

5 fresh oysters

100g unsalted butter

2 free-range egg yolks

1   Soak the beef bones in plenty of cold water to which you have added a good handful of salt. After half an hour, drain and rinse. Using a long thin-bladed sharp knife or skewer, scoop out the marrow. Bring a small pan of water to the boil and blanch the marrow for about 10 minutes until it firms, then drain and plunge into a bowl of iced water. When cold, remove and pat dry.

2   Blanch the *girolles* in a large pan of boiling water for 2 minutes, then drain, rinse in cold running water, drain and pat dry.

3   Preheat the oven to 250°C/Gas 9.

4   Start the *sabayon*. Place the closed oysters on a small tray and when the oven is hot, pop in the oysters for about 2 minutes until they open. Remove and tip the juices into a cup. Pop the oysters into a blender and whizz to a paste. Chill both.

5   Melt the butter in a small saucepan (or a cup in the microwave). Let the hot liquid stand for a few minutes so the solids sink to the bottom, then pour off the buttery oil into a cup or jug. Discard the solids.

6   Put a pan of water on to boil with a heatproof bowl that fits on top. Place the egg yolks and oyster juices in the bowl plus a little seasoning. Place the bowl over the simmering water and, using a small hand-held electric whisk, beat the yolks to a foam that gradually increases in size and becomes pale golden.

7   When the foam is about doubled in volume, and holds soft peaks when the beaters are lifted up, very slowly drizzle in the cooled but still runny clarified butter, whisking as you pour. Do this slowly or the mixture will remain very runny. When all the butter is incorporated, then slowly whisk in the oyster paste. Check the seasoning and remove the bowl from the pan, but keep it warm whilst you cook the steaks and *girolles*.

8   Heat 2 tablespoons of the oil in a large frying pan and when hot stir-fry the *girolles* until lightly browned. Then chop the marrow and mix in with the tarragon, cooking until hot. Check the seasoning and keep warm.

9   Now you are ready to cook the steaks. Heat the remaining oil in a non-stick frying pan and when hot cook the steaks as you like them, around 2–3 minutes each side, more if you like them well done (which I hope you don't). Season in the pan, allow to stand for 5 minutes whilst you plate the rest of the dish.

10 Divide the mushrooms between four warmed plates. If using, stand a marrow bone on the side of each plate and fill with the *sabayon*, otherwise just spoon it around. Put some *girolles* in the centre of each plate. Carve the beef fillet in thick slices, and put on top of the *girolles*.

COOKS NOTES

If you have a meat saw, you might like to cut four neat 10cm lengths from the marrow bones to use them as containers for the sauce. Wash again and pat dry.

The water incidentally should be saved as a light mushroomy stock to be used in soup, so don't waste it.

BEEF ONGLET *with* *MILLAS FRITTERS,* SPROUT *LEAF* SALAD *& MANDARIN* SAUCE

Onglet is a popular 'frying' steak cut in France (equivalent to flank or skirt of beef). You must cook it rare with a crispy outside, when it will still be tougher than you are used to, but it rewards you with a wonderful flavour. This is more of a wintery dish, with polenta fritters and a salad of Brussels sprouts leaves. To make the dish simpler, you could buy some mandarin sorbet from the supermarket, and let it melt. Add all the other flavourings, and you will have a sauce that is nearly as good as my original! (If you can't find mandarin, use orange sorbet: add some grapefruit juice and lemon juice to make it a bit sourer.)

Serves 4

INGREDIENTS

4 x 150g onglet beef steaks

some olive oil

sea salt and freshly ground black pepper

MILLAS FRITTERS INGREDIENTS

1 litre milk

150g instant polenta

1 garlic clove, crushed

1 ½ tablespoons olive oil

2 free-range eggs

2 egg yolks

100g dried breadcrumbs

vegetable oil

MANDARIN SAUCE INGREDIENTS

5 mandarins or clementines

2 tablespoons olive oil

1 tablespoon Meaux mustard (coarse grain)

½ teaspoon Espelette pepper

SPROUT LEAF SALAD INGREDIENTS

100g large Brussels sprouts

2 teaspoons balsamic vinegar

2 teaspoons sherry vinegar

3 tablespoons olive oil

1 Make the *millas* fritters first. Bring the milk to the boil in a large non-stick saucepan and turn down to a simmer. Pour the polenta into the milk with one hand whilst you stir briskly with the other, then add the garlic, the oil and 1 teaspoon salt plus pepper to taste. Simmer gently for 5 minutes, stirring occasionally, then remove from the heat. As the mixture cools, beat together the eggs and yolks and stir into the mixture. Pour on to an oiled baking sheet and spread to a rectangle of about 1cm thickness. Cool until set.

2 For the sauce, peel the mandarins as cleanly as possible. Place in a blender or food processor and whizz until smooth. Pour into a saucepan with the olive oil, mustard and Espelette, bring to the boil, simmer a minute, then remove and cool. Strain through a sieve, pressing down with the back of a ladle. Set aside.

3 Pick the outer leaves off the sprouts until you reach the cores (use the centres of the sprouts elsewhere). Blanch the leaves in a pan of boiling water for 30 seconds, then drain and rinse under a cold running tap. Drain again and pat dry with paper towel. Whisk together the dressing of two vinegars, oil and some seasoning to emulsify and set aside.

4 When the *millas* is set, cut into fingers of 2 x 5cm. Toss in the breadcrumbs, shaking off the excess. Pour vegetable oil into a deep frying pan to a depth of 2cm and heat until a cube of bread browns in 30 seconds. Lower in the *millas* fritters one by one with a slotted spoon and cook for 1–2 minutes until golden brown and crisp on the outside. Drain and keep warm, uncovered, in a warm oven.

5 Cook the steaks. Heat a large non-stick frying pan until hot, pour in a tablespoon or two of olive oil and swirl around the pan. Season the steaks on both sides and cook in the hot pan for 2 minutes each side until they feel firm but still springy. Do not overcook. Remove from the heat and stand for 5 minutes.

6 Reheat the mandarin sauce until simmering. Toss the sprout leaves with the dressing. Serve the steaks with the sauce, *millas* fritters and sprout leaf salad.

POT-AU-FEU
DE MAMAN

Another homely Gascon classic, a boiled beef and vegetable stew, but using the non-traditional beef cheeks and shin cut on the bone, *osso bucco* style. It may take a long time to prepare and cook (my mother would use a pressure cooker and halve the timings), but it is well worth it, as you will have two courses from one pot, and a rich beef stock left over for another time. Another slight departure from tradition is the use of marrow bones; these are poached in the broth, along with some soup pasta, to enrich the soup course. The meats are sliced for the main course served with the *garniture* of vegetables. All you need otherwise are plain boiled potatoes, crushed salt, mustard and gherkins.

Serves 6

INGREDIENTS

800g beef cheeks

400g shin of beef, cut in slices on the bone

2 onions, stuck with 3 cloves each

200g carrots, scrubbed and thickly sliced

200g turnips, scrubbed and thickly sliced

1 large celery stick, thickly sliced

2 leeks, thickly sliced

3 sprigs fresh thyme

a small bunch of parsley stalks

2 bay leaves

4 marrow bones (optional), soaked in cold water for half-hour with some salt

a handful of small soup pasta

sea salt and freshly ground black pepper

1 Place the two meat portions in a large saucepan, cover with cold water to 3cm above, and bring to the boil. Simmer for 30 minutes, skimming off any white deposits that rise to the surface using a slotted spoon. (These are nothing more than harmless meat deposits; skimming helps keep the broth, or *bouillon*, clear.)

2 Then add the vegetables and herbs, return to a gentle simmer and cook for about 3 hours until the meats are very tender.

3 If you have marrow bones, add them about 10 minutes before the end of cooking, which will ensure the marrow is firm. Remove the bones and using a long thin-bladed knife, scoop out the marrow, chop and set aside.

4 For a main course, slice the meats thickly and place on a platter. Surround with the vegetables from the broth, and spoon over a couple of ladles of broth. Cover and keep warm whilst you enjoy the broth as a first course.

5 Stir a handful of small pasta into the broth and simmer for 10–15 minutes until cooked. Stir in the chopped marrow to reheat, then ladle into soup bowls.

6 Serve the meat portions with plain boiled potatoes, gherkins and coarse-grain French mustard.

PRES ET PATURAGES

BRAISED *OX CHEEK* BORDELAISE, *with* PARSNIP & WHITE *CHOCOLATE* PUREE

I am pleased to see ox cheeks appearing more regularly now in butchers' shops. They are lean and meaty but do need long slow cooking to tenderise them. We serve them with a creamy purée of parsnips enriched with some squares of white chocolate. You will need some fresh beef stock for this dish, which you can either buy now from the chill cabinets of supermarkets or make your own using beef bones and meat trimmings (or use the stock left over from your *pot-au-feu*).

Serves 4

INGREDIENTS

800g ox cheeks

a little olive oil

2 tablespoons plain flour

100g sugar

1 x 75cl bottle red wine

500ml fresh beef stock

2–3 sprigs fresh thyme

2 bay leaves

2 fat garlic cloves, crushed

sea salt and freshly ground black pepper

500g shallots, sliced lengthways

4 marrow bones (optional), soaked in cold water for 2–3 hours

1 In a large saucepan, sauté the ox cheeks in hot oil, turning until nicely caramelised and browned. Mix in the flour and sugar. Stir in the red wine and the beef stock, plus the herbs, 1 garlic clove and some seasoning.

2 Bring to the boil, then turn down to a simmer, cover and cook gently for about 4 hours until the meat is tender.

3 Strain a ladle of the cooking liquid into another saucepan. Add the sliced shallots and remaining garlic and simmer until the shallots are softened and the cooking liquid has reduced to a syrupy glaze.

4 If using the marrow bones, drain them and steam over boiling water for 10 minutes, then remove, cool and scoop out the marrow. Chop and set aside.

5 Meanwhile, make the parsnip purée. Quarter the parsnips lengthways and cut out the hard central cores, then chop the flesh. Cook in the milk and cream, with seasoning until softened, about 15 minutes, adding extra water if necessary.

6 Tip the parsnips into a blender or food processor, add the butter and chocolate, broken in chunks, and whizz until smooth and creamy. Scoop into a bowl.

7 When ready to serve, slice the ox cheeks. Reheat the shallot glaze and a little of the cooking *jus*. Spoon the parsnips into the centre of four warmed plates, top with the sliced beef and glazed shallots and drizzle a little cooking *jus* around. If using the steamed marrow, scatter on top. Serve immediately.

PARSNIP PUREE INGREDIENTS

500g young parsnips, peeled

200ml milk

100ml double or whipping cream

50g butter

70g white chocolate

BLOODY MARY PORK *with* ROSEMARY POLENTA *&* TOMATO *TARTARE*

This dish is what we would call 'Modern Gascon', using up-to-date style and ingredients, following in the tradition of punchy flavours and gutsy sauces. And, of course, I must celebrate the fact that possibly the most popular vodka today, Grey Goose, is not only French but it is made in Gascony!

Serves 4

INGREDIENTS

600g tenderloin of pork

100ml vodka (ideally Grey Goose)

750ml milk

1 small sprig fresh rosemary

150g instant polenta

½ teaspoon celery salt

sea salt and freshly ground black pepper

100g butter

20ml olive oil

1 Make the tomato sauce first. Purée half the tomatoes in a juicer for fresh tomato juice. Chop the remaining tomatoes, seeds, insides and all. Put the tomatoes and juice and everything else but the Tabasco into a large saucepan with some freshly ground black pepper. Bring to the boil, then simmer for about 30 minutes. Blitz in a blender or food processor, then rub through a sieve with the back of a ladle. Set aside in a pan ready to reheat later.

2 For the tartare, halve the tomatoes, de-seed, then chop the flesh into neat small dice. Combine with the diced celery and spring onion, olive oil and season with some crushed *fleur de sel*. Roughly chop the celery leaves and mix in. Chill until ready to serve.

3 Cut the tenderloin into four 150g medallions and mix with the vodka. Marinate for 20 minutes whilst you make the polenta.

4 Heat the milk, with the leaves stripped from the rosemary, for about 15 minutes, then whizz in a blender and strain through a sieve into a large non-stick saucepan. Heat it slowly until almost on the point of boiling, then pour in the polenta in a slow stream, whisking vigorously as you pour so the grains incorporate smoothly. Add the celery salt, plus some black pepper to taste. Return to a gentle simmer and cook for 5–7 minutes, partially covered with a lid as polenta plops as it cooks. When smooth and thick add the butter in chunks, beating well in between until it is glossy. Keep warm whilst you cook the pork.

5 Heat the oil in a large non-stick frying pan and brown the medallions, turning until golden brown, then lower the heat, season and continue pan-roasting the meat until it is just cooked but still a little springy when pressed with the back of a fork. I like to serve pork slightly pink and juicy. Modern pork reared in humane hygienic conditions is perfectly safe to eat a little pink.

6 Leave the pork to rest for 5 minutes, then slice each medallion in four or five and place in the centre of warmed plates. Reheat the sauce, add dashes of Tabasco to taste and spoon the sauce around. Sprinkle over the tartare and serve the polenta on the side.

TOMATO SAUCE INGREDIENTS

500g tomatoes, chopped

2 tablespoons tomato purée

½ teaspoon celery salt

100ml olive oil

Tabasco, in careful dashes

TOMATO TARTARE INGREDIENTS

1 medium green tomato

1 medium yellow tomato

1 celery stick, diced

2 spring onions, diced

2 teaspoons olive oil

fleur de sel

a sprig of celery leaves

RACK OF VEAL, POTATO CAKE & RED LILLET SAUCE

A rack of veal is just a larger version of a lamb rack, a prepared loin joint that has been chined and rib-bone tips cleaned (known as French cut). You can use the Continental white veal for this dish, or why not try British rose veal from grass-fed, less intensively reared calves? The potato cake is layered potato, baked with tender cooked chard stems and chopped kumquats, then fried. It takes a time to prepare and make, but is worth it. It also makes a nice and stylish garnish for beef, venison or duck *magret*.

Serves 4

INGREDIENTS

1 rack of veal, about 1.2kg, 'French cut'

40g butter

3 tablespoons olive oil

5 fresh sage leaves

3 garlic cloves, unpeeled

30g sugar

50ml sherry vinegar

200ml red Lillet
(see page 25)

1 tablespoon flour

sea salt and freshly ground black pepper

POTATO CAKE INGREDIENTS

1 bunch Swiss chard

40g butter

3 large even-sized roasting potatoes, e.g. King Edwards

100g kumquats, finely chopped

1 Make the potato cake first. Cut the Swiss Chard's fleshy stems from the leaves. Use the leaves (cooked like spinach) for another meal. Using a swivel peeler peel the ribs of the leaves if they are thick, then boil in salted water with the butter until they are meltingly tender and the liquid has reduced to a buttery glaze. Cool.

2 Peel the potatoes and slice to a 3mm thickness (like a £1 coin).

3 Meanwhile, heat the oven to 180°C/Gas 4. Line a medium rectangular or square baking dish with non-stick baking parchment. Using half the potatoes, place a layer slightly overlapping on the base and season lightly. Top with a layer of chard, then sprinkle with the kumquats. Top with a layer of the remaining potatoes, cover with a sheet of baking paper and place another baking dish of the same size on top to weigh it down. Bake in the preheated oven for 20 minutes. Remove from the oven and cool, still weighted down. Leave until it is quite cold. This can be made beforehand and chilled.

4 To cook the veal, first heat the oven to 250°C/Gas 9. Heat a large roasting pan or frying pan on the hob with the butter and half the oil, the sage leaves and garlic cloves. Sear the veal rack on all sides until nicely browned and then place in the hot oven.

5 Turn the heat down to 180°C/Gas 4 and cook for 30 minutes, basting the joint once or twice with the pan juices, then reduce to 150°C/Gas 2 for a further 15 minutes. The meat should by now be cooked, slightly pink and juicy inside. Remove the meat to a warmed platter to rest for 15 minutes.

6 Whilst the meat is cooking you can start the sauce and finish cooking the potato cake. Put the sugar and half the sherry vinegar in a medium saucepan and heat until dissolved, then raise the heat, add the Lillet and boil until reduced by half. Stir the flour into the roasting pan with the meat juices, then mix in about 150ml or so of water. Mix this into the pan with the sauce base and heat until it thickens. Simmer for a minute or so, then add the remaining vinegar and season to taste.

7 For the potato cake, remove from the dish and peel off the paper, then cut into four squares or rectangles. Add the remaining oil to a hot frying pan and cook the potato until golden brown and crisp on both sides. It is important to have a nice golden colour!

8 Strain the sauce into a jug, cut the meat into chops and serve with the potato cake. A nicely dressed green salad would complete this delicious meal.

PRES ET PATURAGES

FILLET OF VENISON *with* CRUSHED ARTICHOKES *& A VIOLET & POMEGRANATE* SAUCE

This is a great dish, but you must have one particular ingredient, the violet syrup from Toulouse (see page 61). Nothing else will give the unique sweet and spicy, violet coloured and shiny sauce. Pan-fried fillet of lean venison is nicely complemented by pomegranates and blueberries, a similar game and fruit combination to what you might find in Britain. (The pomegranate molasses you can find in Middle Eastern delis.) Here I have accompanied the crushed artichoke garnish with pak-choi, a Chinese member of the cabbage family, but sometimes I add some seaweed or samphire for an oceanic hint.

Serves 4

INGREDIENTS

1 prepared venison fillet, 350–400g

2 teaspoons fennel seeds, roughly crushed

3 tablespoons grapeseed oil

4 tablespoons chilli jelly, ideally Gascon-style (hot and spicy)

2 tablespoons pomegranate molasses or syrup

sea salt, freshly ground black pepper and Espelette pepper

some fresh lemon juice

2 teaspoons plain flour

4 tablespoons violet syrup (see page 61)

a knob of butter

1   Sprinkle the venison with the fennel seeds and plenty of ground black pepper in a shallow dish then drizzle with grapeseed oil. Cover and marinate for about an hour.

2   Meanwhile, cook the artichokes in salted water to which you have added a good squeeze of lemon juice. Simmer for 20–30 minutes until tender. Pour off and reserve 200ml of the cooking water into another pan; drain the rest and set the artichokes aside.

3   Return the artichoke water to the boil and mix in the chilli jelly, molasses, seasoning including Espelette, and another squeeze of lemon. Stir the flour to a thin paste with a little cold water and briskly whisk into the hot liquid. Boil until reduced by two-thirds and stir in the violet syrup. Check the seasoning, the flavour should hover between spicy and sweet.

4   To finish the artichokes, crush with a fork, adding seasoning, including Espelette, plus the dill and a dash of olive oil.

5   Peel the outer leaves of the pak-choi and chop or shred. Stir these into the artichokes. Slice each pak-choi in half lengthways.

6   When ready to serve, heat a frying pan with the butter and when hot add the venison fillet, complete with the crushed spices. Turn in the pan frequently, basting it in the juices until browned on the outside and slightly pink inside, about 15 minutes or so.

7   Remove from the heat and allow to rest whilst you pan-fry the pak-choi for 2–3 minutes in a little more hot olive oil, seasoning lightly.

8   Finally, reheat the artichokes and sauce. Lightly crush the blueberries and season with some black pepper. Spoon the artichokes on to four warmed plates, and sprinkle with the blueberries and pomegranate seeds, if using.

9   Slice the venison into eight to twelve medallions and divide between the plates. Drizzle with the sauce and surround with the pak-choi.

CRUSHED ARTICHOKES INGREDIENTS

400g Jerusalem artichokes, peeled

some fresh lemon juice

2 tablespoons chopped fresh dill

a little olive oil

TO SERVE INGREDIENTS

4 heads pak-choi

½ punnet fresh blueberries

a few fresh pomegranate seeds (optional)

HEARTS *with* SPINACH *&* SORREL SAUCE

Hearts are all muscle, so are very lean and full of flavour. We use little ducks' hearts in our restaurants – as I always say, the Gascons use everything of the duck but the beak! – but of course this option may not be open to you, so I suggest as an alternative the more readily available lamb hearts. Pan-fry them, then coat in a bright green spinach and sorrel sauce, and serve with, if you like, some *confit* potatoes, although sauté potatoes would be equally delicious.

Serves 4

INGREDIENTS

24 ducks' hearts or 4 lambs' hearts

400g Charlotte potatoes

2 garlic cloves, chopped

2 sprigs fresh thyme, leaves stripped off

sea salt and freshly ground black pepper

olive oil

200g baby leaf spinach, washed

a small handful of fresh sorrel leaves

50g butter, chilled and cut in cubes

fleur de sel

8 spring onions, trimmed and sliced

1 Cut the hearts in half lengthways and, using kitchen scissors, snip out the tubes, fat etc, so you have only lean muscle left. If using lambs' hearts, then slice thinly.

2 Heat the oven to 160–170°C/Gas 3.

3 Peel the potatoes, slice thinly, then rinse. Layer in a medium oven-proof dish with the chopped garlic, thyme and seasoning, then trickle over 200ml of the olive oil, ensuring it seeps into the layers. Brush some on the top as well, and grind over some black pepper. Bake in the preheated oven for about 1 hour until the potatoes are golden on top and tender when pierced with a thin-bladed knife.

4 Make the sauce. Heat a large saucepan with a little olive oil and when hot toss in the spinach and sorrel and stir-fry until wilted, adding a splash or two of boiling water, if necessary. Season, then spoon the contents into a food processor or blender and blend until smooth and creamy. Scoop back into the pan and reheat on a medium heat.

5 Using a balloon whisk, drop in the cubes of butter and beat steadily until incorporated into the sauce. Set aside and keep warm.

6 When the potatoes are ready, heat a large frying pan with a little olive oil and sauté the hearts for about 10 minutes until browned and still slightly pink inside. Season in the pan with *fleur de sel* and toss in the sliced spring onions.

7 Put the potato *confit* in the middle of four warmed plates, scatter the hearts on top and spoon over the sauce.

PRES ET PATURAGES

CHICKEN LIVER PARFAITS *with* PORT JELLY

I think this is probably one of the simplest recipes in the book: a light and delicious chicken liver pâté topped with a layer of port jelly. It's a classic French recipe, which we serve at Comptoir.

Serves 4–6

INGREDIENTS

300g chicken livers

200ml double cream, chilled

1 free-range egg

1 egg yolk

½ teaspoon sea salt

a little freshly ground black pepper

200ml + 1½ tablespoons port

½ teaspoon sugar

¼ teaspoon Espelette pepper

2 gelatine sheets, soaked in cold water

1 Heat the oven to 150°C/Gas 2.

2 Rinse the livers in cold water, then pat dry. Snip out any sinews. Then place in a food processor or blender with the cream, egg, egg yolk, salt, some pepper and the 1½ tablespoons port. Whizz until very smooth, scraping down the sides once or twice. Pour this purée through a sieve into a bowl, rubbing through with the back of a ladle.

3 Lightly oil four medium or six small ramekins and pour the purée into them. There may well be small bubbles on top, so here is a neat chef's trick to burst them – wave over a lit cook's blow-torch. Then cover the ramekin tops with oiled foil and place in a roasting pan.

4 Pour in boiling water from a kettle to come two-thirds of the way up the ramekin sides, as a *bain-marie*, and bake in the preheated oven for 17 minutes or until the mixture is still slightly wobbly and lightly set on top. Remove from the pan, still covered in foil and cool to room temperature, then chill lightly.

5 Meanwhile, for the jelly, boil the remaining port with 200ml water plus the sugar and Espelette until reduced by half to 200ml. Slide in the soaked gelatine and stir until dissolved. Cool to room temperature.

6 Pour the cooked jelly on top of each pâté and return to the fridge until set. Serve with hot toasts and *cornichons* or small gherkins.

QUERCY

ROAST VEAL KIDNEYS with CORN & BALSAMIC ONIONS

Veal kidneys are perhaps the nicest ever, almost sweet, juicy and delicious when pan-roasted with the suet fat that encloses them. We like to serve them chopped and mixed with fresh corn kernels and tossed with balsamic onions, parsley and garlic.

Serves 4

INGREDIENTS

2 large onions

100ml balsamic vinegar

2 veal kidneys, in their fat

sea salt and freshly ground black pepper

4 heads corn on the cob

4 sprigs fresh dill, chopped

2 garlic cloves, chopped

a small handful of fresh parsley sprigs, chopped

1   Heat the oven to 100°C/Gas ½.

2   Peel the skins from the onions, then quarter them. Separate out the leaves of the onions and scatter in a small roasting pan. Stir in the balsamic and cook, uncovered, for an hour, stirring once or twice until softened but still a little *al dente*. Remove and increase the oven temperature to 180°C/Gas 4.

3   Remove the hard suet fat enclosing the kidneys and set aside. Peel off the thin membrane over the kidneys, then slice them in half length-ways through the cores. Using kitchen scissors, snip out the cores and cut the meat into bite-sized pieces. Keep to one side.

4   Snip the fat into small chunks also, and mix in a roasting pan with a little salt. Roast uncovered for 20–25 minutes until the fat starts to melt and the pieces become crisp and golden. Remove the pieces using a slotted spoon and keep to one side.

5   Toss the kidney cubes plus seasoning into the fat remaining in the roasting pan. Place the pan on the hob and cook the kidneys on a medium high setting, stirring occasionally, for about 10 minutes until just firm. Remove the kidneys with a slotted spoon to a shallow dish and keep warm.

6   Cut the kernels from the cobs by standing them upright and slicing straight down with a sharp knife. Sauté the corn kernels in the pan juices with some seasoning for 3–5 minutes.

7   Return the kidneys, then mix into the onions and reheat. Add the chopped dill, garlic and parsley at the last minute. Sprinkle with the crisp pieces of fat, and serve hot.

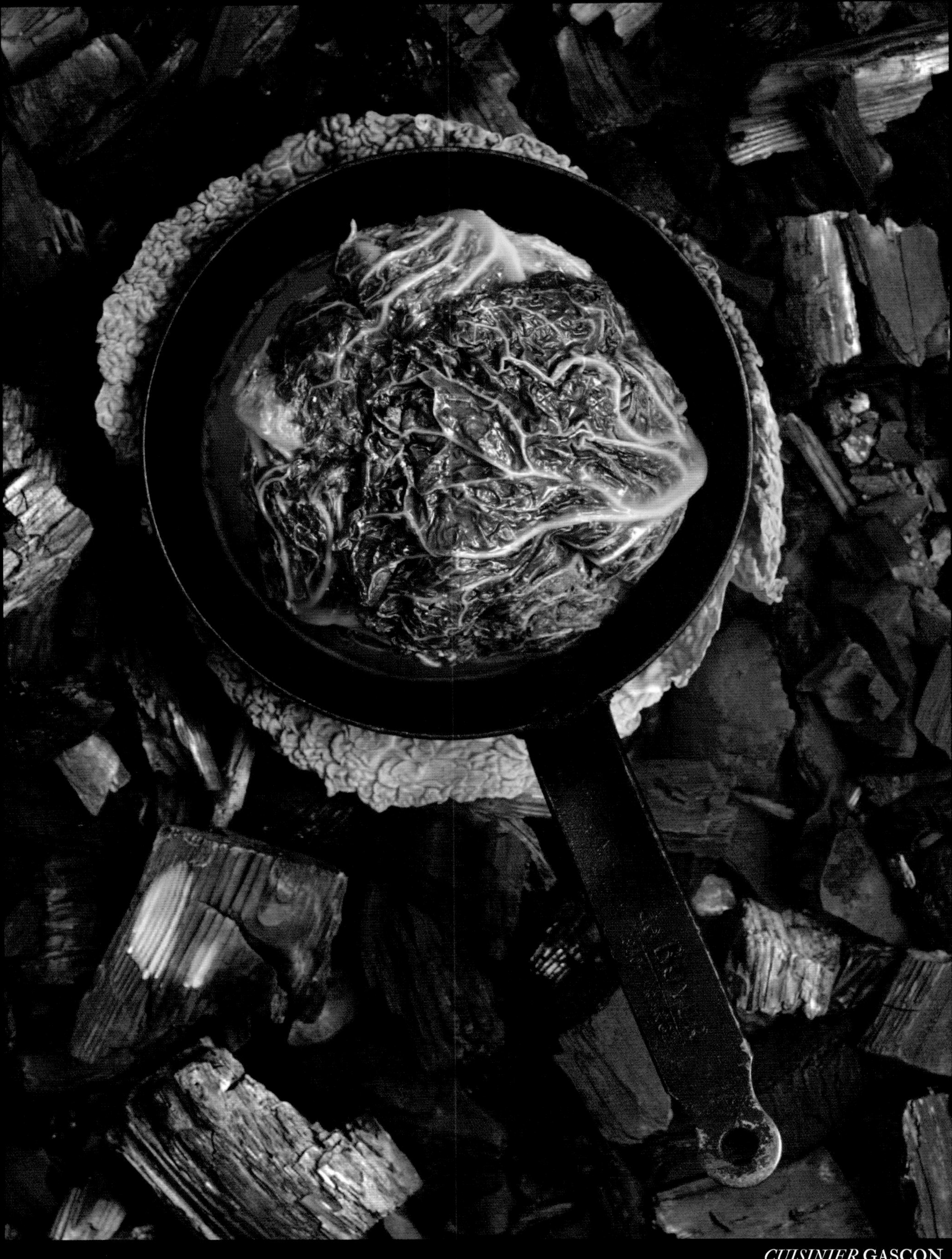

CHOU *FARCI*

This French stuffed cabbage is a way of using leftovers from a *pot-au-feu* (see page 151), using the meat stuffed into a whole cabbage, which is then simmered gently in the liquor. But you could use any cooked beef and beef stock. To keep a neat shape during cooking, you can wrap the cabbage in a large piece of caul fat, the lacy membrane used to wrap home-made sausages, faggots etc., (see below). Otherwise, ensure the cabbage is cooked in a well-fitting saucepan.

Serves 4–6

INGREDIENTS

1 medium green cabbage, ideally Savoy

about 200g cooked beef, finely chopped

400g pork sausage meat

2 garlic cloves, chopped

2 free-range eggs, beaten

sea salt and freshly ground black pepper

a large piece of caul fat (optional, see below)

2 carrots, chopped

2 onions, chopped

100g fat bacon, chopped

1 litre beef stock or cooking liquor from a *pot-au-feu*

1 *bouquet garni* (fresh parsley, thyme, bay and celery)

1 Choose a pan that will hold the cabbage snugly, allowing a little room for the stock etc. Place the cabbage in base-side down, pour over boiling water to cover, then simmer for 10 minutes. Drain off the water, remove the cabbage and cool upside in a colander.

2 Meanwhile, mix together the chopped beef, sausage meat, garlic and egg using a fork, and season, remembering that sausage meat is already seasoned.

3 Pull the centre of the cabbage apart and cut out the heart. Chop this and mix back into the stuffing. Now, using a spoon, separate out the outer leaves, pushing stuffing into the gaps, and filling the hollowed centre. Press the cabbage together to reshape. Wrap in caul fat if you have it.

4 Place back in the saucepan and scatter around the carrot, onion and bacon. Pour over the stock and add the *bouquet garni*. Bring to the boil, then turn down to a gentle simmer. Cover partially and cook for about 3 hours or until all the liquid has evaporated.

5 Remove and serve cut in quarters or wedges.

COOK'S NOTES

CAUL FAT

This is the large spider's web of fat that is wrapped around animal intestines. It is usually pork caul that is available. Sold wet, it should be soaked in cold water before use and not allowed to dry out. Drain it carefully, and unfold.

It may break occasionally but can be easily folded back on itself. It wraps around many sausage-like products, holding the filling together, adding flavour to the whole, and an appetising sheen to the outside.

TOMATES *FARCIES* *COMME* A LA MAISON

This is a true gutsy Gascon dish. It is a dish that is actually famous throughout France, but usually the tomatoes are baked in the oven. Not so in my family. My grandmother cooked her *tomates farcies* in a stove-top pan instead, and although they may not look like much, collapsed and losing their shape, the caramelisation achieved by the slow cooking tastes wonderful.

Serves 4

INGREDIENTS

4 large beef or stuffing tomatoes

sea salt and freshly ground black pepper

2 tablespoons olive oil

50g sugar

1 Cut the top quarters off the tomatoes and chop. Using a spoon hollow out the insides, reserving the juicy pulp, and lightly sprinkle the insides with salt. Drain upside down in a colander for 30 minutes to *degorge*, that is lose some water. Then up-end (there is no need to rinse).

2 Meanwhile, soak the breadcrumbs in the milk, then mix into the sausage meat using a fork, adding the garlic, parsley, egg, chopped tomato and tomato pulp. Season, then spoon into the tomato shells.

3 Choose a heavy-based sauté or frying pan (Le Creuset type) and heat the oil. Place the tomatoes stuffed ends down first to brown, then up-end them. Sprinkle with the sugar and cook on a low heat for about an hour until they are *ésclaffées* (i.e. on the verge of losing their shape and looking a bit rough, virtually 'exploded').

4 Serve straight from the pan.

STUFFING INGREDIENTS

50g fresh breadcrumbs

3 tablespoons milk

150g sausage meat

2 garlic cloves, chopped

3 tablespoons chopped fresh parsley

1 free-range egg, beaten

TOULOUSE SAUSAGE *with SAVORA* MASH & *MUSTARD-PRUNE* SAUCE

Gascon garlicky bangers and mash – perfection! This is something we invented for Croque Gascon, a prune and mustard sauce to go with the wonderful Toulouse sausages. Savora mustard condiment is not strictly speaking a mustard, as most varieties use a blend of about eleven herbs and spices, including mustard seeds. It is mild, sweet and spicy. (The most famous mustard company in Britain says Savora was the first mustard product they ever made.)

Serves 4

INGREDIENTS

500g old potatoes, peeled

100ml milk

200g butter, cubed in small pieces

sea salt and freshly ground black pepper

100g Savora mustard

150g Dijon mustard

100g no-need-to-soak stoned prunes

4 large Toulouse sausages

1 Boil the potatoes in salted water until tender, then drain and tip back into the saucepan over a low heat to dry off. Place the potatoes in a high-sided bowl and mash until smooth and creamy.

2 Heat the milk until on the point of boiling and beat into the potatoes, adding the butter gradually, then season and add the Savora mustard. The purée should be very smooth, almost runny, and the secret is to make sure the potatoes don't lose heat as you beat them. Keep warm.

3 Place the Dijon mustard and prunes into a blender with 3 tablespoons of hot water and whizz to a smooth sauce. Add a pinch or two of salt. Keep warm.

4 Grill or gently pan-fry the sausages until firm but still juicy and golden brown. Don't overcook them. Serve with the creamed potatoes and prune mustard sauce.

5

DISHES *from the* FOREST *&* PRAIRIE

FORET *ET PRAIRIE*

Gascony is generously wooded with many varieties of trees – oaks, elms, limes, chestnuts, and walnuts. In the shade of all these trees grow more of Gascony's culinary treasures – wild mushrooms and, sometimes, truffles, although these are more of a feature further east in the Périgord around Cahors. In the lush meadows, from valleys to mountains, are harvested snails, frogs, eggs and rich milk from cows, sheep and goats used in the making of the few Gascony cheeses. (And can I mention that the French are not the only gourmets to appreciate snails and frogs? They are hugely popular in the Orient, in fact even more so).

La forêt des landes de Gascogne, claimed to be one the largest pine forests in Europe is, astonishingly, man-made, not natural. *'La lande'* means sandy moor or heath in French, and the area of Gascony now known as Les Landes was once covered by desolate sandy moors and marshes. At one time, the only regular inhabitants of the area were huge flocks of sheep and their shepherds, known as *échassiers,* who used to walk through the marshland on stilts, the better to keep their animals within view and their feet dry. It wasn't until the 18th century that work began on reclamation. Resinous trees were planted to drain the water, and by the beginning of the 20th century the area was covered with *Pinus pinaster,* the maritime pine. I find it astounding that what was virtually reclaimed land from the mosquito-ridden 'Sahara of France', should now be so deliciously productive! I even use dried pine needles in my cooking, a style of barbecue smoking we called *éclade* (see page 29).

FORET ET PRAIRIE

FUNGI

TRUFFLES AND MUSHROOMS

There are many kinds of truffle, but the most important to us is the black truffle of the Périgord (*Tuber melanosporum*). This species peacefully co-exists at the foot of oak trees although it will accept hazel and lime trees and Aleppo pines. In addition to finding the right tree base and soil there needs to be the right weather condition, not too cold and not too dry.

Truffles have intrigued us since the times of the ancients with their lumpy veined flesh. A food enjoyed by peasants and nobles alike for centuries, many attempts have been made to cultivate them, but it wasn't until the end of the 18th century that it was discovered that it was spores from the truffles themselves that contained the seeds and that these only grew best under oak trees. But many ancient oaks had already been cut down to make way for vineyards. The outbreak of *phylloxera* in the late 19th century, which destroyed most Gascony vineyards, was an opportunity to replant thousands of hectares with oak. The truffle harvest began to recover and by the end of the century, thanks to improved rail links with Paris, truffles became very much more commercial, appearing in northern markets, food shops and restaurants. Truffles are still found in the wild – principally in the Dordogne or Périgord and the Quercy – but the future seems to rely on private passion and not on commercial cultivation.

If you are lucky enough to lay your hands on a fresh black truffle, treat it with reverence. It is a reservoir of perfume, which can escape very easily; take every precaution to retain this, not letting air get to it too much. You can keep it in a little jar covered with goose or duck fat, or with a fragrance-free oil such as corn or grapeseed (both fat and oil will taste wonderful afterwards). You can peel truffles, as the inside is much nicer than the outside; but keep these peelings, as they too can be used to scent fat or oil.

There was once a fashion for baking whole truffles *sous la cendre*, wrapped in foil and gently warmed in charcoal ashes, or in a pastry case. I have played with this idea in my whole truffle recipe, but it is baked in clay, an idea that came to me when we were first designing Club Gascon. Sophie, the architect in charge at the time, had some clay for moulding, which she stored in the fridge, and I grabbed it! Otherwise, use slivers of raw truffle with potatoes, eggs and in salads and pâtés. A truffle omelette is heaven; my grandmother's *coquillettes* on page 49 would be magic spiked with a little truffle; and you could slip a few slivers of truffle under the skin of a chicken to be roasted.

Legend has it that Rossini, the famous Italian composer and gourmet (he was a friend of Carême), wept only three times in his life: the first time was when his first opera failed; the second time was when he heard Paganini play the violin; and the third time was when a cooked turkey, with slivers of truffle under its skin, fell overboard at a boating party. I think I would have wept too.

FUNGI AND WILD MUSHROOMS

I first went wild mushroom hunting at about fifteen and then after that I would try and be in the woods every autumn!

Gascony is rich in all sorts of wild mushrooms. The most appreciated is the *cèpe* (*Boletus edulis*), *porcini* in Italian and cep or penny bun in English. We can also find *chanterelles* (*Cantharellus cibarius*), horn of plenty (*Craterellus cornucopioides*), *pied bleu* or blewit (*Lepista nuda/saeva*), *pied de mouton* or hedgehog mushroom (*Hydnum repandum*), and a host of others, including the morel (*Morchella*), which likes the sandy soil of eastern Gascony. But, there is one wild mushroom which I associate particularly with Gascony and Les Landes, and that is the pine morel (*Sparassis crispa*). It looks like a sponge, and tastes sweet and nutty (page 174).

Although I am fairly confident about my ability to identify a number of wild mushrooms, I would never go on a mushroom hunt without at least a very good identification guidebook – preferably with someone who is an expert. There are a great many fungi that look edible, but which are very poisonous, so play safe until you learn to confidently identify wild mushrooms. In France you can get advice from a local pharmacist, who may double as a fungi expert.

COOKING FUNGI

When you have gathered your wild fungi, wipe them with a damp cloth. Then cook them as simply as possible, so that their flavours will sing out. My *Cèpes à la Bordelaise* recipe on page 181 is classic: the wonderful mushrooms are simply fried in duck fat with garlic, shallot, and finished with chopped parsley and lemon juice. You could add potatoes to this, to make the dish bigger.

But I also like to blanch them first in boiling water, drain well, then fry them in duck fat or olive oil. This blanching water is full of flavour so don't waste it! I use it is a stock.

left: Monsieur Pebeyre in his factory in Cahors. His family has been selling truffles for 4 generations.

FORET ET PRAIRIE

FORET ET PRAIRIE

MIJOTEE of PINE MORELS

Mijoter is the French word for 'to simmer' or 'to stew'. And this is the way we like to cook the special spongy pine morels of *Les Landes* (*Sparassis crispa*, the cauliflower fungus) that grow at the base of pine-tree trunks. The same recipe works well for the more common morel if you are fortunate enough to find or buy them fresh.

Serves 6–8

INGREDIENTS

1 kg pine morels

100g shallots, thinly sliced

300ml dry white wine

3 tablespoons Noilly Prat or dry Martini

300ml double cream

1 tablespoon well-reduced veal or chicken stock (optional)

sea salt and freshly ground black pepper

1 Pine morels are very spongy and need to be well washed before use. So, slash the bases halfway up and wash the heads and stalks thoroughly under cold running water. Drain into a large saucepan and sprinkle with the shallots.

2 Cover and cook over a medium-high heat in a covered pan until a *jus* is extracted, about 5 minutes. Drain the mushrooms in a colander set over a bowl to retain the *jus*. Return the *jus* to the pan and boil down until reduced by half.

3 Add the wine and Noilly Prat and boil again until reduced by half. Pour in the cream and stock (if using), then return the morels. Add some seasoning and leave to simmer slowly for 20–30 minutes until soft and 'stewy'. Leave to cool in the cooking *jus* then serve with roast or grilled veal, chicken or pork.

PORTOBELLO MUSHROOM *CONFIT*

Like all *confit* recipes, this is one for keeping. Confitting fresh foods in duck fat and salt, then cooking long and slowly is an old Gascon way of preserving food. In this case, heads of large mushrooms can be stored in the fridge ready to serve as an accompaniment to grills or roasts, or to mix into an omelette or scrambled eggs. Ceps would work here too.

Serves 6–8

INGREDIENTS

1 kg Portobello mushrooms

50g coarse rock salt

1 fat garlic clove, thinly sliced

2 shallots, halved lengthways and thinly sliced

200g duck fat

2 tablespoons freshly grated horseradish

1 bay leaf

3 sprigs fresh thyme

1 Preheat the oven to about 100°C/Gas ½.

2 Pull the stalks from the mushrooms (these can be used for stock elsewhere, no need to waste them).

3 Arrange the mushroom heads upside down in a shallow ovenproof dish and sprinkle with the salt, slices of garlic and shallot.

4 Heat the duck fat in a saucepan with the horseradish. Pour over the mushrooms and add the bay leaf and thyme on top. Cover with foil. Cook for up to 4 hours in the preheated low oven until the mushroom heads are soft. Then remove and cool.

5 The mushrooms can be gently transferred to a large Kilner-style jar, covered with the fat and stored, chilled, for 2–3 weeks.

COOK'S NOTES

AGA CONFITS

If you have an old-fashioned Aga cooker, then this recipe is perfect for cooking in the low-heat simmering oven.

FORET ET PRAIRIE

FRICASSEE of WILD MUSHROOMS PERSILLADE

This fricassée is perfect served as an accompaniment to meats or bacon. The *persillade*, a mixture of garlic and parsley, which is added at the last minute, is typically Gascon.

Serves 4

INGREDIENTS

800g mixed wild mushrooms, e.g. *chanterelles*, horn of plenty, *pieds bleus*/blewits, *pieds de mouton*

sea salt and freshly ground black pepper

duck fat

1 medium potato, peeled and thinly sliced (ideally on a mandolin or Japanese food slicer)

1 little gem lettuce

1 large garlic clove, finely chopped

5–6 large sprigs fresh parsley, chopped

1 Wash the mushrooms briefly in a bowl of cold water, then drain. Take care if using *pieds de mouton* not to damage them under the heads. Cut all the mushrooms into bite-sized pieces if necessary, otherwise leave them whole.

2 Put the mushrooms into a large saucepan, cover with boiling water from a kettle and add about 2 teaspoons salt. Return to the boil, cook for about 2 minutes, then drain off the water and reserve it for stock. Leave the mushrooms to drain well in the colander.

3 Cook the potatoes. Heat about 2 tablespoons duck fat in a shallow pan and sauté the potato slices for about 10 minutes until tender and golden brown. Drain and set aside. Shred the lettuce into slices 1cm thick.

4 Heat another 2–3 tablespoons duck fat in the shallow pan and fry the blanched mushrooms for about 5 minutes, seasoning in the pan. Mix in the potato slices and lettuce shreds, then remove from the heat and mix in the chopped garlic and parsley. Do not cook further, just serve.

TRUFFLE VINAIGRETTE

Makes about 100ml

Continuing the theme of truffle fragrance, this is a lovely dressing for salads, warm new potatoes, pasta, eggs etc. You don't have to use a top-quality truffle, canned would do, or even a summer truffle. The vinegar must be the best, though, and I like to use Banyuls vinegar, although sherry vinegar is good too. Never use a balsamic.

INGREDIENTS

5 shallots, finely chopped

3 tablespoons clear honey

2 tablespoons truffle oil

1 tablespoon Armagnac

1 teaspoon Banyuls or sherry vinegar

sea salt and freshly ground black pepper

1 small black truffle, fresh or canned, chopped

1 Place the shallots in a thick-based saucepan with 250ml water and the honey. Simmer very gently until the shallots are meltingly tender, 30–40 minutes, stirring once or twice.

2 Mix in the truffle oil, Armagnac, vinegar and seasoning. Simmer for a minute longer, then place in a blender with the truffle and blitz until smooth.

3 Thin with a little extra water to make it runny, then store in a small jar. It will keep for about 1–2 weeks in the fridge.

PICKLED *CHAMPIGNONS*

It is worth having a jar of this useful pickle in your fridge or larder – it enhances many different meals.

Serves 6

INGREDIENTS

1kg wild mushrooms in season, e.g. ceps, *mousseron, girolles* or Paris (brown button) mushrooms, sliced

100ml sherry vinegar

100ml grapeseed oil

20ml hazelnut oil

2 tablespoons sugar

1 large sprig fresh thyme

2 bay leaves

1 teaspoon sea salt plus freshly ground black pepper

1 Check the mushrooms are clean and free from mushroom compost. They may only need to be wiped with a damp cloth. Cut any large ones in half, if necessary.

2 Place the vinegar, both oils, sugar, thyme, bay, a teaspoon of salt plus pepper to taste into a large saucepan and 200ml water. Bring to the boil.

3 Then stir in the mushrooms. Return the liquid to the boil, stirring once or twice, then simmer for 30 seconds and remove the pan from the heat. Cover and set aside to cool completely. Transfer to a large jar or food container, cover tightly and store in the fridge until required. Will keep for at least 2 weeks.

FORET ET PRAIRIE

CEPES A LA *BORDELAISE*

With their velvety caps and intensely fragrant flavour, ceps are the ultimate gourmet's mushroom, the king of mushrooms. I like to enhance these attributes the Gascon way, classically simple in the true Bordelaise fashion – stir-fried in duck fat and finished with garlic, shallots, chopped parsley and lemon juice.

Serves 4

INGREDIENTS

250g ceps, cleaned

1 tablespoon duck fat

sea salt and freshly ground black pepper

2 garlic cloves, chopped

1 shallot, thinly sliced

2 tablespoons chopped fresh parsley

juice of ½ lemon

1　Pull the stalks from the cep caps (don't waste these, they can be used to flavour stocks). Larger cep caps can be halved, otherwise keep them whole.

2　Heat the duck fat in a large frying pan and, when hot, toss in the ceps and stir-fry them until they soften and become golden brown, about 5 minutes. Season nicely.

3　Remove from the heat, and stir in the garlic, shallot, parsley and lemon juice. Check the seasoning again and serve.

COOK'S NOTES

DUCK FAT

Many Gascon recipes call for duck fat. You can buy this fairly easily in cans (400g size), but if you cook duck portions or whole ducks regularly the fat that drains off is plentiful and perfect. Simply drain it into a heat-proof glass jar, cool and then cover with a screw-top lid. You will be pleasantly surprised how much accumulates. Keep it in the fridge. Goose fat can be stored in the same way.

SOFT MILLAS *with* *TRUFFLE* & PARMESAN

Millas (polenta), truffles and Parmesan seem to have an affinity with each other. Parmesan is a reminder of the truffle, in fact, as both have that pungent meaty and savoury flavour that the Japanese call *umami*. This soft polenta could be served as a starter by itself, or with some fish (delicious with grilled monkfish), fillet of beef, or white meat, but not lamb as it is quite delicate.

Serves 4

INGREDIENTS

400ml milk (or use half chicken or veal stock, or a good mushroom stock)

70g instant polenta

70g butter

1 tablespoons truffle oil

1 small black truffle, grated

50g Parmesan, freshly grated

sea salt and freshly ground black pepper

1   Bring the milk (or milk and stock) up to the boil in a large non-stick saucepan. Sprinkle in the polenta as you stir briskly, then lower the heat to a bare simmer and cook for 10 minutes, whisking occasionally.

2   Stir in the butter, oil, grated truffle and Parmesan. Season to taste, simmer a minute or two longer then serve – either on its own, topped with more Parmesan or as a side dish.

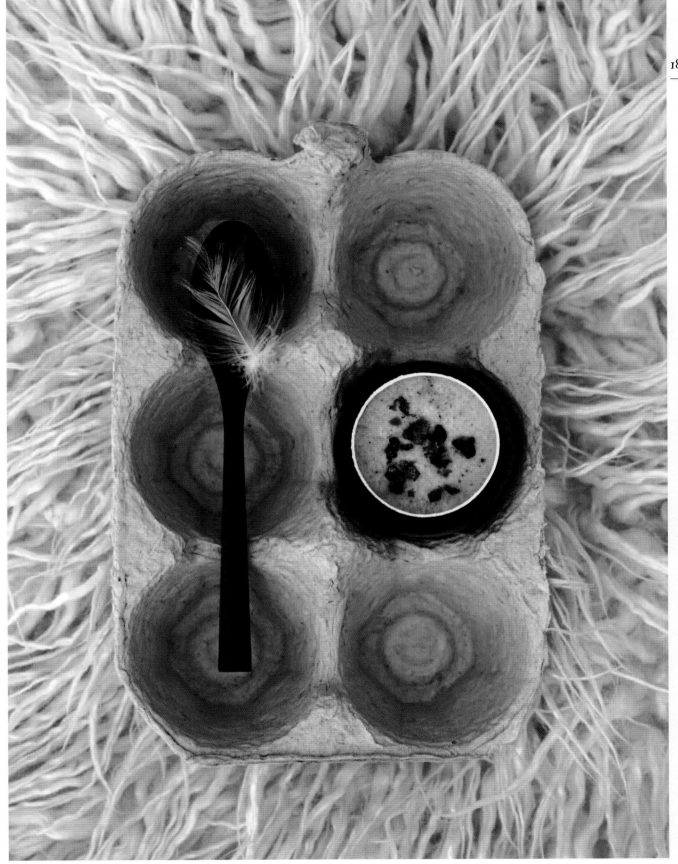

FORET ET PRAIRIE

WHOLE *BLACK* TRUFFLE *BAKED* IN CLAY

If and when you have a whole black truffle, then you might want to try this way of capturing its fragrant essence by baking it whole in clay. This does require that you buy some fresh green clay. In France, this can be found in pharmacies but in Britain you may find it in art suppliers or potters' shops. The recipe is a lot like 'pass the parcel'. You wrap the whole truffle in spinach leaves, then cabbage and finally in a rolled layer of clay. The fun part is breaking the baked clay with a hammer to release the heavenly aromas. How you want to enjoy thereafter is up to you, but I would suggest this is a perfect Christmas treat *à deux*.

Serves 2

INGREDIENTS

500g fresh green clay

4 outside leaves of a whole cabbage, de-stalked

about 6 whole spinach leaves, de-stalked

1 whole black Périgord truffle

fleur de sel

1 Make the compote first. Gently simmer the shallots in a small pan with the butter, sugar and 150ml water until very soft, about 30 minutes. Stir in the honey, pepper and lemon juice and continue cooking until the liquid has evaporated. Remove from the heat and mix in the Armagnac. Set aside to cool.

2 Preheat the oven to 180°C/Gas 4.

3 Roll out the clay between two large sheets of non-stick baking parchment to a round. Set aside.

4 Using a sharp knife, cut out the central stalk vein from the cabbage leaves in a V-shape where it merges into the main leaf. This is so the leaf will mould nicely when rolled. Bring a large pan of water to the boil. Blanch the cabbage leaves first for a minute or two, and then lift them out with a slotted spoon into a large bowl of iced water to cool.

5 Repeat with the spinach leaves, blanching for 1 minute. Drain and cool in the iced water. Then lay out both sets of leaves on a clean tea-towel and pat dry.

6 Lay the spinach leaves on a board overlapping in a large round and spoon half the shallot compote in the centre. Press the truffle in the middle and spoon over the rest of the shallots, moulding around the truffle. Draw up the spinach leaves to make a neat ball.

7 Lay out half the cabbage leaves in a round and wrap up the spinach-covered truffle, then repeat the layering with the remaining cabbage leaves, pressing well into the truffle as a neat ball.

8 Press the ball into the clay and draw up the sides to cover the leaves, shaping with your hands into a neat ball. Pretend you are a potter shaping a masterpiece.

9 Put the ball in a shallow ovenproof dish and bake in the preheated oven for 45 minutes. Then remove from the heat, and stand for 5 minutes.

10 Using a small hammer, gently smash open the clay and peel it away along with the first layer of cabbage leaves. Cut the ball neatly in half to reveal the layers of cabbage and spinach.

11 Complete the perfection with a small mixed leaf salad and some truffle vinaigrette (see page 177).

SHALLOT COMPOTE INGREDIENTS

2 large shallots, chopped

40g butter

1 tablespoon sugar

1 tablespoon honey

½ teaspoon freshly ground black pepper

2 teaspoons lemon juice

2 teaspoons Armagnac

BABY FERN HEADS *with* *MARROW* & TRUFFLE SHAVINGS

Discover the delights of eating new shoots of wild ferns before they unfurl, when the tops look like old-fashioned shepherds' crooks. Popular across Europe and North America, there are a number of varieties that are edible, including the widely available bracken or fiddlehead ferns (*Pteridium aquilinum*) found in woods mid-spring, but you must cook and eat them the same day they are gathered. (And if picking from the wild, take only a few shoots from each plant, to ensure the plant survives.) The flavour is mild and not dissimilar to young asparagus. Nice as a starter or side dish with beef.

Serves 4

INGREDIENTS

3 beef marrow bones

200g freshly picked fiddlehead ferns

30g butter

sea salt and freshly ground black pepper

1 black truffle

a little truffle vinaigrette (see page 177), optional

1 Soak the marrow bones in a big bowl of cold water, changing it two or three times, to extract any blood. Drain and steam over boiling water in a steamer basket for about 5 minutes. Cool the bones, then using a skewer extract the marrow and dice it. Set aside.

2 Peel off the silky covering to the fern heads, then wash in cold water and drain in a colander.

3 Melt the butter in a large frying pan and toss in the fern heads plus about 100ml cold water. Cook for about 3 minutes, stirring once or twice until the water evaporates, then add the diced marrow and cook a couple of minutes more.

4 Season to taste and divide between four serving plates. Shave the truffle on top and drizzle with a little truffle vinaigrette, if liked. Serve immediately.

FORET ET PRAIRIE

OEUFS &
ESCARGOTS

A FULL *FRENCH* with SUNNY-SIDE-UP EGGS

This is our take on the British 'all-day' breakfast. Eggs and bacon with a tomato compote and long sweet green peppers, rather like a *pipérade*. You will note that I add an aniseed flavour with good old English Fisherman's Friend lozenges!

Serves 4

INGREDIENTS

4 long sweet green peppers

2 tablespoons olive oil

4–8 slices back or lean streaky bacon

4 large, very fresh free-range eggs

sea salt and Espelette pepper

1 Make the compote first. Dip the tomatoes into a pan of boiling water for a few seconds, then skin and cut in quarters. Remove the cores and seeds. Chop the flesh and place in a shallow saucepan with 3 tablespoons of the oil, the garlic, tomato purée and sugar.

2 Cook for about 5 minutes, stirring occasionally until the mixture becomes pulpy, then stir in the Fisherman's Friend lozenges until they dissolve. Add the herbs and some seasoning and cook for 5–10 minutes until all the liquid has evaporated. Keep warm.

3 Halve the peppers lengthways, shake out the seeds and trim the inner membranes. Heat the oil in a large frying pan and cook the pepper halves until they soften, turning carefully once or twice. Try and keep them whole, if possible.

4 When ready to serve, dry-fry the bacon in a hot non-stick frying pan until crisp. Remove the rashers and keep warm. Finally fry the eggs in the bacon fat (adding a touch of oil if necessary). Cook them on one side only until the whites are just firm and the yolks soft.

5 Divide the tomato mixture between four warm dinner plates, add the pepper halves on top followed by the bacon and eggs. Sprinkle over some Espelette pepper and serve.

TOMATO COMPOTE INGREDIENTS

1kg ripe tomatoes

3 tablespoons olive oil

2 garlic cloves, chopped

2 tablespoons tomato purée

50g sugar

3 Fisherman's Friend lozenges

2–3 sprigs fresh lemon thyme

1 bay leaf

FORET ET PRAIRIE

ESCARGOTS *A LA* VIGNERONNE

Snails suit good full-flavoured sauces, and so it is no surprise that in one of the great wine regions of the world – Bordeaux – the two are often cooked together. Now, Napoleon may have dismissed parsnips as a British vegetable fit only for horses, but we like to use it as a purée as a base for this delicious French dish.

Serves 4

INGREDIENTS

24 snails, canned or frozen

1 carrot, diced

2 shallots, diced

100g smoked ham, diced

4 garlic cloves, chopped

2 tablespoons olive oil

1 tablespoon tomato purée

½ teaspoon sugar

300ml red wine

300ml ruby port

3 sprigs fresh thyme, chopped

1 bay leaf

sea salt and freshly ground black pepper

1 Make the parsnip purée first. Simmer the parsnip cubes in the milk for about 12 minutes until just tender and the milk has been absorbed. Season and tip into a food processor or blender and whizz to a smooth purée. Then return the purée to the pan and heat gently.

2 Gradually stir in the cream and then the butter. Check the seasoning and set aside to keep warm.

3 Make the *persillade* butter. Place the softened butter in a food processor or blender with the garlic, ham, mushrooms, almonds and cardamom. Whizz to a smooth purée, then add the three herbs and pulse for a few seconds until they are just incorporated but not pulverised. Scoop into a roll on a sheet of clingfilm, wrap tightly and chill.

4 Cook the snails. In a large pan, sauté the carrots, shallots, ham and garlic in the olive oil for about 5 minutes until just softened, then mix in the tomato purée, sugar, wine, port and herbs. Simmer for 10–12 minutes until reduced down by half.

5 Wash the snails well and pop into the pot, cover and cook gently for about 20 minutes. Season.

6 Reheat the parsnip purée if necessary and divide between four wide shallow bowls. Spoon over the snails and sauce. Unroll the *persillade* butter and cut into rounds then pieces. Dot these on top (you won't need all the butter, so re-chill the rest), and serve.

PARSNIP PUREE INGREDIENTS

500g young parsnips, peeled and cubed

200ml milk

100ml double cream

100g butter, diced

PERSILLADE BUTTER

100g butter, softened

2 garlic cloves, chopped

30g ham, diced

25g button mushrooms, diced

10g ground almonds

seeds from 3 cardamom pods, ground

10g each of parsley sprigs, dill heads and chervil leaves

LANDES

DUCK *COQUES with* SEA URCHINS *& SOLDIERS*

If you find sea urchins either in the fishmongers or when fishing from the shore, do try them spooned into soft-boiled duck eggs (*coques*). They may look spiny and impenetrable but, armed with a pair of sharp kitchen scissors and the end of a thin teaspoon, they are quite easy to prepare. You eat the orange tongues inside. To make the dish a little more substantial cook some *crosnes* (or Chinese artichokes) or maybe some thick juicy asparagus spears to dunk in as soldiers. Failing that, thin brown bread toasts.

Serves 4

INGREDIENTS

4 very fresh sea urchins

125g *crosnes* (optional)

4 fresh free-range duck eggs

a knob of butter

sea salt and freshly ground black pepper

1 Prepare the urchins first. Holding an urchin in your hand (covered with a cloth of course), and using sharp kitchen scissors, snip out the central beak. Then tip upside down over a cup to collect the juices from inside. Work your scissors around the top to expose the orange tongues inside.

2 Using the end of a thin teaspoon, scoop out the orange flesh on to a saucer.

3 Scrub the *crosnes*, if using, and trim the ends. Simmer in salted water for 2–3 minutes and drain.

4 Boil the duck eggs for 3 minutes, timing from when the water returns to the boil after the eggs are lowered in. Remove with a slotted spoon.

5 Stand the eggs in egg cups. Cut off the tops and divide the sea urchin tongues between the opened eggs.

6 Tip the saved urchin liquid through a sieve into a small saucepan and bring to the boil. Using a hand-held blender, whisk in a knob of butter to a froth and spoon this over each egg. Serve the *crosnes* as 'soldiers', with salt and pepper on the table.

GULLS' EGGS *with* FREGOLA, WILD ASPARAGUS & SAMPHIRE

This is a dish for the brief season when seagulls' eggs, wild asparagus and samphire all coincide. Make the dish more substantial by serving with the small round Sardinian pasta known as *fregola*, but failing that the giant couscous grains will do.

Serves 4

INGREDIENTS

200g *fregola* pasta

100g fresh or frozen peas

30g butter

4 seagulls' eggs

1 dessertspoon vinegar

1 tablespoon olive oil

200g fresh samphire, washed and stalk ends trimmed

1 bunch wild asparagus or thin-stemmed asparagus (*sprue*)

1 bunch fresh chives, chopped

1 tablespoon truffle oil

1–2 tablespoons fresh dulse seaweed or *wakame*, chopped (optional)

sea salt and freshly ground black pepper

1 Boil the pasta in plenty of salted water for 10 minutes, then drain and set aside.

2 Boil the peas for 3–5 minutes until tender, then drain, reserving some of the water. Tip the peas into a food processor with half the butter and a little of the water and blend to a smooth sauce. For a velvety texture, you can rub the purée through a sieve with the back of a ladle. Set aside.

3 Boil the eggs in simmering water with the vinegar. Time for 1½ minutes from when the water returns to the boil. Drain and place in a large bowl of cold water for a few minutes, then peel.

4 Heat the olive oil in a frying pan and sauté the samphire and asparagus until just wilted but still crisp, 2–3 minutes.

5 Heat the remaining butter in another frying pan and when hot toss in the cooked pasta plus the chopped chives and truffle oil. Toss into the greens (with some dulse or *wakame* if you have any), season and mix well.

6 Divide the mixture between four warmed plates, place a halved egg on top and dribble the pea sauce around. Serve immediately.

BABY ARTICHOKES & SNAILS A LA *BARIGOULE*

Early-to-midsummer artichokes are excellent eating served with a *barigoule* dressing – a classic French recipe – along with some garlicky snails. I am not suggesting you go out picking fresh snails from the garden, a can or jar of ready-shelled and pre-cooked snails is fine.

Serves 4

INGREDIENTS

8 young artichokes, about 7cm in diameter

1 medium onion, thinly sliced

2 tablespoons olive oil

2 tablespoons dry white wine

2–3 sprigs fresh thyme

juice of 1 lemon

1 teaspoon coriander seeds, crushed

sea salt and freshly ground black pepper

1 Halve the artichokes lengthways down the centre and place in a large pan with the sliced onion and 2 tablespoons of olive oil. Heat and cook until the onion is lightly browned, then add the wine, thyme, lemon juice, coriander seeds and some seasoning. Cover and cook on a low heat for about 15 minutes, then remove from the heat and cool.

2 In another saucepan, make the *barigoule*. Sauté the diced carrot, shallots and ham in the oil for about 5 minutes, then add the garlic and tomato on top. Season and cook gently for about 5 minutes, stirring once or twice until the liquid is absorbed.

3 Stir in the snails and cook for 3–5 minutes until hot and bubbling.

4 Remove the artichoke halves to four shallow bowls and scoop out any hairy chokes with a teaspoon. Tear the basil into chunks, mix into the snail *barigoule* and spoon on top of the artichokes to serve.

SNAIL BARIGOULE INGREDIENTS

1 carrot, finely diced

4 shallots, diced

100g Bayonne ham, diced

2 tablespoons olive oil

2 fat garlic cloves, chopped

1 large juicy tomato, roughly chopped

24 large snails, canned or frozen (ideally from Burgundy)

a bunch of fresh basil

FORET ET PRAIRIE

*Gabriel Bachelet
of Fromages des
Pyrennees, Lons*

FROMAGES

SALAD OF *FRISEE, WALNUTS* & CABECOU CHEESE *with* RED WINE *PEARS*

Pears in red wine are not only good as a dessert, they make an excellent relish for serving with salads. This is a colourful starter, using baby-sized soft Cabecou goats' cheeses on toast with a walnut-oil dressed salad.

Serves 4

INGREDIENTS

about 150g *frisée* leaves or curly lettuce or rocket

2 dessertspoons each of walnut oil and olive oil

2 dessertspoons balsamic vinegar

sea salt and freshly ground black pepper

100g fresh walnut halves

4 Cabecou cheeses, unwrapped if in leaves

4 small slices rustic bread (*campagne*/sourdough style)

1 Make the red wine pears first. Peel the pears, cut in half lengthways then score out the core. Cut each pear half in half again for quarters.

2 Boil the wine in a large saucepan for 2–3 minutes, then add the spices and orange zest. Add the pears, making sure they are submerged under the wine, then cover and simmer for about 20 minutes until just tender. Remove the pears with a slotted spoon to a shallow dish.

3 Re-boil the wine until reduced by two-thirds until lightly syrupy, then mix in the sherry vinegar and sugar. Strain over the pears and set aside to cool.

4 When ready to serve, preheat the oven to 200°C/Gas 6.

5 Prepare the salad leaves in a bowl. Whisk together the two oils, balsamic vinegar and some seasoning. Then toss into the leaves and divide between four serving plates. Surround the salad with the walnuts and pears.

6 Place the bread slices on a flat baking sheet and top with the cheeses. Bake in the hot oven for 3–5 minutes until the cheese starts to melt.

7 Remove, place each melted cheese toast on top of the salad, and serve immediately.

RED WINE PEARS INGREDIENTS

4 firm pears

1 x 75cl bottle red wine

3 cloves

2 star anise

¼ teaspoon black peppercorns

3 strips fresh orange zest

2 dessertspoons sherry vinegar

2 teaspoons sugar

COOK'S NOTES:
CHEESES OF THE SOUTH WEST

Outside Gascony only two cheeses are found on the international scene. The most familiar is perhaps Ossau-Iraty, *a sheeps' milk cheese made in the Ossau Valley in the Bearn, and the wooded hills of Iraty in the Pays Basque. (Sometimes seen as Pyrenees Brébis, or fromage de Brébis.) Recognised with an AOC (appellation d'origine contrôlée) since 1980, it is a semi-soft cheese, which becomes firmer and nuttier as it matures. Its flavour actually depends to a large extent on when it is made (from spring or summer milk, the latter is more floral); on where the sheep graze (the lower on the mountain, the more varied their diet); and how long it is aged (for at least 90 days and up to two years). It is made in wheels, often in shepherds' huts (when it is suffixed* fermier). *In fact, it is so sweet and buttery that it is known locally as 'the farmer's dessert'. When it is more mature, and sliced paper thin, it makes a delicious dessert paired by black cherry jam. I like to serve it with fruit.*

CAMEMBERT *with* SPICED *TARTE TATIN* APPLES

Cheese and apples are a popular combination in many European countries, including the UK. This is a Gascon way of serving a mould-ripened cheese with apples cooked *tarte Tatin* style.

Serves 4

INGREDIENTS

3 Golden Delicious or Granny Smith apples

100g golden caster sugar or light soft brown sugar

½ teaspoon ground cloves or 5 whole cloves

120g slightly salted butter, in cubes

1 whole Camembert, about 250g

1 Core the apples, then slice each into eight pieces. You can peel the apples first if you like, but leaving the skins on gives them more character and colour.

2 Preheat the oven to 180°C/Gas 4.

3 Heat a large shallow-based pan with heatproof handles and when hot sprinkle in the sugar in an even layer with 2 tablespoons of water.

4 Leave the pan undisturbed and watch the sugar dissolve into a caramel, adjusting the temperature down if it starts to burn. Resist the temptation to stir until it is a pale caramel, then remove from the heat. Add the cloves, then the butter in cubes, stirring until well mixed in.

5 Scatter in the apple slices, stirring to coat them in the buttery caramel, then place the pan in the preheated oven. Roast for 15–20 minutes until the apples have softened, basting once or twice with the pan juices. Remove from the heat and discard the whole cloves, if using. Cool until warm.

6 Serve the cheese in wedges with the apples alongside.

COOK'S NOTES: CONTINUED

BETHMALE, a cheese from Ariege in the Hautes Pyrenees is a cows' milk. Made in wheels, it has an orange rind, and a firm but creamy flesh with lots of holes.

CABECOU, a goats' milk cheese, is one of France's smallest cheese at barely 40g. The name is derived from the langue d'Oc *(or Occitan), the ancient language of South West France, and is a diminutive word for goat. It is a speciality of the Midi-Pyrenees, ours coming from the*

romantic town of Rocamadour, perched high over a gorge in the Dordogne Valley. Sometimes sold wrapped in chestnut leaves.

However, it is worth noting that the most famous cheese in South West France, ROQUEFORT, comes from the Auvergne just outside the Gascony border. It is made with milk from the same breeds of sheep as Ossau-Iraty so in my book that makes it an honorary Gascon cheese!

OSSAU–IRATY *with* *CARAMELISED* CLEMENTINES *&* A *PIMM'S SAUCE*

Ossau–Iraty is a semi-soft cheese from the Pyrenees, sold in wedges, and often found in British food stores. It is served here with a compote of clementines with celery and mushrooms and a dash of Pimm's sauce. It's an interesting combination, and I like the idea of combining a Gascon cheese with Pimm's, that most British of garden drinks.

Serves 4

INGREDIENTS

4 clementines, seedless and peeled

2 tablespoons caster sugar

1 large celery stick, with leaves

120g Paris or brown button mushrooms, halved

2 tablespoons olive oil

sea salt and freshly ground black pepper

200g wedge Ossau-Iraty cheese

1   Start with the caramelised clementines. Peel all the pith from the fruits, then separate into segments.

2   Heat a non-stick frying pan until hot, then sprinkle in the sugar with a small splash of cold water. Leave the sugar in the pan without touching it over a medium heat until it starts to caramelise. Add the clementine segments and stir well to coat. Remove from the heat and cool in the pan.

3   Pinch off the celery leaves and shred thinly. Peel the thick ribs of celery using a swivel vegetable peeler, then cut the stalk into 1cm diamonds.

4   Heat the oil in another pan, and toss together the celery diamonds, mushrooms and shredded leaves. Add some salt and pepper.

5   Make the sauce by heating the Martini and Pimm's in a small saucepan and flaming it with a lit match. When the flames die down, stir in the lemon juice.

6   Cut the Ossau-Iraty into sticks and divide between four plates. Arrange the celery and mushroom salad around and finish with a dash of the sauce.

PIMM'S SAUCE INGREDIENTS

2 tablespoons red Martini

2 tablespoons Pimm's

juice of ½ lemon

FORET ET PRAIRIE

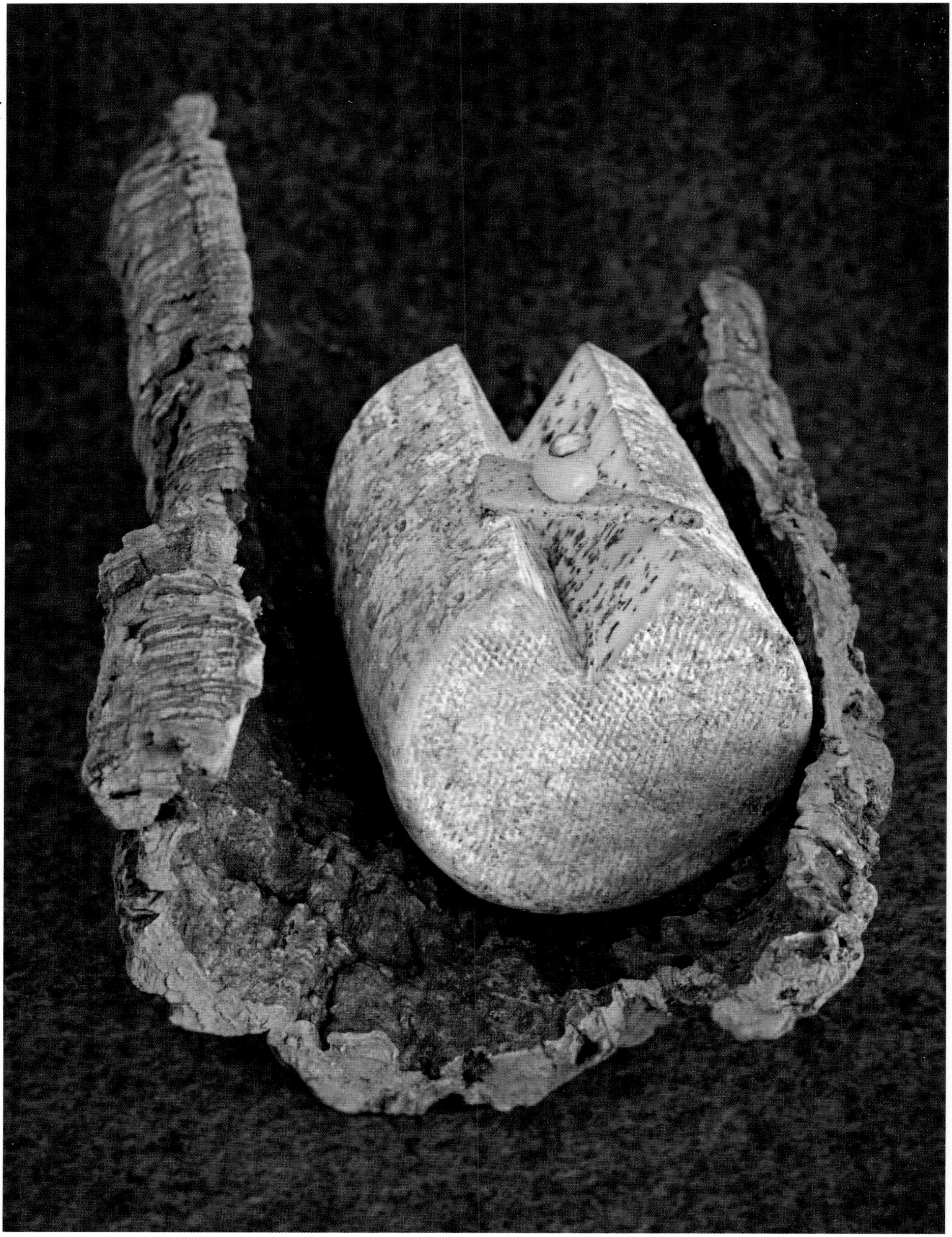

FOURME D'AMBERT *with* PICKLED GRAPES

Fourme d'Ambert is one of France's oldest cheeses, a creamy blue cows' milk cheese from the Auvergne, which we like to serve with an unusual pickle of grapes steeped in a wine and oil dressing. This pickle goes well with many other cheeses, and keeps for up to two weeks in the fridge.

Makes 400g, to serve 10–12

INGREDIENTS

200g Fourme d'Ambert cheese

3–4 tablespoons unsalted pistachios

crackers or sliced baguette, to serve

1   Make the pickle ahead. Ideally, peel the grapes, by dipping them first in boiling water then, after a few seconds, pulling off the skins with your fingernails. However, this is not necessary if the grapes are thin-skinned.

2   Put the vinegar, oil, sugar, thyme and salt into a large saucepan with 200ml water. Bring to the boil and simmer for 1 minute, then tip in all the grapes.

3   Return to the boil, simmer for 1 minute, then remove from the heat and carefully tip into a large heatproof, sterilised preserving jar. Cover and seal, cool and then store in the fridge for at least 24 hours before serving.

4   Spread the cheese on crackers, or slices of baguette, top with 1–2 drained pickled grapes and scatter with pistachios. Leftover pickling liquid can be re-used with more grapes, bringing to the boil and repeating step 2.

PICKLE INGREDIENTS

400g seedless white grapes, pulled from the stalks

100ml white wine vinegar (or 50ml white wine vinegar and 50ml Xipister)

100ml grapeseed oil

3 tablespoons caster sugar

2–3 sprigs fresh thyme

½ teaspoon sea salt

ROQUEFORT PIE *with* *AROMATIC* APRICOTS

This dish is made in a fun way using filo draped over wooden spoons for a rippled wave effect into which you scatter crumbled Roquefort cheese and chopped poached apricots. After baking this is then cut into fingers. If you don't have Roquefort, any other tangy blue cheese will work very nicely.

Serves 4

INGREDIENTS

2 sheets filo pastry

40g butter, melted

granulated sugar

12 *mi-cuit* apricots

2 tablespoons Armagnac

200g Roquefort cheese

50g whole blanched fresh almonds, roughly chopped

1 Heat the oven to 180°C/Gas 4.

2 Brush the filo sheets with the melted butter, in the middle and on top. Then lay four long-handled wooden spoons evenly across a baking sheet.

3 Drape the doubled buttered filo sheets along the baking sheet over the spoon handles so you have ridges and furrows and sprinkle with a tablespoon of sugar. Bake in the preheated oven until golden and crisp, about 8–10 minutes. Remove and cool, still draped over the spoons. When crisp, remove the spoons.

4 Meanwhile, snip each apricot in four and poach in 100ml water with a teaspoon of sugar and the Armagnac for 5–10 minutes until softened and the liquid is all absorbed. Cool, then scatter over the filo.

5 Crumble the Roquefort and sprinkle over the pastry, along with the almonds. To serve, snip into long fingers using kitchen scissors along the furrows as fingers.

FORET ET PRAIRIE

HOME-MADE CHEESE BISCUITS

One of our young travelling chefs introduced us to this delightful recipe, which we make to serve with our cheese course. The Japanese dried peas add protein and texture to the mix.

Makes about 12

INGREDIENTS

50g sunflower seeds

30g poppy seeds

1 teaspoon fennel seeds

25g Japanese dried peas

110g wholemeal flour

½ teaspoon bicarbonate of soda

½ teaspoon fine sea salt

25g caster sugar

160g butter, softened to room temperature

1 free-range egg, beaten

1   Grind together the three seeds and peas to a fine powder. Tip into a mixing bowl and add the flour, bicarbonate, salt and sugar. Stir very well to mix thoroughly, then rub in the butter to fine breadcrumbs.

2   Drizzle in the egg, and stir briskly with a fork or wooden spoon to blend to a firm but not dry dough. Knead lightly until smooth, and form into a ball.

3   Lay a large sheet of non-stick baking parchment paper on a worktop and top with the ball of dough, and then another parchment sheet to match. Using a rolling pin roll the dough to a 5mm thickness. Lift the whole thing carefully on to a flat tray and freeze until cold and solid.

4   Preheat the oven to 180°C/Gas 4.

5   Remove the top sheet of paper and cut out from the dough rounds of whatever size you like, but maybe 5cm diameter would be best. Line a baking sheet with the top sheet of baking paper and place the rounds on top.

6   Put the baking tray into the preheated oven and bake for 8–10 minutes until the biscuits become a little golden around the edges, then remove and cool still on the tray until they firm up. Slide them on to a wire rack to cool completely. Store in an airtight container until required.

6

SWEETS & *SPIRITS*

GOURMANDISES

Gourmandise is a French word indicating a taste, an appreciation of good food. In the old days, it meant gluttony (from the Old French *gormant*, glutton) but, nowadays the word is used much less contentiously, and in the plural, to mean sweets or desserts.

I trained originally as a pastry chef, so this section is one I feel quite passionate about. It is a course our diners greatly enjoy. Now one thing I have learnt since moving to London is that the British pride themselves on their strong dessert and cake tradition. When it comes to the sweet course and tea time treats, they love to beat and bake whilst we French, back home, tend to buy a tart or gâteau from the local patisserie. But, true pâtissière is not just confined to professional pastry cooks, many of the great traditions are kept alive in homely kitchens. I am fortunate to have the friendship and co-operation of a wonderful country cook, Madame Sarran, who makes the best traditional Gascon fruit tart ever, *Tourtière*. She even came over to spend time in the Club Gascon kitchens when we first opened over ten years ago, see the following gatefold after page 216.

I would class British desserts as 'sweet comfort food' and so I have gathered together similar recipes from the length and breadth of Gascony - Toulouse, Biarritz, Bordeaux - in humble homage! These are in the main baked and quite creamy, some of which use yeast as a raising agent instead of baking powder. A few contain apples or prunes (true Gascon fruits) plus some simple cakes, large and small, pastries, baked egg custards (one of which is deep-fried) and a chocolate and walnut fondant spiked with Espelette pepper, perhaps one of the original chocolate and chilli desserts which are now so popular. I think maybe we Gascons thought of this marriage of flavours first!

DIGESTIFS

ARMAGNAC

Many orchard fruits flourish in the *Sud-ouest* – apples, plums, pears, raspberries and walnuts, all of which are turned into *eaux de vie* by many small farm producers who may make anything from a few dozen to hundreds of bottles that are offered for sale to passing travellers, displaying *'dégustation'* signs beckoning one to stop, try and buy. Commercial brands of fruit *eaux de vie* to look out for are Brana (*poire William*), Cazotte for a selection of fruits, and Manzana Verde, a green apple liqueur (see my lovely recipe for a parfait of Manzana, page 243).

There is also a tradition of making herbal liqueurs. Izarra is perhaps the best known, a sweet liqueur from the French Basque country made since 1835, in St. Jean de Luz. With two varieties, yellow and green, it is quite powerful – Izarra Horia (*Jaune*) at 40% proof contains the essences of 32 Pyrenean herbs with an overlying flavour of almonds; Izarra Berdea (*Vert*) at 48% proof has 48 herbs and an overlying peppermint flavour.

These regional *digestifs* are generally only available in France so bring back a bottle or two from your trips there.

At Club Gascon we have also created our own *digestif* coffee – the Biberon Gascon. To replicate it at home, you first need to have caramelised condensed milk (see below). Pour strong espresso into a cup, stir in a teaspoon of brown condensed milk, add a shot of Armagnac and top with a spoon of hot milk froth.

COOK'S NOTES

CARAMELISED CONDENSED MILK

Caramelised condensed milk is made by boiling an unopened tin of condensed milk, totally immersed in water, for up to 2 hours. Or you could use ready-made brown condensed milk sold as Dulce de leche.

Armagnac is perhaps the ultimate *eau de vie* of the south-west of France, and alongside Cognac, classed as one of the best brandies of the world. Its quantity of production however, is significantly lower than that of Cognac, around six per cent of the output of Cognac. This is to do with the nature of the production because, to a very large extent, Armagnac is still mostly distilled on small farms, or by small firms, and consequently has nothing like the global spread and international influence of Cognac. It is this 'old' style production, adhering to the traditions of the past, which I like very much.

Although Cognac is better known on the world stage, Armagnac has a longer history and was being distilled at least 200 years earlier than its more northerly rival. In fact, the art of distillation in France is believed to have originated over the Spanish border as early as the 12th century via Moorish influences. The great Navarre king, Henri IV of France, born in Pau in 1553, was said to have had his new-born lips wetted by his grandfather at his baptism with a dash of Armagnac brandy and a smear of garlic to root him to his birthplace and give him 'wisdom and strength' for his whole life. I'm pleased to say the tradition still survives for all newborn infants of the area.

This Gascon *eau de vie* was first produced by monks, priests and apothecaries for its 'medicinal properties', and then by individual wine producers and small farmers. During the 17th century, Dutch merchants found a ready market in their homeland for this delicious *'brandewijn'* (burnt wine) shipped from the Garonne to Holland, and soon the word spread to other countries.

Many of the famous Armagnac houses were founded by 1850 and the spirit became increasingly popular around the rest of Europe - even, for a few years, overtaking Cognac, whose vines had been attacked by the deadly virus *phylloxera*. But in 1878, the virus caught up with the Armagnac vineyards, destroying most of the vines, and it wasn't until after the end of World War II that production picked up and began to grow again.

Right: Martine Lafitte, owner and 3rd generation producer of Domaine Boingneres, the world famous Armagnac.

CUISINIER GASCON

GATEFOLD 6: PASTRY MASTERCLASS

PASTRY MASTERCLASS

*Makes 2 tarts,
to serve* 8–10

800g plain flour, plus
extra for dusting

a good pinch of fine
sea salt

olive oil

1 free-range egg

FILLING

1kg apples, e.g. Granny
Smiths (about 4)

125g butter, plus extra
for greasing

3 tablespoons orange-
flower water

3 tablespoons Armagnac,
plus a little extra

1 teaspoon ground
cinnamon

200g caster sugar

TOURTIERE LANDAISE AUX POMMES DE MADAME SARRAN

Light, crisp apple pastries have been
popular in the Gascony region for centuries.
The pastry is very like the Arab filo in that it
is made with oil, probably influenced by the
Moorish tradition from over the Spanish
border. Also the elastic dough is not rolled but
stretched by experienced hands over a cloth-
lined table until it is gossamer thin. You need
to start this at least 24 hours ahead to allow
the dough to rest and roll. (If you do not have
the time to make the light pastry then, at a
pinch, you could use sheets of good-quality
filo pastry.)

PIERRETTE SARRAN

*We have known Madame Sarran since
the very earliest days of Club Gascon.
She came to us for a week to talk about
the menu, and to give us a demo of her
tourtière – the one above, for which she
is famous in France. She has been back
many times since to talk to new members
of our team, and has been of invaluable
help to us. (Her son Michel has three
restaurants in Toulouse, and has two
Michelin stars.)*

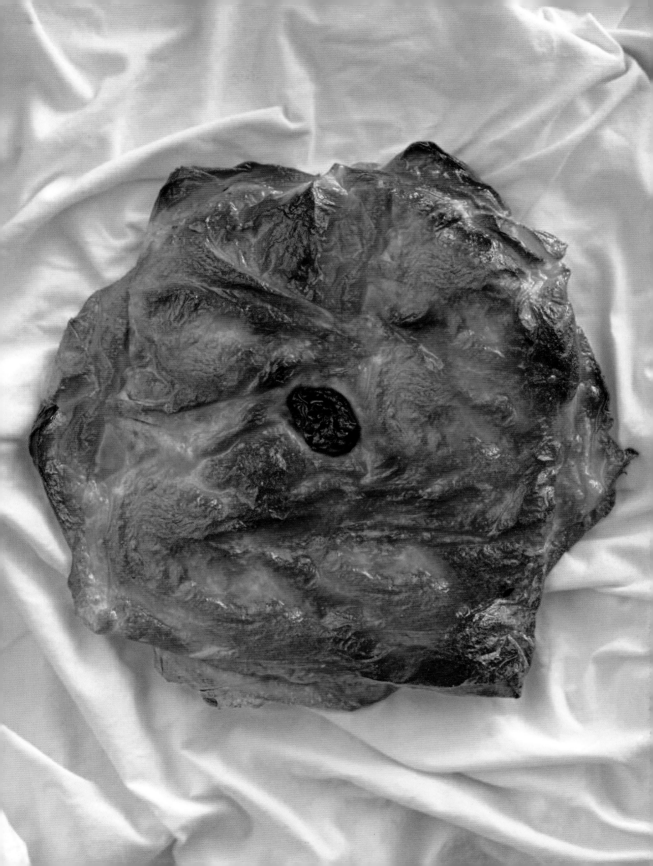

CLASSIFICATIONS OF ARMAGNAC

There are three *terroirs* within the Pays d'Armagnac – covering parts of three French *départements* – mainly the Gers and, to a lesser extent, Les Landes and Lot-et-Garonne. These determine the variations and qualities of Armagnac, perhaps the clearest example of *goût de terroir* ('taste of the earth'), a combination of soil, vine, temperature and weather, elements of which all contribute to the finished product.

Bas-Armagnac is the most westerly *terroir*, nearest to the sea with a sandy soil (*sable fauve*, or 'fawn sand'). Its westernmost point, referred to as 'Grand' Bas-Armagnac, produces what many think of as the supreme Armagnacs – light, fruity, tasting of plum or prune; they are also known as 'Armagnac Noir', because of dark forests of oak and pine surrounding the vineyards.

Ténarèze lies in the middle part of Armagnac, and its clay and limestone soil produces rich, full-bodied and perfumed brandies that take time to reach maturity.

Haut-Armagnac, in the east of the region, the furthest from the sea. The vineyards lie on hills of chalk, giving rise to the name 'Armagnac Blanc'. The brandies from here are perhaps more rustic and good for bottling fruit.

To merit the appellation 'Armagnac' the *eau de vie* must be distilled from wines produced in specific areas, with vine varieties strictly controlled. The official legal existence of Armagnac goes back to 1909, when it was awarded an *Appellation Contrôlée* and Armagnac was granted *Appellation d'Origine Contrôlée* (AOC) status in 1936. This meant distillation of the wine can only take place in two types of still.

The first was a pot still, which was based on double distillation (as in Cognac), but this was superseded by a continuous, single-distillation still known as the *alambic Armagnacais*, which operated at a lower temperature. Armagnac purists insist that the best *eaux de vie* come from the single distillation method, the lower temperature helping the spirit retain more of its fruit character.

After the distillation, the spirit is aged in huge new or little-used casks made from local tannin-rich oak. One of the three major stages of the spirit's ageing, the extraction of tannin from the barrels, gives Armagnac its oaky flavour and scent, as well as its colour. Once the required time has been spent in the barrels – from two to three years – the spirit is transferred to casks made from wood that has already passed on all its tannins, and is left to age, for anything from ten to fifteen up to forty years. The cellar-master might blend various vintages. If a bottle says twenty or twenty-five years on its label, this refers to the youngest brandy in the blend.

I love a good aged Armagnac, and it never ceases to surprise me how different in flavour various vintages are. I have distinguished chocolate, cream, plums and prunes, melon, tropical fruit such as papaya and banana - even toasted almonds and black treacle. I am very fond of a small glass of Armagnac after a good dinner – it is the perfect *digestif* – but I also use it quite a lot in my cooking especially for *foie gras* and desserts.

YOU MAY ALSO COME ACROSS THESE CATEGORIES ON LABELS.

***	(Three crowns or stars) - the Armagnac has been in the cask for at least 1 year.
V.O.	Very Old
V.S.O.P.	Very Superior Old Pale
RESERVE	Armagnac in the cask for at least 4 years.
X.O.	Extra Old, Napoleon, Vielle Reserve, the Armagnac has been in the cask for at least 5 years, often longer.

GASCON MESS

Our tribute to the great classic English summer dessert, Eton Mess – marinated prunes stirred with crushed meringue in a crème Chantilly. A great party dish.

Serves 8–10

INGREDIENTS

4 egg whites

240g caster sugar

1 litre double cream

25g icing sugar

100ml Armagnac

MARINATED PRUNES INGREDIENTS

300g Agen prunes, soaked if not semi-soft or ready-to-eat

50g sugar

1 cinnamon stick

1 star anise

5 cardamom pods

grated zest 1 orange

1 If the prunes are not semi-soft, then they should be blanched first in a pan of boiling water for 1 minute, then drained. If they are semi-soft there is no need to blanch them. Make a syrup with the 50g sugar and 150ml boiling water in a saucepan adding the cinnamon stick, star anise, cardamoms and orange zest. Stir in the prunes and simmer 3 minutes, then remove and cool. Remove the stones if they are not already stoned. Leave to marinate overnight.

2 Heat the oven to 100°C/Gas ½. Cover a large baking sheet with non-stick baking parchment.

3 Whisk the egg whites in a large (grease free) bowl and using a balloon whisk or electric beater beat the whites until you have a white foam that holds firm peaks with soft tops.

4 Then gradually beat in 240g of sugar until the foam becomes a glossy and thick meringue. Drop tablespoons of the mixture onto the baking sheet in mounds, allowing a little space between, then bake for up to 3 hours until crisp and a very pale golden. Cool.

5 When ready to put the dessert together, whip the cream with the icing sugar until softly stiff, then gradually whip in the Armagnac until the cream is firm but not dry.

6 Drain the prunes but leave them still a little juicy, then cut them in halves or quarters. Roughly crush the meringues and fold all the elements together. Serve nicely chilled in glass bowls or sundae glasses. We serve a little red berry coulis and candied julienned orange strips on top.

GOURMANDISE

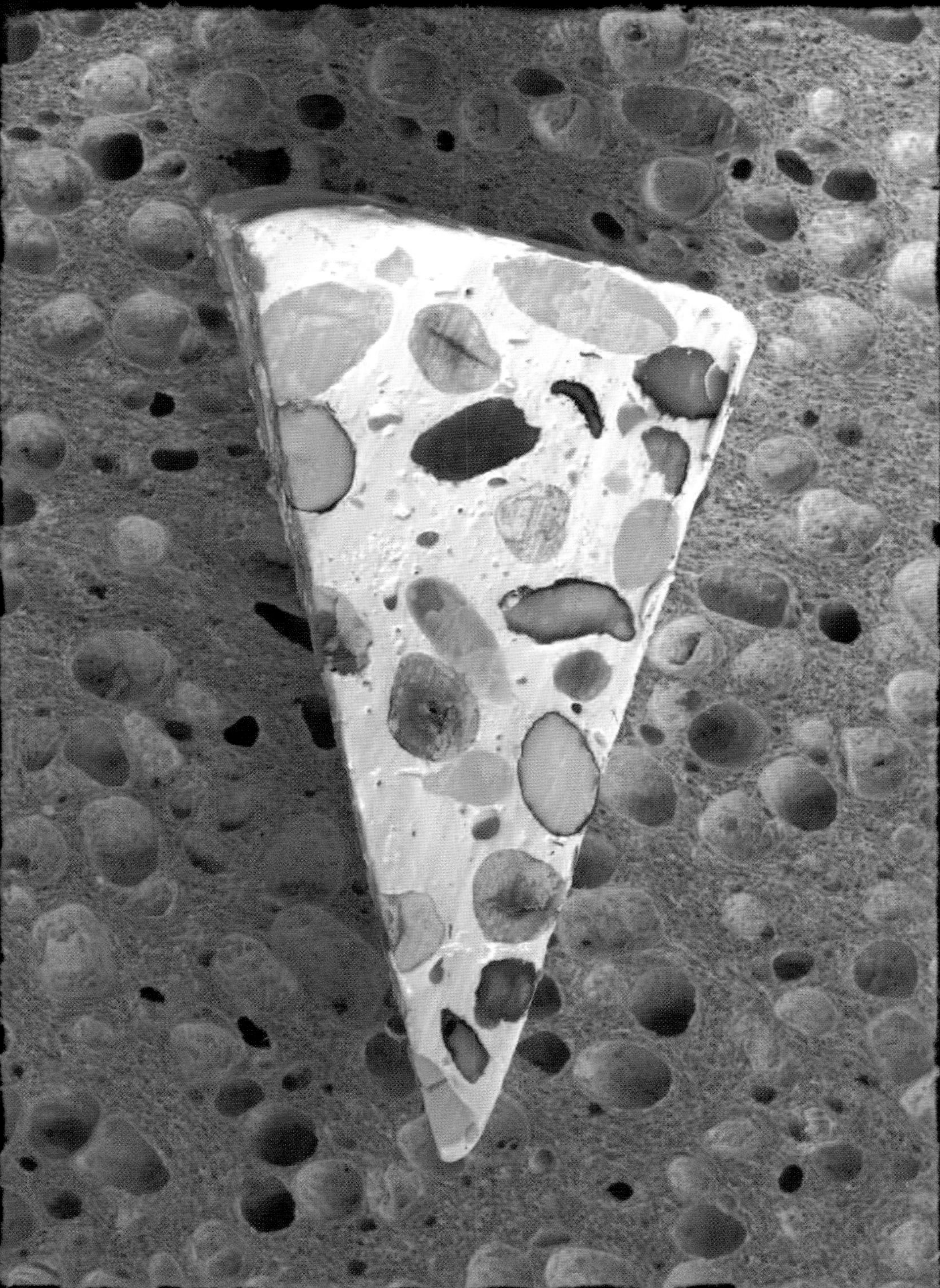

NOUGAT

One of our Club Gascon specialities, which we serve as a treat. Once made, it can be stored in air-tight tins for several months.

Makes 10 *portions*

INGREDIENTS

60g green shelled pistachios

125g shelled almonds

125g shelled hazelnuts

3 tablespoons honey

3 tablespoons golden syrup

250g sugar

2 free-range egg whites

1 Heat the oven to 150°C/Gas 2. Spread the three nuts out onto a baking tray and roast in the oven for 20 minutes, stirring once or twice. Meanwhile, heat the honey and syrup in a pan and keep warm.

2 Place the sugar in a medium size saucepan with 3 tablespoons of water and heat gently until the sugar dissolves and starts to turn a light golden colour.

3 Meanwhile, whisk the egg whites in a heatproof brown with an electric beater until it forms firm peaks. Pour on the hot honey syrup, beating as you pour.

4 By this time the sugar would have become a light golden caramel colour. With the beaters still running, pour on the caramel syrup and keep it hot on the heat, beating until the mixture starts to come away from the pan sides.

5 Remove the pan from the heat and mix in the roasted nuts, then scoop out the mixture onto a flat sheet lined with baking parchment. Spread to an even neat rectangle and allow to cool. Cut in wedges to serve.

GATEAU *BASQUE*

This gâteau is more a rich almond custard pie than a cake, with versions that abound all over France. My Gascon recipe is a light crisp pastry case filled with a *crème patisserie* flavoured with dark rum and almonds. It is best made ahead, then served at room temperature and I like to serve a small shot glass of freshly crushed Granny Smith apple juice to go alongside

Serves 4–6

PASTRY INGREDIENTS

100g caster sugar

50g butter, softened

100g plain flour + extra for rolling

½ teaspoon baking powder

20g ground almonds

a pinch salt

1 teaspoon brown rum

3 drops vanilla extract

2 egg yolks

1 tablespoon milk

COOK'S NOTES

DARK RUM

Our favourite brand is Negrita. Dark or brown aged rums are almost as popular in Gascon cooking as Armagnac.

1 Make the pastry. Put all the pastry ingredients into a bowl, except for 1 egg yolk and the milk. Mix together to a smooth, soft dough using a large wooden spoon. Knead gently, then cover in cling film and leave to rest in the fridge for about 4 hours.

2 Meanwhile make the cream filling. Heat the milk with the vanilla pod in a non-stick saucepan and leave for 10 minutes. Whisk together the flour, 1 egg yolk, 2 tablespoons caster sugar and rum in a heatproof bowl. Remove the vanilla from the milk and reheat it until almost boiling, then pour gradually onto the whisked mixture, beating until smooth. Return the mixture to the saucepan and cook gently until thickened, stirring. Pour back into the bowl, cover and set aside to cool.

3 At the same time, beat together the 40g softened butter and 40g caster sugar until creamy, then mix in the second egg yolk, ground almonds, Pernod or Ricard and almond essence. When the custard has cooled to room temperature fold in the almond cream and chill the mixture in the fridge until firm.

4 When the pastry has rested for 4 hours, remove it from the fridge and leave for about 30 minutes to come to room temperature. Line a flat baking sheet with non-stick paper, then place a tartlet ring on top, about 16cm diameter and 3cm high. Cut off two-thirds of the dough and knead gently into a round, then roll out on a lightly floured board until large enough to fit inside the ring, lifting gently over the pin. Press in carefully to the sides, making sure you don't tear the dough and allowing a little overlap around the sides.

5 Beat together the remaining yolk and tablespoon milk as a glaze. Brush this around the top edge of the pastry case, then spoon the filling into the centre, levelling the top. Roll out the remaining third of dough and lift on top, pressing the edges together to seal firmly. Use a sharp knife to trim the edges neatly of excess dough. Then using the prongs of a fork, draw a grid over top and brush evenly with the remaining glaze. Make a small steam hole in the centre.

6 Set aside to rest whilst you heat the oven to 170°C/Gas 3 then bake for 30–40 minutes until golden brown and firm. Cool until just warm and serve in wedges.

CUSTARD & ALMOND CREAM INGREDIENTS

140ml milk

½ vanilla pod, split in half lengthways

1 tablespoon flour

2 egg yolks

2 tablespoons caster sugar + 40g

2 teaspoons dark rum *

50g butter, softened

50g ground almonds

1 teaspoon Pernod or Ricard

½ teaspoon almond essence

OLD-FASHIONED FRENCH FRUIT CAKE

The French, like the British, are fond of a nice slice of fruit cake, except ours is not as dense and dark and has a nice crisp outside. Yeast is used as a raising agent but the dough is not kneaded.

Makes an 18cm square (or 20cm round) cake, for 10–12 portions

INGREDIENTS

50g raisins or sultanas

50g currants

40 g chopped mixed peel

2 tablespoons dark rum, e.g. Negrita

125g butter, softened

80g caster sugar (try golden caster for a nice flavour)

250g plain flour

a good pinch fine sea salt

1 sachet easy blend yeast (or 8g of fresh yeast, crumbled)

3 free-range large eggs

3–4 tablespoons milk, warmed until tepid

1 Put the three dried fruits into a small pan with the rum and heat gently until hot, then set aside until cooled. Grease and line an 18cm square deep-sided cake tin (or a 20cm round one) with non-stick baking parchment.

2 Beat together the butter and sugar until light and creamy. Sift together the flour and salt and easy blend yeast, if using. (If using fresh yeast, then mix it with a tablespoon warm water until creamy.)

3 Gradually beat in the eggs, one at a time, into the butter sugar mixture, adding spoonfuls of flour if the mixture starts to curdle. (If using fresh yeast, then mix it in at this stage.) Finally fold in the rest of the flour and beat gently until smoothly incorporated, adding the tepid milk at the end to loosen the dough.

4 Spoon this into the prepared tin and level the top. Leave to rise for about 35–40 minutes whilst you preheat the oven to 150 °C/Gas 2.

5 Bake the cake for 5 minutes before increasing the setting to 180°C/Gas 4 and continue baking for 30 minutes until golden brown and firm when pressed. Cool in the tin for 15 minutes before turning out. Cool, then cut in wedges.

CANELES

These famous light-as-a-feather cakes from Bordeaux are traditionally baked in little ridged copper moulds, which you buy from specialist kitchenware suppliers (or bring back a set when you go on holiday to Gascony!). But shape apart, the mixture rises nicely in dariole or brioche moulds or muffin tins but for best results, let the mixture mature in the fridge for 3–4 days before baking.

Makes 12

INGREDIENTS

500ml whole milk

1 vanilla pod, split lengthways

50g butter + extra softened for greasing the moulds

2 free-range eggs

2 egg yolks

250g icing sugar

4 tablespoons brown rum

100g plain flour, sifted

1 Scald the milk with the seeds scraped from the vanilla pod plus the actual pod, then mix in the butter, stirring to melt. Remove from the heat and cool.

2 Beat together the eggs, yolks, icing sugar, rum and flour to a thick batter (this can be done in a food processor). Then strain on the buttery milk and beat (or whizz) until smooth.

3 Chill the batter in the fridge for 3–4 days if liked.

4 When ready to bake, heat the oven to 200°C/Gas 6.

5 Brush the insides of the moulds with extra softened butter, place on a flat baking sheet to hold them steady, then pour in the chilled batter almost up to the top edges.

6 Bake for 15 minutes, then turn the oven temperature down to 190°C/Gas 5 and bake on for another 30 minutes or until the little cakes are crisp on the outside and set. Remove from the oven and cool 5 minutes, then turn out to serve warm.

COOK'S NOTES
VANILLA PODS

Don't waste scraped vanilla pods. These can be rinsed and wiped dry and used to flavour sugar in a storage jar.

CREPES *DE SIMONE*

This is my mother's favourite recipe for light and lacy pancakes – one that I grew up with. Her secret is always the same easy formula of a rounded tablespoon of flour to each egg. You can either use the batter straight away or leave it for up to 2 hours in the fridge and thin it down with a little water.

Makes about 6–8 crêpes

INGREDIENTS

1 large free-range egg

1 rounded tablespoon of flour (approximately 20g) + pinch of sea salt

200ml milk

1 tablespoon Armagnac or dark rum

1 tablespoon orange flower water

a little sunflower oil, for greasing the pan

caster sugar, for serving

1   In a mixing bowl, whisk the egg with the flour, then gradually beat in the milk, next the Armagnac and orange flower water.

2   Heat a crêpe pan, about 20cm round, and lightly brush with a little oil. (My mother uses a fork wrapped with a little cotton cloth.) When you can feel a good heat rising from the pan, pour in a small ladle of batter (about 50ml) and quickly swirl the pan to coat.

3   Cook until thin and lacy. When the batter sets on top, loosen the edges of the crêpes and flip over for a few seconds to brown the underside.

4   Then slide the crêpe out onto a clean tea towel or sheet of kitchen paper. Reheat the pan and repeat with the oiling and cooking. Stack the crêpes up on each other to keep them moist and serve simply sprinkled with caster sugar.

LES BUGNES

In southern France, where Mardi Gras and carnivals are celebrated, these crisp enriched doughs were fried in oil before the long lean days of Lent set in. Tradition has it that they were a speciality of the Romans, who of course loved feasting and festivals, but nowadays we enjoy them as doughnuts, or *beignets*. The dough can be shaped in several different shapes depending on the region. We cook ours as slim pencils dusted with sugar.

Makes about 40

INGREDIENTS

500g plain flour + extra for dusting

½ teaspoon baking powder

10g fresh yeast, crumbled or 1 teaspoon easy-bake dried yeast

50g caster sugar

4 free-range eggs

2 tablespoons orange flower water

2 tablespoons dark rum

2 tablespoons Armagnac

grated zest and juice 1 lemon

250g butter, at room temperature

1 litre grapeseed oil, for frying

sifted icing sugar, for dusting

1 Put all the ingredients, from the flour to the lemon juice, in a mixer or food processor and beat until blended, then add the butter in small cubes mixing until incorporated and the dough becomes smooth, shiny and elastic.

2 Tip the dough out onto a worktop dusted with sifted flour and knead into a ball. Place in a bowl, cover with cling film and chill for about 4 hours.

3 After this, dust the worktop again with flour and roll out the dough ball to a rectangle of 1cm thickness. Cut out 1 cm wide 'pencils' of dough and place them on a flat baking sheet lined with non-stick baking paper.

4 Leave to rise for 30–45 minutes in a warm room until doubled in size. Heat the oil in a wide saucepan to 170°C and carefully drop in the dough pencils 4–5 at a time and cook 2–3 minutes until golden and crisp. Drain with a slotted spoon onto kitchen paper and repeat until all the dough is cooked, reheating the oil in between if the temperature drops. Dust with sifted icing sugar and serve freshly baked.

LE *RUSSE*

This almond meringue gâteau was created in the nineteenth century by a local baker, Adrién Artigarrade, in the little Pyrenees town of Oloron Sainte Marie, near the Franco–Spanish border. Why the Russian name? Because Artigarrade used fragrant almonds from the Crimea, and dusted with icing sugar, it made him think of the snowy plains of Russia.

To serve 8–10

INGREDIENTS

4 large egg whites

150g caster sugar

150g ground almonds

A little icing sugar, for dusting

1 First make the *crème patisserie*. Beat the sugar, yolks and cornflour together in a heatproof bowl until creamy. Scald the milk in a small non-stick saucepan with the vanilla and pistachio paste, or ground nuts. Pour the hot nutty milk onto the egg and sugar, whisking as you pour so the mixture blends smoothly.

2 Pour this back into the saucepan and reheat gently, stirring with a wooden spoon until smooth and thick. Pour this back into the bowl you beat the yolks and sugar in, and cool for a minute or two. Then beat in the butter, cover the bowl with clingfilm to prevent a skin forming and cool, whilst you make the meringue.

3 Heat the oven to 200°C/Gas 6. Line a large flat baking tray with non-stick baking paper. Whisk the egg whites to firm peaks in a large grease-free bowl using a balloon whisk or an electric beater, then gradually whisk in the sugar until thick and glossy. Fold in the ground almonds.

4 Spread the meringue out in a large 32cm square and 1 cm thick. Bake 18–20 minutes until firm, browned and crisp. As you remove the meringue sheet from the oven, spray the hot tray with cold water which will help moisten the meringue yet leave the outside crisp. Cool, then slide off the paper onto a chopping board and cut the square into two.

5 Place one meringue half upside down on a serving plate or board and spread with the cream. Top with the other meringue half. Chill for half an hour, dust with sifted icing sugar and serve, cut in slices with some soft red berry fruits.

CREME PATISSERIE INGREDIENTS

30g caster sugar

2 egg yolks

10g cornflour

100ml milk

¼ teaspoon vanilla extract

50g pistachio paste, or very finely ground unsalted pistachios

100g butter, melted

GOURMANDISE

LEMON TARTLETS

French lemon tarts rule the culinary world and this is my recipe. But in honour of my adopted country, Britain, I also have a quick and easier version, filling the centre with creamy lemon posset instead of curd. This is my contribution to gastronomical *Entente Cordiale*.

Serves 6

PASTRY INGREDIENTS

50g chilled butter, cubed small

125g plain flour + extra for rolling

50g caster sugar

a good pinch fine sea salt

2 egg yolks

LEMON FILLING INGREDIENTS

100ml fresh lemon juice

2 free-range eggs

1 egg yolk

80g caster sugar

90g chilled butter, cut in small cubes

Grated zest 1 lime

1   Rub the butter into the flour either by hand or in a food processor, until it resembles fine breadcrumbs. Then stir in the sugar and salt.

2   Beat the egg yolks and stir into the flour until a smooth dough, adding splashes of cold water if the mix seems a little dry. Knead gently until smooth, cover with clingfilm and chill for about 2 hours.

3   Remove the dough and knead gently again until soft enough to roll out thinly on a lightly floured worktop to the thickness of a £1 coin. Cut out 10–12 cm rounds to fit into six 8cm tartlet tins, trimming to fit and re-rolling trimmings if necessary to cut out more pastry to fit. Return to the fridge to rest for 10-15 minutes whilst the oven preheats to 170°C/Gas 3. Bake the pastry cases for 10–12 minutes until just firm and pale golden. Remove and cool then press out the tartlet cases from the tins.

4   Make the lemon curd filling. Strain the lemon juice into a heatproof bowl and whisk in the lime zest, eggs, yolk and sugar. Then place the bowl over a pan of gently simmering water and continue whisking or stirring until the mixture starts to thicken like a custard. Do not allow to overheat or it will curdle.

5   Remove the bowl from the pan and drop in the butter cubes, stirring until melted and smooth. Remove from the heat, cool and chill, then spoon into the tartlet cases and sprinkle with the grated lime zest. Remove from the tins.

COOK'S NOTES

LEMON POSSET TARTS

Instead of the curd filling use this recipe. Whisk 300ml double cream and 90g caster sugar until forming soft peaks then whisk in the grated zests and juice of 1 lemon and 1 lime. When thickened spoon into the tartlet cases.

CREME *FRITES*

These are crispy fritters of rich crème pâtissière
served with a dipping sauce of marmalade.
Another of my Anglo-British offerings.

Makes 8–10 fritters

INGREDIENTS

2 vanilla pods

500ml double cream

60g cornflour

75g caster sugar

4 free-range eggs

6 egg yolks

3 tablespoons ground
almonds

3 tablespoons flour

1 litre grapeseed oil

icing sugar, to dust

pinches of ground
cinnamon

half a pot of marmalade,
warmed until runny

1   Split the vanilla pods lengthways, then scrape out the sticky seeds
and place in a deep non-stick saucepan with the cream.

2   Bring slowly to the boil, then set aside. Meanwhile, whisk the
cornflour, sugar, 2 eggs and all the yolks in a heatproof bowl and
slowly pour over the hot cream, whisking as you pour. Heat gently
until the mixture starts to thicken and remove immediately so it
does not overheat and curdle.

3   Line a shallow rectangular container with clingfilm and pour in the
cream. Cover with another sheet of clingfilm and freeze until solid.

4   When ready serve, remove the frozen cream from the freezer and
thaw until softened enough to cut into fingers about 10 x 1cm.
Beat the remaining eggs thoroughly in a shallow bowl and mix
the almonds and flour in another bowl. Heat the oil in a shallow
saucepan to a temperature about 160°C.

5   Now take the finger and dip into the egg to coat completely, laying on
a plate, then dip into the almond and flour so they are evenly covered.
Lay the fingers on a clean plate, then lower gently about 4–5 at a time
into the hot oil and cook for 2–3 minutes until golden brown. Repeat
with the remaining fingers, reheating the oil in between. Drain the
fingers on paper towel and dust with icing sugar and the cinnamon.
Serve immediately with some warmed marmalade.

CREME CARAMEL MONBAZILLAC *with* GLAZED GRAPES

Like the Spanish Basques and Catalans, we call a rich set custard with a caramel topping a 'flan'. But our recipe flavours the custard with Monbazillac, a sweet dessert wine from the Dordogne and served with roasted black grapes.

Makes 6

INGREDIENTS

200g caster sugar + 50g for the custard

1 free-range egg

3 yolks

250ml double cream

225ml Monbazillac wine

125g black seedless grapes

1 tablespoon sifted icing sugar

1   Heat the oven to 100°C/Gas ½. Lay out 6 medium size ramekins on a tray. Heat the 200g sugar in a hot non-stick saucepan, without stirring until it melts, swirling the pan a few times but not stirring the sugar. Carry on heating until the melted sugar turns brown, then immediately pour into the ramekins and swirl the caramel in the ramekins to coat the bases and sides. Leave until set.

2   Whisk the egg, yolks and 50g sugar in a heatproof bowl until thick and creamy. Heat the cream and 125ml Monbazillac in a pan until on the point of boiling, then slowly pour onto the whisked eggs stirring until smooth and incorporated.

3   Pour the custard through a fine sieve into the caramel-coated ramekins. Place the ramekins into a roasting pan and pour enough boiling water around to come halfway up the sides of the dishes as a *bain-marie*. Bake for 25–30 minutes until a skin forms on the top of the dishes. Remove and cool, then chill until firm.

4   Meanwhile, peel the grapes, if you want to, using long fingernails if you have them. (If the grape skins are thin then this is not necessary.) Place the grapes into a frying pan over a medium high heat and sprinkle over the icing sugar. Cook until the sugar begins to melt and caramelise, then pour in the remaining 100ml of Monbazillac.

5   Demould the ramekins by running a blunt table knife around the inside and shaking out the caramel custards onto dessert plates. Scatter each with the glazed grapes and serve.

CREME CATALANE

A simple caramel custard that highlights the shared
Catalan and Gascon cuisine enjoyed a lot throughout
South West France. The custard is cooked on top of
the stove, then allowed to cool in ramekin dishes.
Sprinkle with demerara sugar and caramelise with
a cook's blow torch crème brulée style.

Makes 6

INGREDIENTS

500ml single cream

100ml milk

thinly peeled zest from
1 lemon

1 cinnamon stick

80g caster sugar

2 large egg yolks

Demerara sugar,
to sprinkle, optional

1 Scald the cream and milk in a saucepan and pour into a jug with the
lemon zest strips and cinnamon, cool, then chill for 3–4 hours in the
fridge to infuse. Remove the lemon and cinnamon.

2 Heat a medium size non-stick saucepan and sprinkle in the sugar,
heating until it starts to caramelise and turn a mid brown. Immediately pour in the infused creamy milk, beating fast with a wooden
spoon until it dissolves the caramel. (Take care this does not splurt
upwards.)

3 Place the egg yolks in a heatproof jug or bowl and pour over the hot
caramel cream, whisking as you pour until incorporated, then return
the liquid to the pan and over a low heat, stir with a wooden spoon
until the mixture begins to thicken slightly when you can draw a
line across the back of the spoon coated in the custard. If you have
a thermometer the temperature should read 86°C.

4 Line 6 medium size ramekins on a tray and strain over the hot custard.
Cool then chill until set.

5 If you like you could sprinkle teaspoonfuls of Demerara sugar over the
top of each custard when set, then caramelise the sugar with a cook's
blow torch or under a flaming hot grill and serve as crème brulées.

CUISINIER GASCON

OLD BOYS' JAM

Steeping soft fruits in a spirit syrup appears in many parts of Europe. It deals with the gluts of berries and spreads the pleasure of summer eating throughout the year. *Confiture des vieux garçons* ('old boy' recipes) appear in many parts of France. Gascon cooks enrich the syrup with Oriental spices, then top it up with Armagnac. The recipe is easy to tweak to suit, adding extra fruit at later stages.

Makes 1 litre preserving jar

INGREDIENTS

400g caster sugar

10 cardamom pods

10 cloves

10 star anise

800g–1 kg mixture of fresh berries – choose from blueberries, raspberries, blackberries and blackcurrants in equal measure

300ml Armagnac

1 Put 600ml boiling water into a large saucepan, stir in the sugar over a low heat until dissolved.

2 Tie the spices in a small muslin bag and add to the pan along with the fruits. Return to a simmer and cook for a minute or two stirring very gently with a thin metal spoon.

3 Remove from the heat, stir in the spirit and pour carefully into a large heatproof Kilner-style jar. Seal with a screw top and leave for a few days or longer if liked. The spice bag can be discarded after a few days.

4 Perfect to spoon over ice cream, whipped Chantilly cream or alongside chocolate cake.

PRUNES IN *ARMAGNAC*

This makes a nice preserve to have on hand when you want a quick dessert with cream or ice cream, or to give as gifts. It is a variation of the prunes from Gascon Mess (see page 218).

Makes a large preserving jar (1 litre size)

INGREDIENTS

500g Agen prunes

1 green-tea tea bag

200ml Armagnac

200g sugar

grated zest 1 orange

5 cloves

1 cinnamon stick

4 star anise

1 Pour 500ml boiling water in a bowl with the tea bag and stir in the prunes. Cover and leave to steep for 24 hours, then drain off the tea and discard the bag. Stone the prunes if necessary but leave whole and drop them into a large preserving jar.

2 Pour the Armagnac over the prunes, making sure they are pressed under the alcohol, cover and chill in the fridge for 10 days, then remove and allow to return to room temperature.

3 After that, combine 300ml boiling water with the sugar in a saucepan with the spices. Bring to the boil, simmer 1 minute, then pour over the prunes, including the spices. Cool, seal and leave to marinate for at least a month. Not only are the prunes quite delicious, the syrup makes good drinking after a fine dinner.

RED-HOT CHILLI BERRIES

I often think of the flavours and colours of Bordeaux and the Basque country as all red and spicy, and these have been the inspiration for one of our more exciting deserts combining piquillos peppers with fruits and cream. We also make thin *tuile* sheets with peppers and sugar served as a sandwich with fresh raspberries, flavour Chantilly cream with them and freeze them in a *granita*. You could spoon on a spoonful or more of Old Boys' Jam (page 235) alongside for extra colour.

Serves 4

INGREDIENTS

100g piquillos peppers, drained weight

50g icing sugar + a little extra to sweeten

150ml double cream

250g fresh raspberries

a little Old Boys' Jam berries (optional, page 235)

1   Make the *granita*. Place the 40g piquillos in a small blender with 125ml water, the caster sugar, lemon juice and a good pinch of Espelette. Whizz until very smooth, then scoop out into a small freezerproof box and freeze, stirring with a fork two or three times as it freezes down to crush the ice mixture.

2   For the *tuiles*, pat the piquillos dry with paper towel, then blitz in a blender or food processor with the icing sugar. Reserve a tablespoon of the pulp and set aside. Heat the oven to 150°C/Gas 2.

3   Line a flat baking sheet with a silicone cooking mat (Silpat). Using a thin palette knife, spread the remaining piquillos paste over the Silpat in a wafer-thin sheet, ensuring there are no holes.

4   Then bake for 9–10 minutes until the paste hardens. Tear a sheet of non-stick baking parchment and lay on the worktop.

5   Up end the Silpat with the *tuiles* mixture upside down on the paper and using a palette knife, prise off the sheet of pepper mix onto the paper and allow to dry. Then break or cut into eight even-sized pieces to match the size of your dessert or side plates.

6   When ready to serve, remove the *granita* from the freezer to soften a little. Whip the cream and when thick stir in the reserved piquillos purée, plus a little extra icing sugar to sweeten, if liked. Set this spiced Chantilly cream aside. Lay four broken *tuiles* on four plates, scatter with the berries, then dollop the piquillos Chantilly cream over the berries and finish with another piece of *tuile*.

7   Scrape shavings of *granita* with a spoon and put onto each plate alongside small spoonfuls of Old Boys' Jam, if liked.

GRANITA INGREDIENTS

40g piquillos peppers

25g caster sugar

juice ½ lemon

good pinch Espelette pepper

M. DUCLOS' *PASTIS*

Is this a cake or enriched bread? Well, it is certainly eaten like a cake in wedges, with a delicious, aromatic coffee alongside, but it is yeast-raised, old-style bread using a starter levain. In a way, it is Gascony's answer to Pannetone, complete with crushed pearl sugar on top but differs in that it is soaked in vanilla syrup. This recipe is based on one given to me around ten years ago by a Monsieur Duclos when we first set up Club Gascon. You can make this in a straight-sided deep cake tin, but we prefer the more traditional slightly sloping sided *moule a manqué* tin.

Makes a 20cm cake, to serve 6

INGREDIENTS

350g plain flour

¼ teaspoon fine sea salt

10g fresh yeast, crumbled

100ml milk, warmed until tepid

1 vanilla pod

80g butter, softened

5 free range eggs

100g caster sugar + 100g for syrup

1 teaspoon vanilla extract + ½ teaspoon for syrup

1 teaspoon Pastis e.g. Pernod or Ricard

a handful pearl sugar or crushed sugar lumps

1 First, make the levain in a small mixing bowl by beating 100g flour with the salt, yeast and warm milk to a thick batter, then cover with clingfilm and leave in a warm place until it rises until doubled in size, about 30 minutes.

2 Split the vanilla pod lengthways and using the tip of a sharp knife scrape out the sticky seeds. Put the seeds into a mixing bowl and reserve the pod. Add the softened butter, eggs, and 100g sugar, vanilla extract and pastis. Stir well to combine until smooth.

3 Then beat in the remaining flour and the risen levain. Mix vigorously for at least 3 minutes. This whole action can be done in a food mixer using a dough hook. Cover the smooth, elastic dough with lightly oiled clingfilm and leave to rise until doubled in size for about 45 minutes at room temperature.

4 Meanwhile, grease a 20cm diameter and 10cm deep cake tin and line the base with non-stick baking paper, if liked. Preheat the oven to 150°C/Gas 3.

5 When the dough is raised, scrape it out of the bowl gently using a large spoon or palette knife into the tin ensuring it doesn't deflate too much.

6 Bake for 35-40 minutes until risen and light golden brown and the top sounds hollow when you knock it with a crooked finger.

7 Meanwhile, make a syrup by dissolving the 100g sugar in 100ml water then add the empty vanilla pod and ½ teaspoon vanilla extract. Bring to the boil then simmer 1 minute, remove the vanilla pod shell and cool.

8 As soon as the cake comes from the oven, slowly pour over the syrup until it is all absorbed, whilst at the same time sprinkling over the pearl sugar so it sticks to the syrupy top. When cool, demould from the tin onto a wire rack, using a table knife, run round the perimeter. Cool and serve in wedges.

CHOCOLATE & *WALNUT FONDANT*

This rich chocolate and crushed walnut recipe, spiked with a little Espelette pepper, comes from our Knightsbridge restaurant, Le Cercle. You can make them ahead, then bake and serve with red berries or a scoop of sorbet. The insides will be slightly runny when spooned into, so there is no need for extra cream, unless of course you want to gild the lily. You will need some metal baking rings for this, approximately 6cm diameter and 4–5 cm high.

Makes 6

INGREDIENTS

100g dark chocolate, 55–60% cocoa solids

100g unsalted butter, in chunks + 20g extra, melted and cooled

a little sifted cocoa powder, to dust

2 egg yolks

2 whole free-range eggs

55g caster sugar

25g plain flour, sifted

60g ground walnuts

a good pinch Espelette pepper

1   Break up the chocolate into a heatproof bowl and add the butter. Place over a saucepan of gently simmering water, stirring once or twice until melted. Then remove and cool.

2   Brush the insides of six metal rings, 6cm wide and 4–5 cm deep with the 20g melted and cooled butter, brushing from the top to the bottom in stripes then dust the insides with cocoa powder, shaking off the excess. Chill until ready to fill.

3   In another larger bowl, whisk together the yolks, eggs and sugar using a balloon whisk or hand-held beater until the mixture becomes thick and pale golden and leaves a trail when the whisk or beaters are lifted up.

4   Scoop the chocolate into the whisked egg gently folding in a figure of eight with a large metal spoon, then when that is almost incorporated fold in the flour and walnuts.

5   Line a flat baking sheet with cling film and place the cocoa dusted rings on top. Spoon the chocolate mixture into the rings, filling right up to the top. Tap the baking sheet lightly on the worktop to settle the mixture and run the back of a knife over the tops to level. Chill for at least 6 hours, or overnight, until ready to bake.

6   To bake, heat the oven to 200°C/Gas 6. Cut 6 squares of non-stick baking paper about 8cm square and set aside. Slide the filled rings one at a time onto a non-stick metal baking tray using a flat spatula. (If liked you could line the sheet first with baking paper.) Then place a paper square on top of each ring and bake 5–6 minutes.

7   Serve immediately by sliding a palette knife under each ring and transferring immediately onto a serving plate. Remove the baking paper tops and serve, with some berries or sorbet, or both.

PARFAIS GLACE MANZANA

Iced parfaits are easy ice creams that you whisk and set in the freezer without having to use an ice cream machine. After a little thawing they are easy to spoon into. This recipe contains Manzana, an apple flavoured liqueur but you could also use Izzara liqueur for another Gascon flavour.

Makes 6 portions

INGREDIENTS

4 free range egg yolks

50g caster sugar

3 tablespoons Manzana

220ml double cream, chilled

sifted icing sugar, to dust

1 Put the egg yolks and sugar in a large bowl and whisk with electric beaters until you have a pale golden firm foam that forms soft peaks. Then whisk in the Manzana.

2 Whisk the chilled cream in another bowl until forming soft peaks also and gently fold into the yolk mixture using a spatula.

3 Divide the mix between six medium-large ramekins, spreading the tops to level, then freeze overnight until firm. When ready to serve, remove from the freezer about 15 minutes beforehand and dust with icing sugar.

ARMAGNAC
MADELEINES

Originally created by the Madeleine nuns, these light shell-shaped sponge fingers were made to raise money for their order. I like to add a Gascon flavour with Armagnac and orange-flower water. You will need the classic shallow shell moulds in which to bake the creamy batter, then serve them with coffee or a fruit compote and cream.

Serves 24

INGREDIENTS

2 large free-range eggs

120g caster sugar

100g plain flour, sifted with 1 teaspoon baking powder

grated zest ½ lemon

100g butter, melted and cooled + a little extra for greasing

1 tablespoon Armagnac

2 teaspoons orange-flower water

1 Heat the oven to 200°C/Gas 6. Whisk the eggs and sugar in a large bowl with a balloon whisk or electric beater until thick and creamy, then fold in the flour and lemon zest.

2 When smoothly incorporated, trickle in the melted butter and gently fold again, adding the Armagnac and flower water at the end.

3 Use a little more melted butter to brush the shell mould tin and spoon in about a dessert spoon of batter in each mould. Bake 10–12 minutes until risen and pale golden and lightly firm when pressed.

4 Cool for 5 minutes, then loosen each Madeleine with the tip of a table knife and remove to cool on a wire rack. Repeat with more greasing, filling with batter and baking twice more. Serve warm and freshly baked.

INDEX

ACKNOWLEDGEMENTS & THANKS

There are many people I would like to thank – those who have helped me put this book together and those who over the past ten years or so contributed to the success of our Gascon restaurants.

The book team – Jean Cazals (photography), Roz Denny (editing), Matthew le Maistre Smith (art direction and design) and Jon Croft, my publisher who has given me the opportunity to fulfil my dream of producing my first book. Most particularly, I must pay tribute to my head chef Thierry Beyris and Nicolas Belorgey, our pastry chef who supplied recipes as well as advice for the book.

Then there are my indispensable, loyal and hard working teams of staff from Club, Cellar, Comptoir, Croque and Cercle who have, from the very earliest days, contributed their efforts and talents to help the company evolve. And others who have made a special impact in the restaurants: Christian Haller, Franck, Bastien, Arnaud, Yann, Kate, Damien, Max, Pierre, Romuald, Andy and the two Juliens.

A good restaurant needs the lifeblood of dedicated suppliers with top quality produce to maintain consistent standards. Some of the artisans from France who bring us the best of their products are – the Biraben family (foie gras), Gabriel Bachelet (cheeses), Accocebery (charcutier-conserveur-traiteur), Caviar d'Aquitaine et poissons transformes, Pebeyre truffles, Salaisons Pyrénéennes, Masse, Boucherie Aimé, Axuria, Charairre (vegetables), Joel Dupuch (oysters), Champiland (mushrooms) and Maison Barthouil.

On our photography trip around Gascony I have special thanks for Madame Sarran, Martine Laffite of Boingnères Armagnac, Dominique from Cabane de l'Aiguillon, Le Pastis d'Amélie, and Eric Treuille from Books for Cooks, and a big thanks to Jean Pierre Xiradakis from La Tupina.

I have personal thanks for the people who helped us to set up the company, particularly Fabienne Labeyrie, Mourad Mazouz, Jonathan Laredo and Vincent Dahinden. Then there are the people from the trade in France who trusted me and believed in my motivation to become a chef, from Louis Marzin to Guy Savoy, from Gérard Vié to Yafa Edery, from Yvan Zaplatilek to Alain Dutournier.

And, of course, a big thank you to Pierre Koffmann for writing the foreword to my book.

Finally, I would like to thank my family for their support, our customers who encourage us to be better, and I could not have done any of this without my best friend and business partner, Vincent Labeyrie.

Pascal Aussignac, *Londres, Octobre,* 2009

SUPPLIERS LIST

FOIE GRAS ET CANARDS, PRODUITS DU TERROIR

Maison Biraben

63 Rue Ribere

64800 Beuste

www.biraben.fr

JAMBONS ET PRODUITS DERIVES

Salaisons Pyreneennes

2 Rue Anatole France

65320 Borderes sur L'echez

www.salaisons-pyreneennes.com

ARMAGNAC

Domaine Boingneres

Earl Lafitte

40240 La Bastide d'Armagnac

TRUFFLES

Maison Pebeyre

66 Rue Frederic Suisse

46000 Cahors

CHARCUTIER-CONSERVEUR-TRAITEUR

Accoceberry

64250 Espelette

www.accocebery.fr

Pierrette Sarran

Tourtiere et Conseil

Hauresat

32110 Saint Martin d'Armagnac

CAVIAR D'AQUITAINE ET POISSONS TRANSFORMES

Ste Sturgeon

Claudia Boucher

21 Rue de la Gare

33450 Saint Sulpice et Cameyrac

www.kaviar.com

FROMAGES

Gabriel Bachelet

3 Av Marcel Dassault

64140 Lons

www.fromagesdespyrennees.fr

PATISSERIE ARTISANALE

Le Pastis d'Amelie

64230 Mazerolles

www.lepastisdamelie.com

Fabienne Labeyrie

Lecons de Cuisine du Sud -Ouest

263 Bd De La Plage

33120 Arcachon

Fabiennelabeyrie@hotmail.fr

ONLINE SALES OF SPECIFIC PRODUCT FROM SOUTH WEST OF FRANCE

www.gasconline.com